Accounting with Sage for Windows
Version 3

Accounting with Sage for Windows
Version 3

David Royall

An imprint of **Pearson Education**

Harlow, England · London · New York · Reading, Massachusetts · San Francisco · Toronto · Don Mills, Ontario · Sydney
Tokyo · Singapore · Hong Kong · Seoul · Taipei · Cape Town · Madrid · Mexico City · Amsterdam · Munich · Paris · Milan

Pearson Education Limited
Edinburgh Gate
Harlow
Essex CM20 2JE
England

and Associated Companies throughout the world

Visit us on the World Wide Web at:
http://www.pearsoneduc.com

First edition published in Great Britain 1996

© Pearson Professional Limited 1996

British Library Cataloguing in Publication Data
A CIP catalogue record for this book is available on request from the British Library.

ISBN 0 273 62307 9

The right of David Royall to be identified as author of
this work has been asserted by him in accordance with the
Copyright, Designs and Patents Act 1988.

All rights reserved; no part of this publication may be reproduced, stored
in a retrieval system, or transmitted in any form or by any means, electronic,
mechanical, photocopying, recording, or otherwise without either the prior
written permission of the Publishers or a licence permitting restricted copying
in the United Kingdom issued by the Copyright Licensing Agency Ltd,
90 Tottenham Court Road, London W1P 0LP. This book may not be lent,
resold, hired out or otherwise disposed of by way of trade in any form
of binding or cover other than that in which it is published, without the
prior consent of the Publishers.

10 9 8 7 6 5 4 3
04 03 02 01 00

Typeset by Pantek Arts, Maidstone, Kent
Printed and bound in Great Britain by Redwood Books, Trowbridge, Wiltshire

The Publishers' policy is to use paper manufactured from sustainable forests.

CONTENTS

Preface   vii

1 Introduction   1
Identifying the need for a computer · The benefits of using computers · Computer systems · Printers · Staff training · The Data Protection Act 1984 · Installing Sage on your system

2 The customer accounts   14
Introduction · Creating customers · Customer invoices and credit notes · Extracting customer reports · Discounts · Exiting Sage · Exercises

3 The supplier accounts   37
Introduction · Creating suppliers · Supplier invoices and credit notes · Extracting supplier reports · Backing up your data · Exercises

4 Bank transactions   61
Introduction · Control accounts · Creating bank accounts · Nominal bank payments and receipts · Transferring funds between accounts · Recurring bank entries · Bank reconciliation · Bank statements · Exercises

5 The Nominal Ledger   79
Introduction · Looking at double entry · Nominal Ledger organisation · Double entry summarised · Petty cash transactions · Exercises

6 Advanced ledger work   100
Introduction · Managing the Sales Ledger · Managing the Purchase Ledger · Managing the Nominal Ledger · The financial year · Exercises

7 Stock control   129
Introduction · The structure of Sage Stock Control · Preparing stock records · Stock assembly · Stock movements · Extracting stock reports · Product transfers · Re-ordering stock · Exercises · Appendix

8 Sales invoicing   146
Introduction · The structure of the invoicing function · Preparing documents · Printing invoices · Updating the ledger · Conclusion · Exercises

9 Sales and purchase order processing — 163
Introduction · Sales order processing · Purchase order processing · Exercises

10 Advanced Sage utilities — 183
Introduction · Generating reports · Generating graphs · Multiple companies · Maintenance of data files

11 Case studies — 202
Introduction · 1 Brighter Light Ltd · 2 Future Stationery Supplies · 3 Nationwide Appliance Supplies PLC

Index — 223

PREFACE

This book gives students and practitioners a sound knowledge of the Sage Sterling for Windows Version 3 package – referred to throughout the book as Sage – developed to work within the Windows environment. It also helps to develop skills in bookkeeping and financial analysis.

The book introduces all the features of the Sage package and has been set out in such a way that you are able to begin working with the package and developing the required bookkeeping skills straight away. Anyone in business, particularly in a small organisation with limited resources for this kind of development, will find this book extremely useful and will probably be able to implement Sage accounts while working through the book.

Three case studies are included, which show how actual companies have tackled the computerisation of their accounting functions using the Sage package. The case studies are varied in order to demonstrate a wide range of experience as well as differing approaches to implementation.

Although some basic computing skills would be an advantage in learning computerised accounts, no previous computing knowledge is assumed. With computerised accounts, you will soon appreciate that bookkeeping and accounting skills are more important than computering skills. Consequently, this book seeks to cover as much bookkeeping and accounting as it does computing. It is very much a 'teach-yourself' guide.

This book offers practical help to Sage users by covering the use and application of the package away from the computer, as well as structured guidance on using the package on the computer. Planning and organising systems to support the package are as important as learning the techniques involved in using Sage.

This book has been written with a semi-tutorial approach and can be read in chapter sequence with access to a Sage package. In addition to the Sage package, you will require a computer that has Microsoft Windows installed on it. (If you have the DOS version of Sage (Bookkeeper, Accountant, Accountant Plus or Financial Controller) then there is a similar book by the same author entitled *Accounting with Sage* which is better suited to these versions.)

Chapter 1 gives an introduction to the concepts of computing, and the basic requirements which a business ought to adopt to computerise accounts using this package and these methods. It also explains how to install the package on your computer. In the following chapters you will then work through the Sage facilities, one by one, in a way that develops your skills and understanding, both of the package and the basic functions that Sage attempts to computerise.

This book will be of particular help to those students of accounting who are working for a qualification with one the accounting professional boards such as the AAT, ACCA or ICMA. It not only deals with fundamental bookkeeping and accounting principles, but also deals with computing and data processing concepts in an integrated manner – a requirement of almost all accounting qualifications.

It will also serve as a useful text for students and tutors involved with NVQ Levels 2 and 3 in Accounting, BTEC National and Higher National in Business and Finance, Pitman Qualifications' Computerised Accounts Levels 1 and 2, and those studying Small Business Systems and Concepts on BTEC courses in the business and computing areas. With the growing emphasis on the need to integrate many business and information technology skills in a practical way and to make more learning competence-based, this text and the appropriate computing resources offer a method of meeting such requirements.

By the time you have worked through this book, you should have gained an insight into the way a business information system operates, as well as invaluable skills in computerised accounts.

David Royall

CHAPTER 1

Introduction

Using a computer to manage a set of accounts and a stock system is not in itself the answer to all those problems typically encountered when running a business. One of the first points to consider is whether the business can significantly benefit from using a computer and, if it can, what the best way of going about computerisation is. When considering the purchase of a computer system and associated software, there are a number of procedures to follow.

IDENTIFYING THE NEED FOR A COMPUTER

This can be a difficult need to assess if you are not aware of what a computer can and cannot do. It is always wise to gain a little experience by attending exhibitions, short courses at the local college of further education, or even contacting business associates who use a computer in order to benefit from their experience. For most businesses a computer, if properly used and administered, can be of great benefit to the accounting and financial management function.

An important first requirement is to assess exactly what work you want the computer to do. Furthermore, by establishing the amount of work that has to be done, you will help the supplier to ensure that an adequate system is provided to meet your needs. When a business decides to purchase a motor vehicle, there must be some idea of the amount of work such a vehicle has to do and the amount of freight it has to carry, in order that a vehicle that is capable of handling the work is purchased. Exactly the same applies to a computer system.

Having established these requirements, it is a good idea to put such details in writing and to send them to a number of potential suppliers to see what they can offer. Such a document may include:

- the nature of the business;
- what a computer would be expected to do;
- the amount of information processing expected from a system;
- the number of staff currently doing the work and approximately how much time is spent on such processing activities.

Of course, a more experienced person could purchase a complete system through a magazine, catalogue or high street shop and make a success of using it.

However 'ideal' a system might be, its success will depend upon the way it is installed and maintained.

The essence of a computerised accounting system is no different to that of a manual system. The introduction of calculators has not altered the basic rules of arithmetic and mathematics and, likewise, the introduction of computers has not altered the basic rules of bookkeeping and accounts – just our approach.

One of the most difficult aspects of using a computerised system will be the process of setting it up. In most businesses, transactions are being generated on a more or less continuous basis and details about such things as stock quantities, customer accounts and so on would be difficult to assess accurately at any given point of time. When setting up a computer system, it is necessary to begin by entering all the details about the state of a company's accounts. The problem is that by the time all the required information has been compiled and entered on to the system, it has become out of date. The problem is the classic one of trying to alter a moving target.

Many of the above issues will be raised later in this book, but we shall begin in this chapter by installing the Sage package on your computer. Ways of overcoming some of the problems and dilemmas facing a business which wishes to computerise an accounting system and then operate it will be tackled in later chapters.

THE BENEFITS OF USING COMPUTERS

Speeding up transactions processing and the production of a series of reports are the more obvious benefits a business would expect from computerising accounts. The basic structure of any accounting system is depicted in Fig. 1.1.

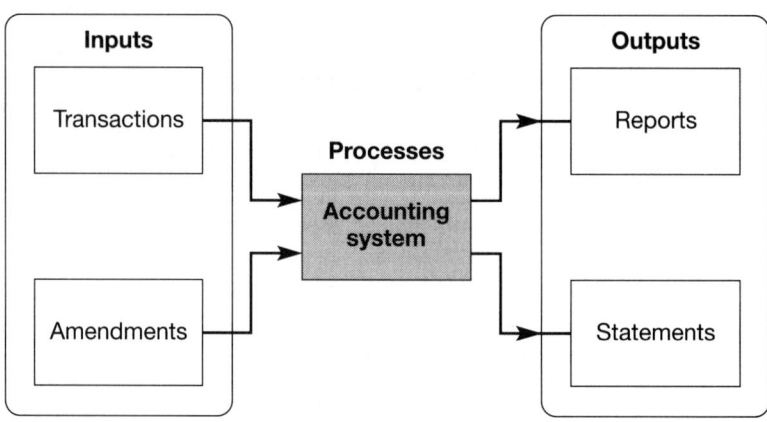

Fig. 1.1

The aim of a computerised accounting system is to perform the processing stage electronically; this should be completed much more quickly than if it were done manually. However, transactions and amendment details have to be input into the process in the correct form, in the correct order and in a timely manner. Although there is scope for using electronic methods of data entry, a good deal of human input and initiative is required, as well as an organised way of doing things. Further time-saving can be achieved by automatic output of reports – such as details about whether the firm is making a profit or loss, customer statements, sales analyses, cash and bank statements. Such reports and statements can be produced by the computer searching through information already generated and saved by the accounting system.

Effective reporting improves the decision-making process. For example, a computer system should be capable of detecting when a customer appears to be running up excessive debts with the company, allowing action to be taken before these get out of hand. Another area is the need to remain within budgets. Many business expenses can become too great, if they are not checked at regular intervals. A computerised accounts system should be capable of an activity called *exception reporting* – a process of issuing early-warning messages to operators when something appears to be out of order. In a manual system, errors or unwanted transactions often go unnoticed until too late or until they have already incurred unnecessary costs to the firm.

For many businesses, the necessary production of monthly and annual returns – such as VAT and payroll – can be time-consuming, tedious and unrewarding. The use of a computer system can be an effective tool to speed up the process and facilitate the production of lengthy reports with large amounts of figure work. In many cases, firms find that they can use computer printouts or even data on computer disks instead of having to complete official forms.

Improved accuracy may be another of the more obvious benefits of any kind of computer system; this is especially the case with accounting, where numerous calculations have to be carried out.

More job satisfaction and more effective use of operator time can be added bonuses with computerisation. For example, if a firm computerises its stock records, the job of the operator who maintains the records will be much the same as with a manual system. However, with instant reporting facilities available – such as a list of all stock items that may be in short supply – the operator can extract and produce details much faster. This will allow the operator to keep a much closer check on stock levels. Furthermore, if time can be saved in producing stock reports, the operator may have more time to 'chase up' suppliers who are not delivering on time or to 'shop around' the market for better suppliers and products.

Many more benefits of computerisation will become apparent throughout this book. It is worth noting that the extent of the benefits will vary from business to business, with each one deriving different benefits. It may even be the case that a business can derive no benefit at all from computerisation because there is insufficient data processing to justify the cost and effort.

Once a computer system is working properly, managers will often find themselves extracting reports that could not be achieved under a manual system within a timescale that would serve a useful purpose. The improved reporting and analysis that can be achieved by computerisation should enhance the whole decision-making process within an organisation.

COMPUTER SYSTEMS

When choosing a computer system, you will need to consider both the hardware and software. In most instances, a decision about the software will be made first. Software instructs the computer system regarding the processing of data. There are three distinct categories of software.

1 *The computer's operating system.* This software, as its name suggests, will operate all parts of the computer system, including keyboard input, screen output, printing, and the internal processing and storage of data inside the computer itself. All computer systems have an operating system, but not necessarily the same operating system. Operating systems include Microsoft Disk Operating System (MS-DOS), Operating System/2 (OS/2), UNIX and Novell. These operating systems are designed for different computer systems and are constantly changing in nature. As computers become more advanced and their operating environment alters, the operating system must also change.

2 *Microsoft Windows.* This software has been developed in order to give the operating system a better presentation. Consequently, the operating system itself will be accessed via the Windows environment – hence, the title of this book *Sage for Windows.*

3 *The applications package.* This adds to the Windows software by offering the added features required to perform specific tasks, such as accounting. When purchasing an applications package, such as Sage, it is important that the correct version is purchased that is compatible with Windows and that the computer does, in fact, have Windows. In other words, compatibility must exist between all levels of software.

Deciding on the hardware needed will become easier once the software decision has been made and the amount of work required of the system is clear. The type of system that would normally meet the needs of a small to medium-sized business would either be a stand-alone system or a network system.

Stand-alone systems

A stand-alone system consists of one screen, one keyboard, one disk drive and enough memory to run Windows. For a firm with relatively small data processing needs and no requirement for more than one operator to be at a keyboard at any time, such a system could prove quite adequate. For a business considering such a system, it will be essential to have a system with a hard disk, and advisable to purchase a system where the operating system and Windows are already loaded.

Network systems

A network system allows the linking up of microcomputers in such a way that they can share information and the data processing system can be centralised. In other words, someone working on a computer on a network system can update information on a customer and at the same time another person on another machine which is also on the network can view the update if the customer's account is accessed. Such a linked system is of particular use in larger organisations that require the accounting and related data processing function to be divided among a number of staff. It also gives management the facility of extracting reports without disturbing the accounts staff.

Such networks are not fixed in size. They can vary according to the requirements of the organisation – from a network of two microcomputers to one linking a very large number of microcomputers. Firms should always take advice when deciding on the number of microcomputers to network together. Too many on a network may lead to congestion.

PRINTERS

All users of computerised accounts will need to print information, such as customer statements, invoices, order forms, audit trails, or reports. It is worth noting that computerising the accounting functions is unlikely significantly to reduce the amount of paper used. In fact many new users have found that the computer results in more paper being used, not less.

Different types of printers are available for computer systems. Any firm using computers will need to assess how many printers are required and the quality of printing that needs to be achieved.

One of the most commonly used printers is the *matrix printer*. This prints character images onto paper by dot patterns, one character at a time. Most matrix printers are capable of printing a full page (A4 size) of text in under a minute and at a very reasonable quality. For most accounting functions' printing output, this kind of printer is both economic and adequate. Stationery for such printers includes continuous paper, which is a cheap way of acquiring printed output. Matrix printers are now available in both black and white and colour models.

For improved output quality and speed, a *laser printer* is another option. The quality of print is better, the machines are not as noisy and they accept standard-sized single sheets of paper. For graphics output and good quality letter production, a laser printer may be a sensible option.

A third common printer now in use is the *ink jet printer*. It offers high quality at low cost. Compared with a laser printer, it is as quiet, but slower. For those wanting colour output, ink jet colour is also available at low cost.

Other types of printer serve differing types of needs. The term *hard copy* is often used to refer to printed output, as opposed to *soft copy*, which refers to screen output.

STAFF TRAINING

Another major issue in implementing computerised accounts will be the need to ensure that staff are adequately prepared and trained. This can be done in a number of ways:

- Purchase a system and the required software from a company which also offers staff training.
- Send a member of staff on a course. Such courses are available at differing times of the year from both private institutions and local colleges of further education.
- Employ someone who is already trained.
- Hope that employees can learn the package and computer system as they implement it, giving them time to research and experiment. (Although this option is extremely risky, it is all too often used.)

Staff training is an expense often overlooked. Poorly trained staff can lead to the downfall of any system – computerised or not.

In conclusion, anyone responsible for computerisation should be aware that a certain amount of time and patience is required. Computerising a manual bookkeeping system cannot be done overnight; it may well take weeks or months. In Chapter 11 there are three case studies which will put this into some kind of perspective and offer a much more detailed analysis for implementing computerised accounts.

THE DATA PROTECTION ACT 1984

Most firms that make extensive use of computers for accounts, payroll and any other applications that involve details of personal individuals would be well advised to register with the Data Protection Board.

The Data Protection Act 1984 defines a *data user* as being someone who makes use of personal data that is on a computer. Basically, *personal data* is data held about individuals. A *data subject* as defined by the Act is any person who has data about them on a computer. Such data on a computer has to be processed by the computer's software before it serves the purpose of information. It is this information that the Data Protection Registrar wants to know about.

Essentially, the data users must declare what information they have access to on a data subject and the uses to which they will put that information. The main objective of the Act is to ensure that individuals are aware of what is being held about them on business computers and to allow them access to this information. There are many exemptions, however, such as medical records, criminal records and information deemed necessary to be kept secret in the national interest.

If a business is only using the Sales Ledger or Purchase Ledger for preparing and sending invoices and statements and does not use the comment details as a contact name, then registration may not be necessary. Furthermore, if customers and suppliers are companies, and individuals cannot be identified in the data, registration is not necessary. With respect to wages, in the same way, if all a data user does with the data is to pay wages and prepare statutory returns, registration is not necessary.

If customer and supplier lists are used for sending out sales promotions, the data user must register; likewise, if data on the payroll is used for management information about staff sickness or any form of staff monitoring.

Forms for registration are available at any main post office. These forms require the business to reveal the kind of data it holds on individuals and the purpose for which it wants to use it. The business must also give details on how data subjects can find out what data is held on computer about them.

In addition to the possible need to register, businesses must comply with certain practices with regard to holding personalised data on computer. Briefly, these are:

- Data must be obtained fairly and lawfully.
- Data can only be used for the specified purpose set out in the original submission to the Registrar. If the business wishes to change the way it uses such data, then it must re-apply.
- Data must not be disclosed to unauthorised parties. Again, authorised parties must be stated within the original application. Sage for Windows allows you to create a password to assist you in this.
- Data held must be adequate, relevant and not excessive for the purposes for which it is being held.
- Data must be kept accurate and up to date. This principle should really apply to all data in an accounting system if the system is being managed and run properly.
- Data must not be kept longer than is necessary.
- Any data subject must be allowed to see the data held on him or her in readable and legible form. This means businesses must have the mechanism

for extracting a complete profile kept on an individual in the event that it is requested. If a data subject does approach a data user requesting such information, the data user can demand a fee to cover any administration costs.
- A data user must have appropriate security against unauthorised access. Again, passwords will help here. However, in addition to this, back-up disks should also be kept secure from unauthorised access.

If a firm is in doubt, then it should always register (the cost of registration is small). The information sent to the Registrar is available to any member of the public for inspection.

INSTALLING SAGE ON YOUR SYSTEM

Having acquired the hardware and Sage software, you need to install it onto your system. Many businesses purchasing a complete system may well have had this done for them.

The need for a package like this to be installed onto a system comes about because the package was not written for a specific system or for a specific business. The installation of the package will put your system on to your hard disk, which matches the computer system you are using and is set for your type of business. The installation will also create an easy way of accessing it through Windows by creating the required 'icons' needed.

When your software arrives, you will receive:

- a number of floppy disks (usually three) containing your software; and
- a reference manual.

Extra disks may also be supplied that offer you additional software. This extra software normally offers you additional features to further enhance the Sage accounting software you already have. This book will only deal with the Sage for Windows package. The disks you need for this purpose will be labelled Disk 1 of 3, Disk 2 of 3 and Disk 3 of 3.

Assuming you have a hard disk system or are using a network, then to install the software, start by switching your computer on and make sure Windows is running. Place the disk marked Disk 1, or Installation, into your floppy disk drive. If you have two drives, then it should go into the one your system refers to as A: drive.

If you are a Windows 95 user, then click on **Start** and then **Run**. Alternatively, click on the **File** option from the Windows manager and then on **Run**. Type in the program name to run as **A:SETUP.EXE**. Figure 1.2(a) shows the Run dialogue box entry required. When this has been entered, click on the **OK** button and, after a few moments, the Setup screen will appear as in Fig. 1.2(b).

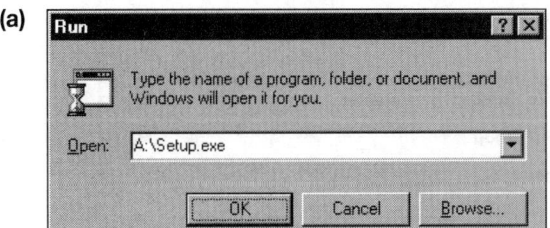

Fig. 1.2

The Setup dialogue box needs to know where on your disk to place the software. The default settings will appear, and unless you require the software somewhere else on your disk, you can simply click on the **Continue** button to proceed to the next stage of installation. Sage will also inform you about disk space. If there is insufficient space on your disk, Sage will inform you of this and stop the installation process. If you have any problems at this stage, then either free up some space on your disk or consult your computer manager, technician or dealer.

The next stage will be for Sage to determine a Windows icon for you and a Windows group into which the icon can be placed. Figure 1.3(a) illustrates how this appears on your screen, with the defaults appearing automatically for you.

Again, unless you have any particular preference, click on the **Continue** button to proceed with installation. One by one, Sage will ask for each of the disks it requires to install Sage. Enter the disks only when required, click on **OK** each time you change the disk.

When this stage is complete, your software has been placed on your disk and a Windows group will have been created for you with the required icons to activate your software. Figure 1.3(b) illustrates this.

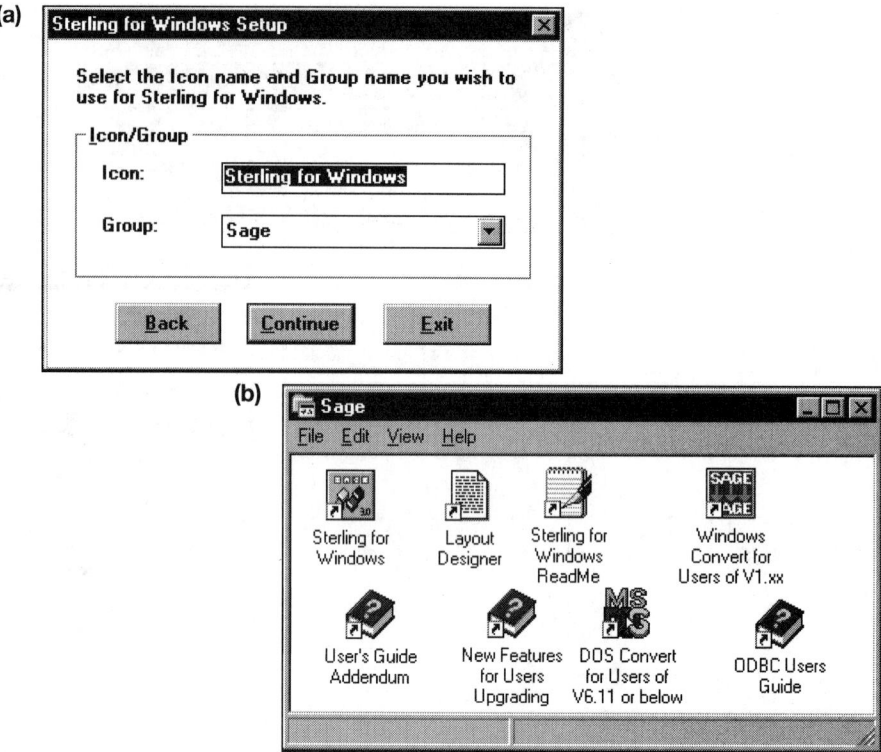

Fig. 1.3

At this stage you are ready to enter Sage for Windows for the first time. Before you work on a company, you will be required to enter some initialisation details required by the program. Click on the **Sterling for Windows** (Sage) icon to enter the program. As this is the first time you have used the program, you will be required to enter two special codes via a Startup Wizard dialogue box. Figure 1.4 shows such a screen.

The serial number and activation key will be unique to each user. Your codes will appear in your User Guide or on a separate document. As you enter the activation key code, Sage will show asterisks. This conceals the code and prevents an onlooker from discovering your code. Click on each box and enter the codes.

When these have been entered, click on the **Next** button to reveal the next stage of initialisation.

Now you will need to enter the company details via another Startup Wizard dialogue box. Figure 1.5 shows such a setting for a fictitious company called Megaxan Sterling Sports – a company that will form the basis of a case study to assist you through the book. The company details simply contain the

Introduction 11

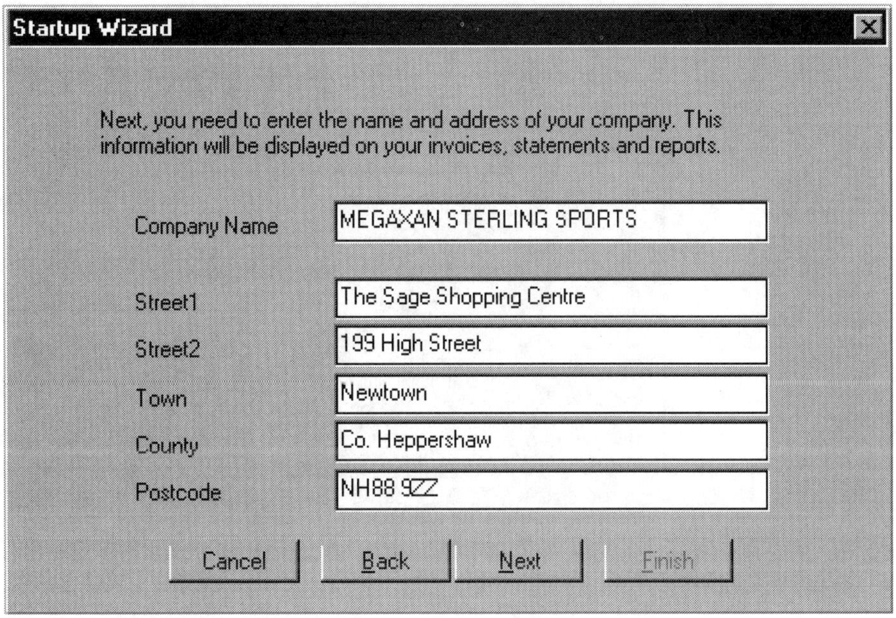

Fig. 1.4

Fig. 1.5

company name and address. If you are using Sage supplied stationery, then this will be used when your company address is needed on the stationery. The top line of the address will appear frequently on your screen when you use Sage. Click on each address line and enter the details required. When this is done, click on **Next** for the next stage of initialisation.

In the next dialogue box you need to enter the date for the start of the financial year. This may not be the current month. Figure 1.6 illustrates the dialogue box that has the settings for the financial year.

If at any point you need to go back because you have missed something out or have made an error, then clicking on the **Back** button at the foot of the dialogue box allows you to do just this. Alternatively, if you wish to abandon the whole installation exercise, then click on the **Cancel** button. Click on **Next** to proceed to the end of installation.

You are now ready to go.

If you have installed the software incorrectly, then you can always re-install it. To do this, you can run the **Setup** program again in exactly the same way as you did before.

After initialisation, the Sage introductory screen will appear momentarily, as shown in Fig. 1.7, before you enter the opening screen.

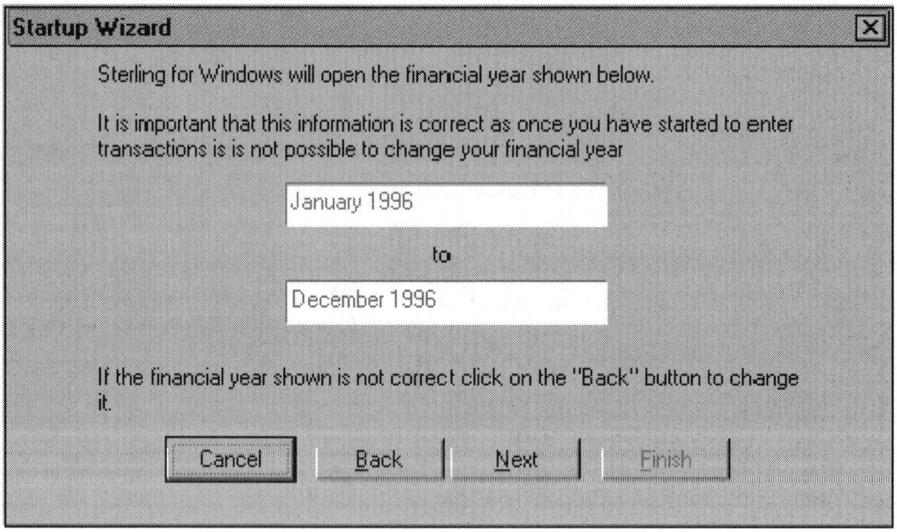

Fig. 1.6

Introduction 13

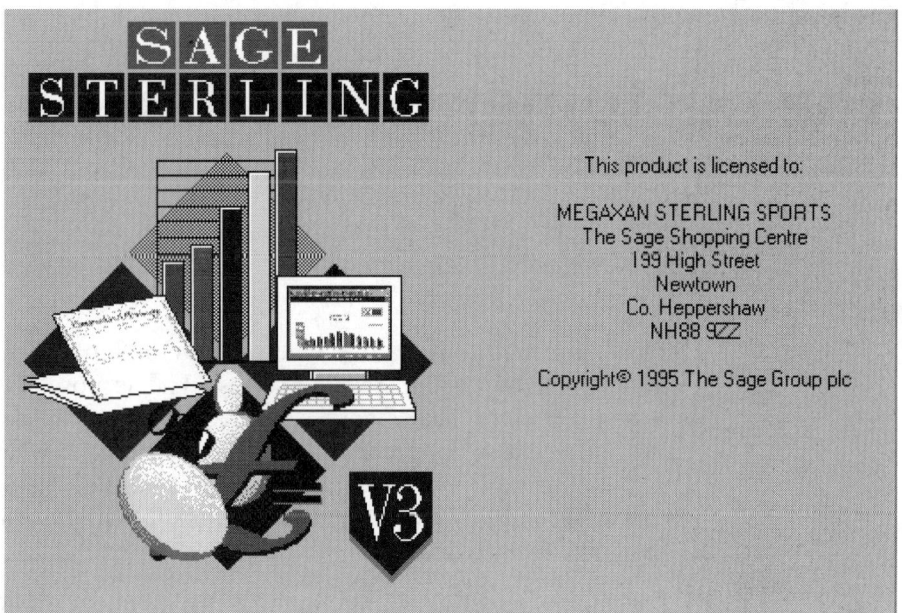

Fig. 1.7

To enter the Sage package in future, simply click on the **Sterling for Windows** icon and you will enter the opening screen without having to go through the initialisation procedures again. If you wish to set up another company set of files, however, you will need to repeat the initialisation procedure. You should, therefore, keep your serial number and activation codes in a safe and secure place for future reference.

CHAPTER 2

The customer accounts

INTRODUCTION

This chapter introduces the Sage package by looking at the way it handles trading with the customers of a business. The purpose of customer accounts is to help a business keep a good set of records about the dealings it has with its customers. These customer accounts will be stored in what is often referred to as the *Sales Ledger*. When considering the use of the Sales Ledger, we are concerned primarily with those customers to whom we sell on a credit-term basis, rather than for cash.

For most of us going about our shopping, payment would normally be made in cash. From the business point of view, the retailer would not need the Sales Ledger for such cash transactions. In practice, it is mostly non-retailing businesses and retailing businesses that deal with mail order which need the Sales Ledger.

The Sales Ledger is a collection of customer accounts. With a customer who deals with the business on this basis, the goods will normally be ordered by the customer, the business will deliver the goods and will then send an invoice for payment. At a subsequent date, ranging from a few days to a few weeks, the customer will make a payment. The Sales Ledger will play a crucial role in managing the customer accounts. Those customers owing the business money are called *debtors* and are regarded by accountants as an asset to the business, as they will provide money to it.

At this point you ought to be aware of the documents used in sales transactions:

- An *invoice* is used to indicate to a customer what has been bought, how much has been bought and the amount it is costing the customer.
- A *credit note* is used to reduce the amount the customer owes the business. Such a document is often issued when goods are returned to the business or the business decides to reduce the amount it wants its customer to pay.

Further documents will be introduced later in the book, but these are the two most important documents when considering the Sales Ledger in the first instance.

The Sales Ledger can be used just as effectively for services rendered as it can for goods sold (or a combination of both). The facilities offered by a Sales Ledger must allow the user to create, delete and amend customer details on the ledger, as well as record all transactions between the business and the customer.

A good reporting system on the Sales Ledger is also necessary to ensure the business is aware of how much is owed to it and by whom. Another important function of the Sales Ledger for many businesses is to give information on VAT collected from its sales income.

Figure 2.1 gives an overview of the function of a Sales Ledger, with input activities showing the maintenance of customer records and entry of transaction data. The output activities consist of the customer statements, audit trails and reports.

The Sales Ledger also provides details of sales, receipts and debtors to the *Nominal Ledger*. This will be dealt with in some length in Chapters 5 and 6.

In addition to supplying the organisation's needs, it is necessary for the system to supply information to those customers and clients to whom the organisation is selling. Such information may include details of invoices sent to them in the past and regular statements of account. A statement of account gives details of all transactions undertaken with the firm over a specific period of time. Sage refers to these reports as *transactions histories*.

The Sage Sales Ledger section of the package (Customers) will meet these requirements along with many others. There are other reporting facilities available for management information in particular which will be dealt with in Chapter 6.

As a useful tip, when operating a Sales Ledger, it is often a good idea to *batch process* much of the work. For example, when adding transactions to the Sales Ledger, it is often best to do a few at the same time (say, weekly) rather than entering them to the Sales Ledger on an *ad hoc* basis (as each one comes in). This will save both time and possible confusion caused by making a large number of visits to the computer to enter small amounts of transactions data.

The *audit trail* is a series of lists indicating all the data that has been entered into the Sales Ledger during the current period. This will be required for checking omissions and errors, and also for subsequent auditing purposes.

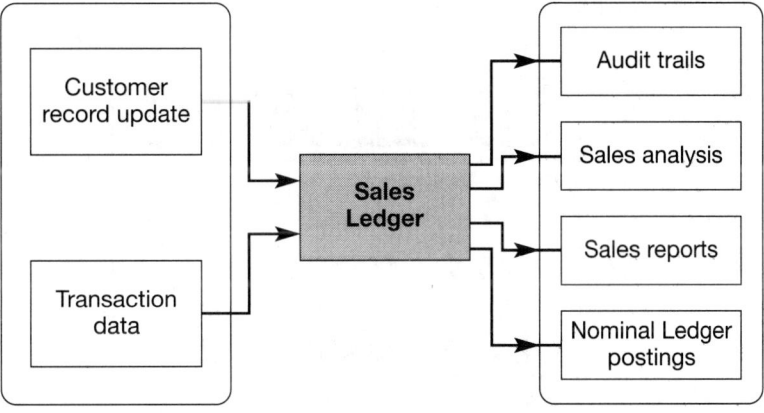

Fig. 2.1

CREATING CUSTOMERS

If you have not installed your Sage package onto your computer, then you will need to do so now by referring to Chapter 1. Once your package is installed, you are ready to start. When you have loaded Windows onto your computer, you need to activate the Sage package by placing the mouse pointer over the **Sterling for Windows** icon and double clicking your right mouse button. If you entered a password when creating your company, then you will first need to type in this password. At this stage, type in the password that was assigned during installation or find out the password from your computer manager. As you type in the password, the screen will display a series of asterisks (*) rather than reveal the password to an onlooker.

Once Sage is loaded and you have typed in your password, you will see an opening Sage window such as the one in Fig. 2.2. The top row shows the title bar naming the package and the name of the company. The Sage window in Fig. 2.2 has been maximised by clicking on the **Maximise** button that appears in the top right-hand corner of the screen, on the title bar. These buttons vary depending on the version of Windows on which you are running Sage. At this stage, you should make yourself familiar with these icons (*see* Fig. 2.3). The **Maximise** button will set Sage so that it fills your screen, while the **Minimise** button will reduce Sage to an icon on your Windows screen. The **Normalise**

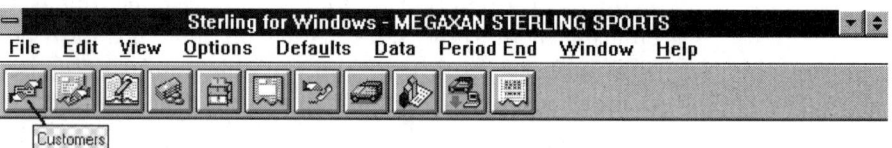

Fig. 2.2

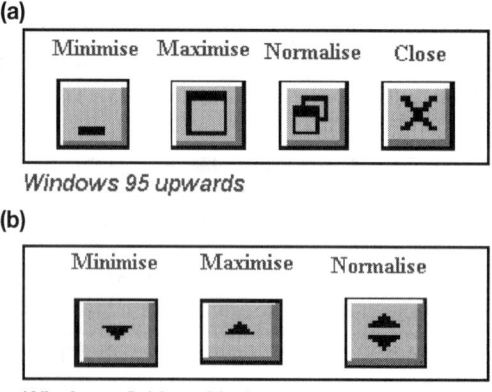

Fig. 2.3 The title bar icons

button will create a window for Sage showing the Windows screen around the edges. Windows 95 has an additional button – **Close** – to allow the speedy closing of the whole program.

The second line on the opening screen (*see* Fig. 2.2) is a pull-down menu. As you work through this book, you will see that these pull-down menus will allow you to perform a whole range of functions.

The third line shows a row of icons which are used in conjunction with your mouse. Such icons are used as an alternative, and often a short cut, to using the pull-down menus.

Point your mouse pointer at the far left icon labelled **Customers** and click. This will display the Customers part of the package by filling up the lower part of the screen. This now creates a window appearing on top of a window. If you click on the **Maximise** button that appears in this window, it will fill more of the screen.

At this stage you will not have any customer records to work with. Consequently, the first stage will be to enter some customers so that you can begin to carry out some transactions. The icon that will allow you to enter your customers is the far left icon labelled **Record**. You will see from Fig. 2.4 that a box has appeared showing some text (Customer Record) giving brief details about what this icon will activate.

To achieve this, place the mouse pointer over the icon without pressing any button on your mouse. This should reveal the box with the text. Sage uses this technique throughout the package and you will find it useful when working

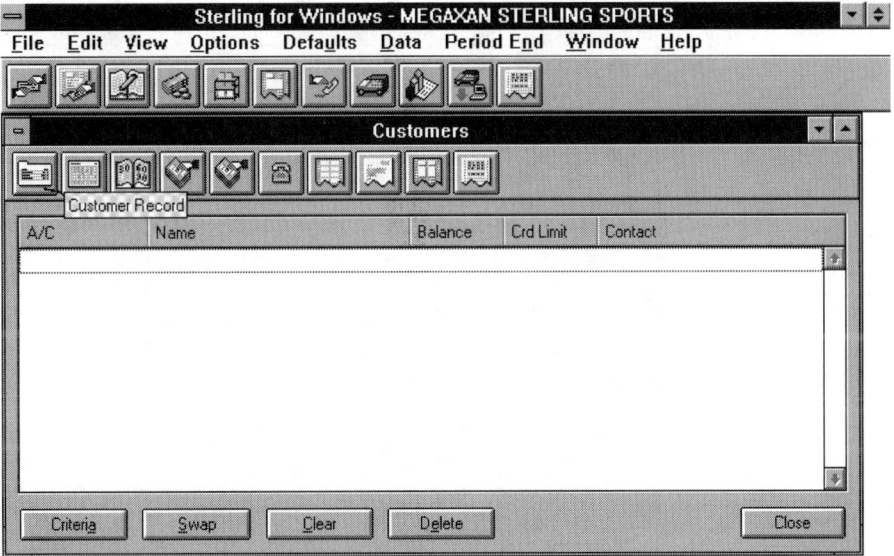

Fig. 2.4

through the package for the first time. When you let go of the mouse button, you will activate an input dialogue box which will serve as the screen for entering details of a new customer or editing details of existing ones.

Figure 2.5 shows part of a customer record that has been completed. When you see this screen blank for the first time, the pointer will be on the **A/C** box requesting an account number for your first customer. Type in an account number for your first customer. It is important to note that each customer has to have a unique account number to distinguish one customer from another. Such a field in a record is often referred to as a *key field* in that it is the key that identifies the customer record. Consequently, no two customers can have the same account number. When the account number is typed in, the words 'New Account' will appear to the right of the account number to indicate that a new customer record is being created rather than an amendment to an existing one. A customer account number can be a combination of letters and numbers. In the example shown in Fig. 2.5, the account number SL0010 has been used to indicate a Sales Ledger account.

When this has been typed in, click on the **Name** box. You should now type in the name of the customer – that is, the name as it would appear on its address details. Exactly the same applies to the five address lines that follow. The **Contact Name** in the box below the address will be used for future reference if you need to contact the customer. The **Telephone** number will also be used for the same purpose. The **Fax** number, if known, can also be typed in and can be

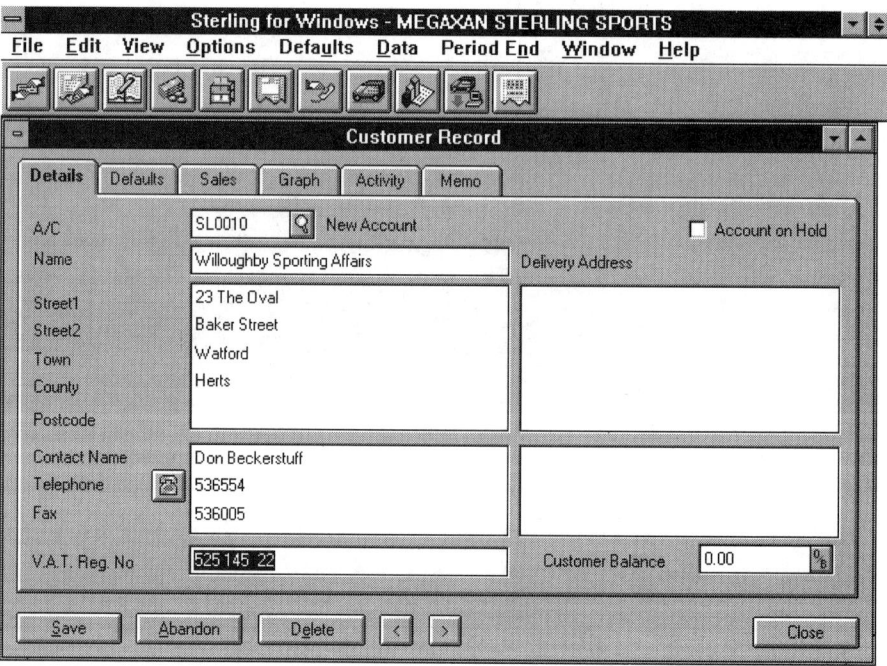

Fig. 2.5

used to send a fax to a customer. Sage allows you to use your computer to send a fax to a customer automatically, providing your computer has the facilities to do it. The use of fax will be covered in Chapter 10.

To the right of the dialogue box is a **Delivery Address**. If this is different from the main address already entered, then this needs to be completed as well. This will mean that goods will be delivered to the delivery address while all correspondence will go to the other address.

Invoices sent to customers will also require the business's **VAT Registration Number**. As all businesses (with the exception of very small ones) need to register, this code should be readily available. When entered, Sage will print this on all invoices produced.

A number of tabs appear at the top of the Customer Record dialogue box. The **Details** one is highlighted to indicate where you are in the customer record. **Sales**, **Graph** and **Activity** will be worked on later. For now, click on the **Defaults** tab to reveal another dialogue box. Figure 2.6 shows an example of one that has been completed.

The **Credit Limit** will set the amount of credit you wish to allow a customer – the maximum amount you want owing to the business by the customer. When this amount is reached, Sage will warn you that the limit is to be exceeded and that you should request some payment from your customer before issuing more goods or services to that customer.

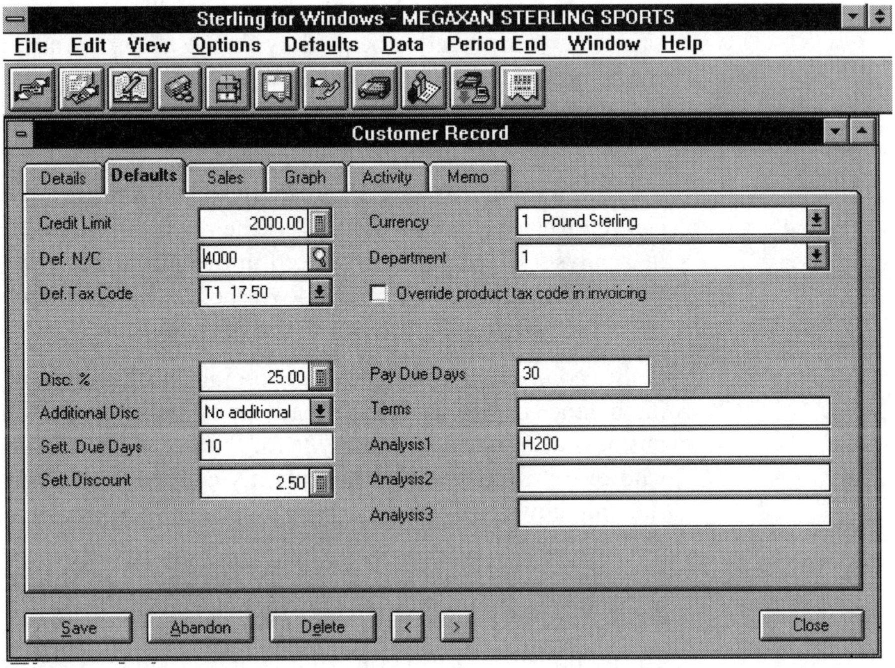

Fig. 2.6

The **Default Nominal Code – Def. N/C** – will ensure all sales data are posted to this nominal account (to be dealt with in Chapter 5). The **Default Tax Code** has been set with T1 17.50. This represents a tax rate of 17.5 per cent that appears in a predefined table, which can be altered should VAT rates change.

The **Currency** box has been set at pounds sterling for this customer. By clicking on the down arrow to the right of this box, you can select from a list of currencies. Sage will also allow you to add to this list.

The **Department** box allows you to select from a list of predefined departments. At this stage they only appear as numbers, but Sage allows you to attach names to these numbers. In Fig. 2.6, this customer has been assigned to Department 1.

The **Disc. %** figure of 25.00 indicates that this customer is entitled to a trade discount of 25 per cent. If this is left blank, you will still have the option of offering a trade discount to the customer. The effect of this is to offer such a discount on the whole invoice amount by default. An **Additional Discount** can also be set, which can be allowed on either quantity of goods sent or their value.

Sett. Due Days is a settlement term where, if payment is made within these days, then the customer will be allowed the stated settlement discount set out in the **Sett. Discount** box below. In the example in Fig. 2.6, if the customer pays this invoice within ten days a 2.5 per cent discount can be claimed.

Pay Due Days is the number of days within which you expect the invoice to be settled. If you type in 30 in the box, this will appear on the invoice and indicates that you expect to be paid by the customer within 30 days of the date of the invoice. The **Terms** box allows you to type in up to 14 characters of text that specifically set out terms; these will be written as they appear here on your invoices.

The **Analysis 1**, **Analysis 2** and **Analysis 3** boxes are used for developing special reports that can be tailored to the needs of the business. H200 appearing in Analysis 1 represents produced information that tells us something about the customer. This information will be used in subsequent chapters to illustrate the reporting features of the Sage package.

Before completing this customer, you may at this stage wish to enter an opening balance if the customer already owes money to the business. In practice, a business using the Sage accounts for the first time will have existing customers who owe it money and, consequently, will have to enter an opening balance showing how much the customer owes. For the purpose of demonstration, we shall assume that this particular customer has an outstanding balance with the business of £650. Click on the **Details** tab in order to return to the dialogue box you started with (*see* Fig. 2.5).

To the bottom right of this dialogue box appears a **Customer Balance** box. Click on the small **O/B** icon that appears to its right to reveal a small dialogue box. Figure 2.7 illustrates the kind of information that you can now type in.

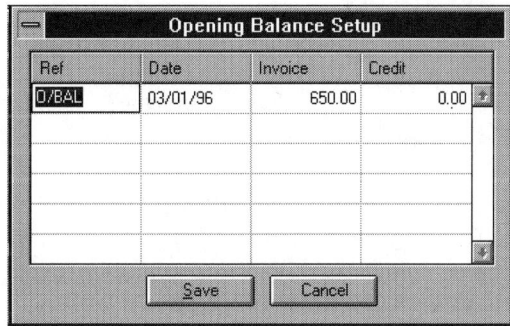

Fig. 2.7

The first **Ref** line has had **O/BAL** typed in it to indicate it is an opening balance. If you wanted to type in an invoice number, then this could be typed in. The **Date** will be generated by the computer, but can be altered by typing in a new date in the format dd/mm/yy (the date in Fig. 2.7 being 3 January 1996). The **Invoice** column records the amount the customer owes. In this example a single amount owing has been typed in as 650.00. Many businesses would prefer to type in details of all invoices currently outstanding. This can be done by typing in line details for each invoice. The same also applies to credit notes, except the amount is typed into the **Credit** column. When you have completed this dialogue box, click on the **Save** button to record the details and return to the Customer Record dialogue box. The **Cancel** button will take you back to the Customers screen without recording any of the details you have typed in.

The **Memo** tab is used to type in any details you wish about this customer – such as a brief history of the customer, or briefing notes about what kind of customer you are dealing with.

At this stage, ensure you are at the **Details** page of the customer and then click on the **Save** button to both save the customer record you have entered and create a new blank form for the next customer.

PRACTICE

Type in details of a few more customers into the customer records so that you have some data to work with. The following list gives some suggestions, but you should add some of your own to gain the practice needed. Set all the defaults as you did with Willoughby Sporting Affairs, unless otherwise stated.

Wantworth Cricket Club
A/C: SL0020
Address: The Sports Centre, Hydean Way, Perth
Contact: Debbie Jones
Tel: 0199 727233
Fax: 0199 977712
Opening bal: £300
Credit limit: £4000
Analysis code: H200

Jackson General Sports
A/C: SL0050
Address: 100 High Street, Glasgow
Contact: J McAllister
Tel: 0188 282823
Fax: 0188 233422
Opening bal: £500
Credit limit: £3000
Analysis code: H200

Harriers Football Club
A/C: SL0030
Address: The Sports Centre,
                Tackle Lane, Hull
Contact: Jack Todd
Tel: 0177 277732
Fax: 0177 377773
Opening bal: £3000
Credit limit: £3500
Analysis code: H100

Sports Super Centre
A/C: SL0040
Address: Sports Arena,
                Doncaster Road,
                London
Contact: Mary or Jack
Tel: 0171 222333
Fax: 0171 333222
Opening bal: £1000
Credit limit: £3500
Analysis code: L100

Dipple Store
A/C: SL0060
Address: The Oval, King
                Street, Manchester
Contact: Bill
Tel: 0132 123222
Fax: 0133 929232
Opening bal: NIL
Credit limit   £3000
Analysis code: H100

Howell Gym Centre
A/C: SL0070
Address: Global Leisure Park,
                Spring Avenue,
                Bexley
Contact: Janet Brown
Tel: 0181 238484
Fax: 0181 292992
Opening bal: £800
Credit limit: £4000
Analysis code: L100

When entering records it is important that you click on the **Save** button each time before you type in the next one. When you have completed each customer record and have saved the last record, click on the **Close** button to return to the main Customers window. A list of your customers will appear in the window. Such a list of customers will prove useful when processing records in future.

Before you enter transactions, it is worth obtaining from the computer a list of the names of the customers. From the main Customers window, click on the **Report** icon. A Customer Reports dialogue box will appear similar to that shown in Fig. 2.8.

The **Layout** panel shows a list of reports available to you. The **Description** column describes in a few words what the report will contain. The **Status** column indicates that the reports are all fixed – that is, they are a permanent feature of your Sage package and cannot be altered. The **Filename** column indicates the file name that the report has been given on your disk. The number of reports can be added to by creating your own, or deleted if they are not wanted.

To the right of the **Layout** panel is a scroll bar. Either click on the down arrow or slide the small box down the bar to reveal more of the list of available reports. You will see a report described as **Customer List**, as highlighted in Fig. 2.8. Click on this one to highlight it.

The customer accounts 23

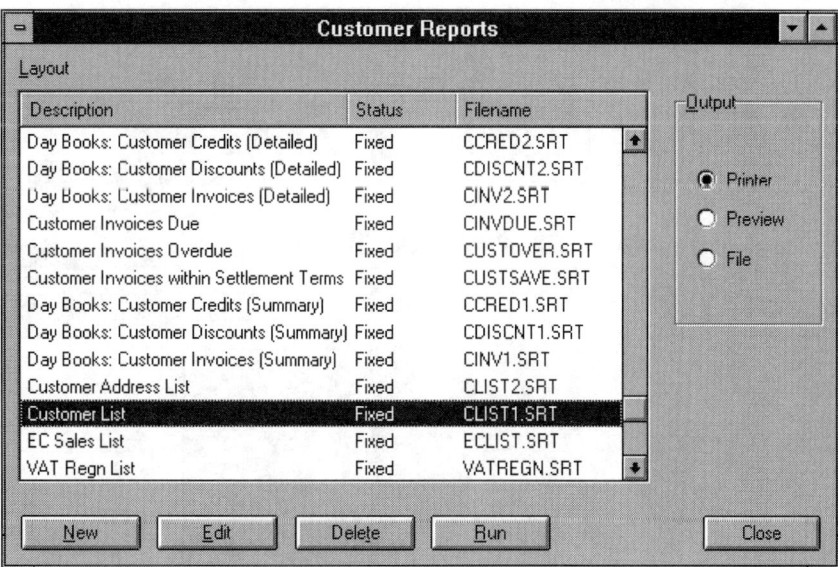

Fig. 2.8

To the right of the **Layout** panel is the **Output** panel offering you three options. **Preview** allows you to see the report on your screen as it would appear on paper from your printer, while **Printer** will send it to your printer. The **File** option sends the information to a file for future processing. Each of these will be dealt with in some detail later in the book. For now, click on the **Printer** option.

Once the options have been set, you need to click on one of the buttons at the bottom of the Customer Reports dialogue box. Click on the **Run** button. Figure 2.9 shows three dialogue boxes that depict in turn the stages that will be gone through to print your report.

The first dialogue box, shown in Fig. 2.9(a), is the Additional Report Filter. This allows you to define the starting and finishing accounts you want on your report. If you entered the exact customers in the sample in this chapter, then the **From** would be SL0010 and the **To** SL0070. Leaving them both as they are, however, will print a list of all customers. Click on the **OK** button now to proceed.

The next dialogue box that will appear is Creating Report, as appears in Fig. 2.9(b). This shows the report being created in preparation for printing.

The Print dialogue box will then appear, as in Fig. 2.9(c), which will vary according to how your Windows has been set up. Check that you have a printer connected and click on the **OK** button to start printing. The result should be a report listing your customers, contact names, telephone numbers and fax numbers.

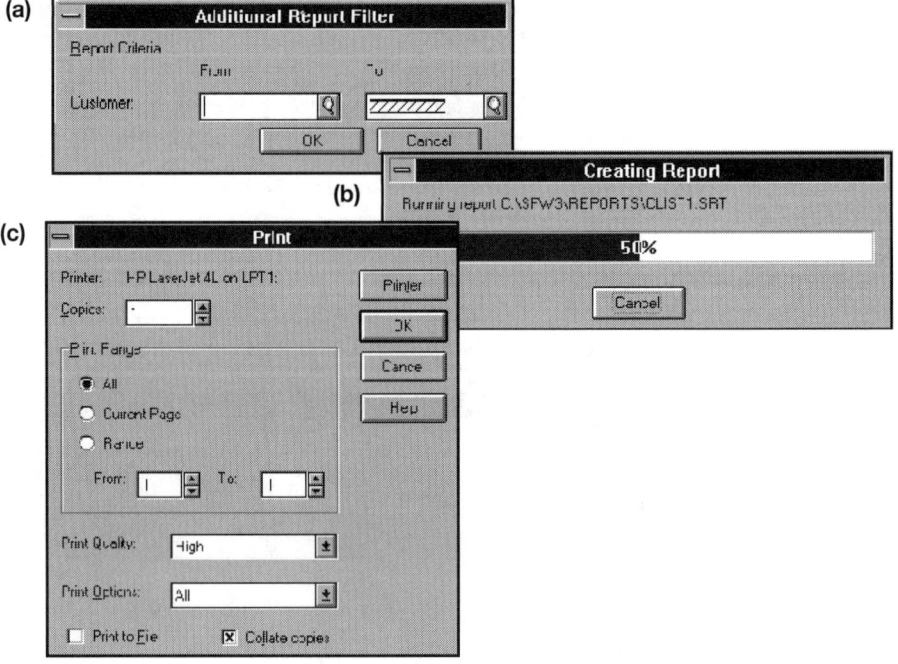

Fig. 2.9

PRACTICE Controlling where information is output is a feature of the Sage package and you should try to become familiar with it as soon as possible. Try some of the other reports in the same way.

When you have finished with the customer reports, click on the **Close** button to return to the main Customers screen.

CUSTOMER INVOICES AND CREDIT NOTES

Before you can enter details of invoices that have been sent to customers and any credit notes, you will need to make sure that the system is aware of the VAT rate to be charged. If a business is registered for VAT then it is obliged to charge its customers VAT and pass this sum on to HM Customs & Excise. At the time of writing, the following VAT rates apply:

- zero rate on some items, such as food and children's clothing;
- standard rate of 17.5 per cent;
- exempt items.

Zero-rated items are those goods and services that the UK government chooses not to tax, while exempt items are those that cannot be taxed under European Union regulations. It is the responsibility of the business to ensure the correct amount of VAT is applied to the goods and services it provides. Most businesses will be aware of this from the outset. What is required for the purpose of running the Sage package is to let the computer become aware of this. Figure 2.10 shows two screen portions that are activated separately but show you what is required when setting up VAT rates.

Make sure that you are now in the main Customer Record menu. The pull-down menu mentioned earlier appears on the second line from the top of your screen. One of the options on the menu bar is **Defaults**. Click on this option to pull down a small menu (*see* Fig. 2.10(a)). It should now be clear why this is referred to as a pull-down menu.

From here, select the **Tax Codes** option to reveal the Tax Codes dialogue box as shown in Fig. 2.10(b). To change the VAT rates table, highlight the code you want altered with your mouse, and then click on the **Edit** button. The screen will then show a dialogue box allowing you to enter the different rates. You may also observe, that codes can be set up for customers who are based in other countries of the European Union. When exporting to other countries in the European Union, you will have to charge customers their own domestic rates of VAT which are often different to those of the UK. When selling to countries outside the European Union, no VAT need be charged. (Overseas trade will be dealt with in a later chapter.) Whether selling within or outside the UK, it is important to note that *all* charges of VAT must be recorded and later declared. VAT is a tax imposed on consumers that must be collected by the business and later passed on to HM Customs & Excise. Without recording whether VAT is charged or not (and how much), the business is unable to report properly what it has collected.

(a) 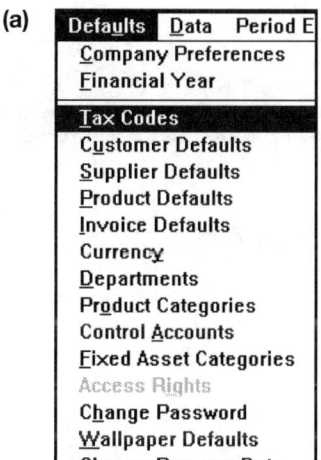   (b)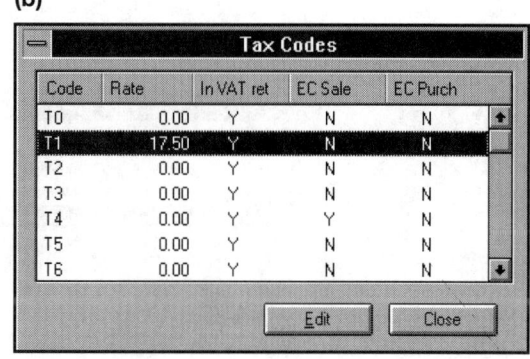

Fig. 2.10

Entering invoices

You are now able to enter invoice details against a customer. When entering invoice details to customer records, it is important to understand that at this stage you will not be generating invoices that can be sent out to customers. What will be entered are details of invoices that have already been created. Chapter 8 will show you how to use Sage to create invoices.

From the main Customers menu click on the **Batch Invoice** icon. The next stage will be to determine against which customer you want to set an invoice. From Fig. 2.11, you will see that Sage allows you to select the customer from a list. A small icon, called a **Finder**, appears next to the **A/C** box. Click on this as shown in Fig. 2.11 to reveal a list of customer accounts.

Now click on the customer required – say, SL0030 Harriers Football Club – and then click on **OK** to start the processing. The main Customer Invoice screen requires summary details about the invoice as shown in Fig. 2.12.

Once the **A/C** box has had an account number entered in it, the **Account Name** will automatically be shown. The **Date** will default to that of the computer system, but you should enter the date shown on the invoice if this is different. The **Ref** box is for an invoice reference, usually the invoice number. Each invoice issued by a business must have a unique invoice number or reference to distinguish it from all other invoices.

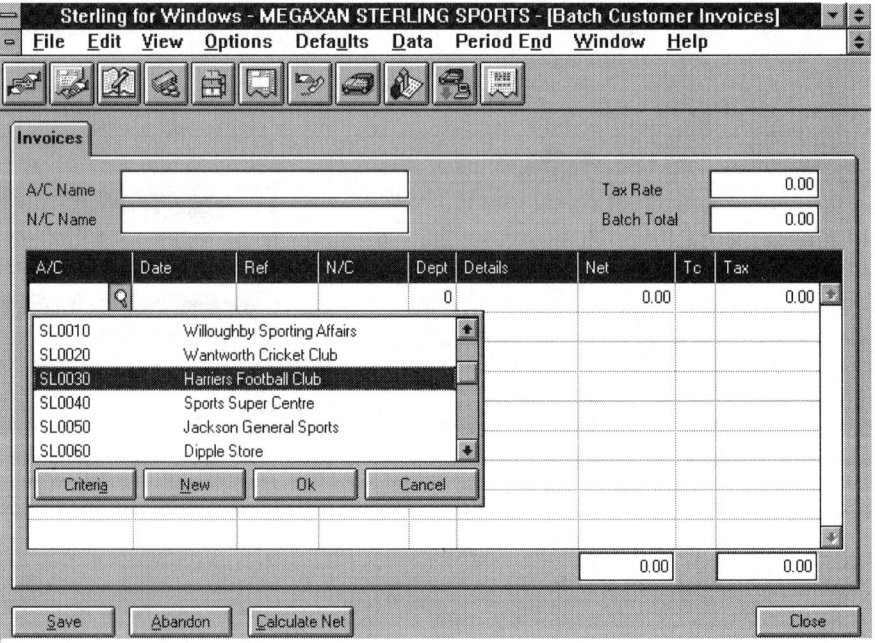

Fig. 2.11

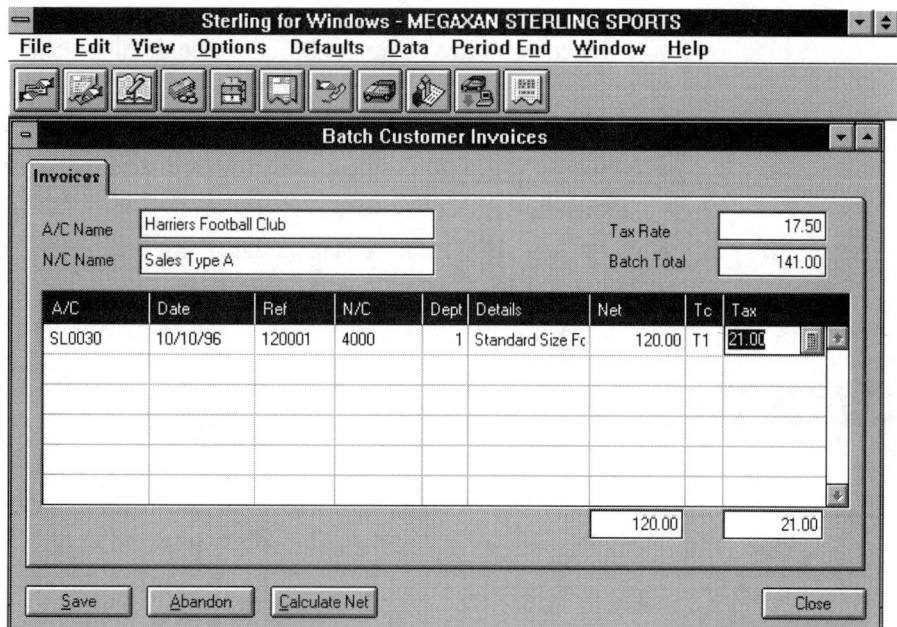

Fig. 2.12

The invoice lines then appear below beginning with the **N/C** column. Each line can represent a different product. The **N/C** column refers to a nominal code. These nominal codes refer to an account that has been set up in the Nominal Ledger (covered in detail in Chapter 5). The code 4000 that appears in Fig. 2.12 is an account code that will be used to record all sales figures, net of VAT. Irrespective of the customers to whom the invoices are being sent, sales information can be stored in this way. For now, it is suggested you use this 4000 code for all invoice lines. When the **N/C** code (4000) has been entered, the name of that account (Sales Type A) is automatically shown – this being the name of the nominal account.

The **Details** column is for your own use and is there for future reference so that you know what you are selling. The **Net** amount is then entered – that is, the amount exclusive of VAT (£120 in Fig. 2.12). The VAT is then calculated for you, based on the rate that was set earlier against the code placed in column **Tc**, and automatically entered in the **Tax** column when you press Enter.

If you have the gross amount (i.e. the amount including VAT) but have not calculated VAT, then Sage has the facility to calculate the VAT for you. To do this, enter the *total* invoice amount in the **Net** amount box and then click on the **Calculate Net** button that appears at the foot of the dialogue box. The effect will be to calculate VAT and deduct this from the gross amount entered.

As each line is entered, the totals of Net, VAT and Gross are calculated for you. When you have completed the invoice details, click on the **Save** button to record the invoice details and update how much the customer will now owe the business. The result of this transaction, therefore, is to:

- increase the amount the customer owes by the gross figure;
- record the VAT collected;
- record the amount of sales (this figure not including VAT);
- update the audit trail (*see* Chapter 10).

PRACTICE

From the list of invoice details in Table 2.1, enter these as invoices to your customers adding a few of your own through the invoices options from the Customer Records.

Table 2.1

A/c	N/C	Date	Ref	Dept	Details	Net (£)	VAT (£)
SL0030	4000	101096	120001	1	Standard size footballs	120.00	21.00
SL0010	4000	101096	120002	1	Cricket balls	30.00	5.25
SL0010	4000	101096	120002	1	Sports bags	17.02	2.98
SL0020	4000	101096	120003	1	Cricket sets	220.00	38.50
SL0020	4000	101096	120003	1	Scarves	25.00	4.38
SL0020	4000	101096	120003	1	Soccer balls	40.00	7.00
SL0030	4000	101096	120004	1	Shirts and shorts	468.09	81.91
SL0040	4000	101096	120005	1	Bat, ball and pads	320.00	56.00
SL0050	4000	101096	120006	1	Hats, scarves	88.00	15.40
SL0050	4000	101096	120006	1	Squash balls	17.02	2.98
SL0060	4000	020296	120007	1	Shirts and shorts	350.00	61.25
SL0060	4000	020296	120006	1	Footwear	200.00	35.00

These transactions will have the effect of debiting each customer's account by the net and VAT amounts. In other words, the size of debtors to the business will have increased. Eventually, customers will begin to pay off some or all of their accounts and this will have the effect of seeing their accounts credited.

As a useful tip, when you are typing in details that are a repeat of the line above, you can use the repeat key, **F6**, instead of typing in the figure again.

When you have entered the invoices, click on the **Close** button to return to the main Customer screen in preparation for entering some credit notes.

Entering credit notes

A credit note has the effect of crediting the customer's account in the same way as it would if the customer paid. Consequently, the effect of issuing a credit note to a customer is to reduce the amount the customer owes. It is also worth noting, that when an account is credited in this way, it will also reduce the amount of VAT that has to be passed on to HM Customs & Excise. There could be a number of reasons why a credit note entry has to be made:

- A customer has returned goods. In this instance you should use a nominal account for goods returned inward to distinguish it from a sale.
- A subsequent discount may be offered for some reason.
- You may want to correct an overcharge made on a customer or counteract an invoice against a customer that should not have been issued.

This activity works in almost the same way as entering an invoice. To enter a credit note, click on the **Credit Note** icon from the Customers screen and, using the example shown in Fig. 2.13, enter a credit note against a customer.

You will see from Fig. 2.13 that a new account in the Nominal Ledger has been created in order to record all sales returns. To do this, click on the small icon to the right of **N/C** to reveal a new dialogue box containing a list of nominal accounts. Click on **New** to indicate you want to create a new nominal account. From here enter the details as **Account Number** 4010 with the **Account Name** as Sales Returns. Then click on **OK** to return to the Batch Customer Credits dialogue box.

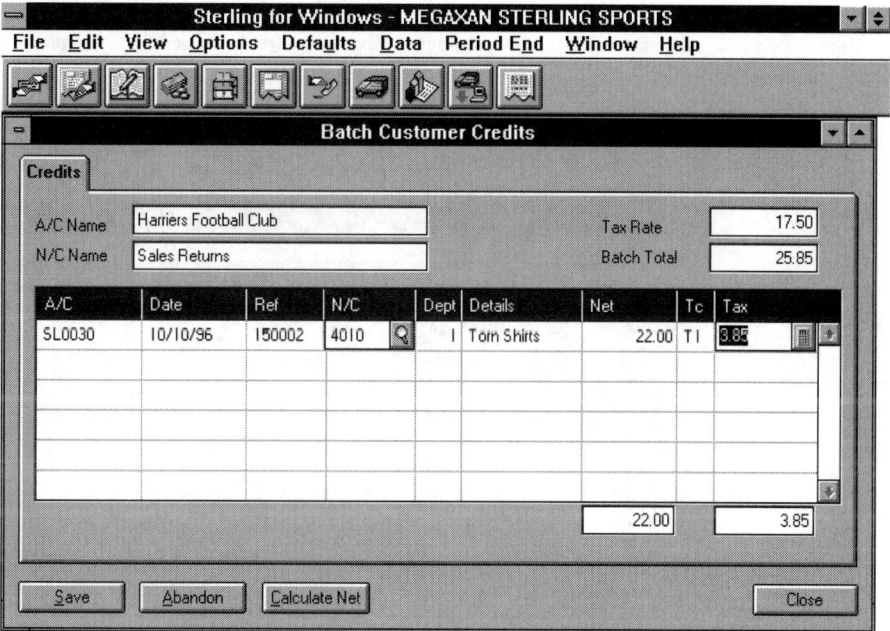

Fig. 2.13

When completed, click on **Save** to record the credit note transaction and **Close** to return to the main Customers screen.

Entering receipts

For any business to survive, it will need to receive payment from its customers. In order to enter a receipt from a customer, you will need to enter a different part of the program. At this stage, make sure you are back at the Customers main screen. The screen should show two rows of icons – the lower being the Customer icons and the higher being the main program icons.

Now click on the **Bank** icon from the upper row of icons to reveal a new set of icons that are related to banking transactions.

At this stage, a new part of the program has shown a Banking window placed over the Customers window. In Chapter 3, you will investigate this window arrangement a little further.

In order to enter details about a customer making a payment, you will need to click on the **Customer Receipt** icon from the set of banking icons. This will reveal a new dialogue box that has to be completed in a similar way to that shown in Fig. 2.14.

Before you can enter details about which invoices are being paid, you must enter the account reference (**A/C**) of the customer. You can access a list of customers as you did before by clicking on the **Finder** icon to the right of **A/C**.

Fig. 2.14

The **Name** of the account will be displayed automatically when you have entered the account reference. The **date** is generated automatically from the computer's system date (change if you wish). The **Ref** box can be filled in according to whatever the business wishes and could, for example, hold the customer's cheque number. The **Amount** will be the amount the cheque has been made out for.

When the top of the screen has been completed, it is now a matter of determining which invoices the cheque has been sent to cover. In the example shown in Fig. 2.14, the cheque received amounts to £520 and is going to settle an amount of £540 – the difference being a cash discount granted to the customer. To do this, enter the 290.00 in the **Paid** box of the first row and 10.00 in the **Discount** box. When the **Bank Balance** figure in the bottom left-hand box equals the **Amount** of the cheque entered, the system will allow you to click on the **Save** button at the bottom of the screen to record the transaction. To complete this process, enter 230.00 in the **Amount** box of the second row and 10.00 in its **Discount** box, then click on the **Save** button. Clicking on **Pay in Full** will have the effect of paying an invoice in full, providing there is sufficient to pay it.

A quicker way of settling invoices would be to enter the amount of the cheque and, instead of entering the amounts against each invoice, click on the **Automatic** button at the bottom of the screen. The effect of this will be to settle the longest outstanding debt first and to carry on through the list of invoices until the whole amount has been accounted for. It will not, however, enter any cash discounts you choose to offer the customer.

If a customer has been issued a credit note, then this credit note can be used to settle an invoice in exactly the same way as a cheque was used. All that is required is to click on the **Credit Note** line to highlight the transaction and then click on the **Pay in Full** button.

If you click on the **Wizard** button, Sage will take you through a sequence of events automatically. This guidance is further supplemented with help on what to do as you go through the required stages.

When payments and credit notes have been allocated against invoices, the account balances will have been reduced accordingly.

PRACTICE Before moving on to the next section, enter a few more payments and credit notes.

EXTRACTING CUSTOMER REPORTS

In the final section of this chapter, you will extract three reports that will give you details about the transactions you have entered against your customers. Each of the reports can be extracted through the Customers part of the program. If you are still in the Bank part of the program, you will need to exit from this. You can either click on the **Close** button or, holding down the **Ctrl** (Control) key, press the function key **F4**.

There are many reports available in this section but the main ones you will look at are customer activity reports, aged debtors lists and customer statements.

Customer activity reports

While in the main Customers window, click on the **Activity** icon to reveal a Defaults dialogue similar to that shown in Fig. 2.15. This allows you to define what transactions you want to examine (**Transaction Range**) and between which dates (**Date Range**).

By clicking immediately on the **OK** button you will accept the defaults given and work on all transactions entered so far. When this has been done, you will see a Transactions window for the first customer on your list (*see* Fig. 2.16).

This produces a detailed summary of a customer account with a list of the business undertaken with that customer. The top part shows the account number (**A/C**), account name (**Name**) and the **Credit Limit**. The **Credit Limit** was set when the customer record was created. The **Balance** figure is the amount the customer now owes the business and will include VAT. The **Amount Paid** figure is the total paid by the customer to date. The **Turnover YTD** represents the total value of sales excluding VAT.

VAT, although collected from customers and passed on to HM Customs & Excise, is still owed by the customer if the invoice has not been settled. With the exception of small firms, the VAT is owed by the business to HM Customs & Excise when the invoice is issued rather than when the money is actually collected. In terms of the sales figures, the business will need the amounts net of VAT if it is to eventually determine whether it is making a profit or not.

Now move on to the transaction details.

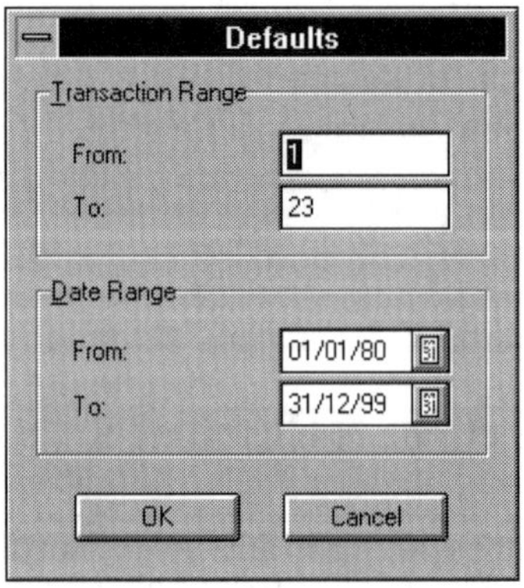

Fig. 2.15

The customer accounts

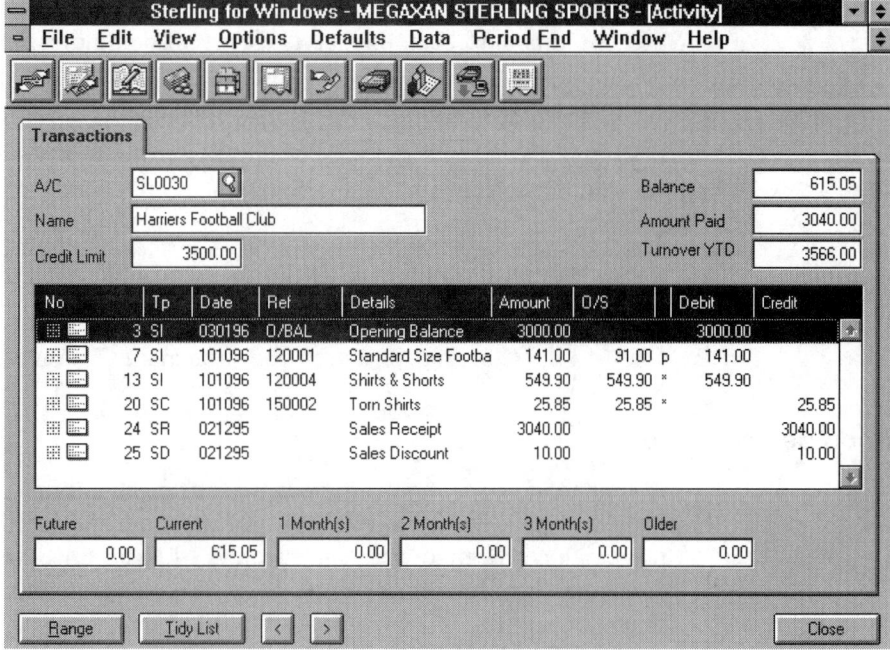

Fig. 2.16

The number that appears in the first column (**No**) is the transaction number. Each transaction you have entered will have been given a separate number in the sequence in which the transaction was carried out.

The second column (**Tp**) indicates the transaction type. These types are shown as:

- **SI** Sales Invoice
- **SC** Sales Credit
- **SR** Sales Receipt
- **SD** Sales Discount

The **Ref** and **Details** columns were entered when the details were originally entered. The **Amount** column shows the value of the transaction.

The **O/S** column is the amount outstanding on the transaction, where appropriate. In the case of Transaction 7, the customer has been debited by a total of £141 for standard size footballs. Part of this invoice amount has been paid, as indicated by the small 'p' next to the value. This has left £91 still to pay on this invoice. Transaction 13 shows that nothing has yet been paid, as indicated by the * (asterisk) beside the **O/S** figure. The **SC** (Sales Credit) figure has not yet been used to offset an invoice amount. The sum of the debits less the sum of the credits will give you the balance, which is the amount the customer owes.

At the foot of this panel is a summary of what is outstanding and how long the amounts have been owing. The **Current** box indicates that £615.05 is now outstanding and is to be paid. If a figure appears in the **Future** box, this indicates the amount appears on post-dated invoices.

If you click on either the < or > buttons at the bottom of the dialogue box, you can move from customer to customer.

The **Tidy List** button has the effect of removing sub-items from view while the **Range** button allows you to select another range of transactions in the sales history of the customer.

Click on the **Close** button to return to the main Customers window.

Aged debtors reports

Rather than supplying a simple statement of how much each customer owes, Sage will produce an aged debtors report giving details of how long customers have been owing the money. Making sure you are in the main Customers window, click on the **Aged Balances** icon and a window similar to that shown in Fig. 2.17 will appear.

The first column shows the account number only. The next two columns will show both the year-to-date (**YTD**) turnover net of VAT and the customer **Credit Limit**. The **Balance** column is the amount owed by the customer as

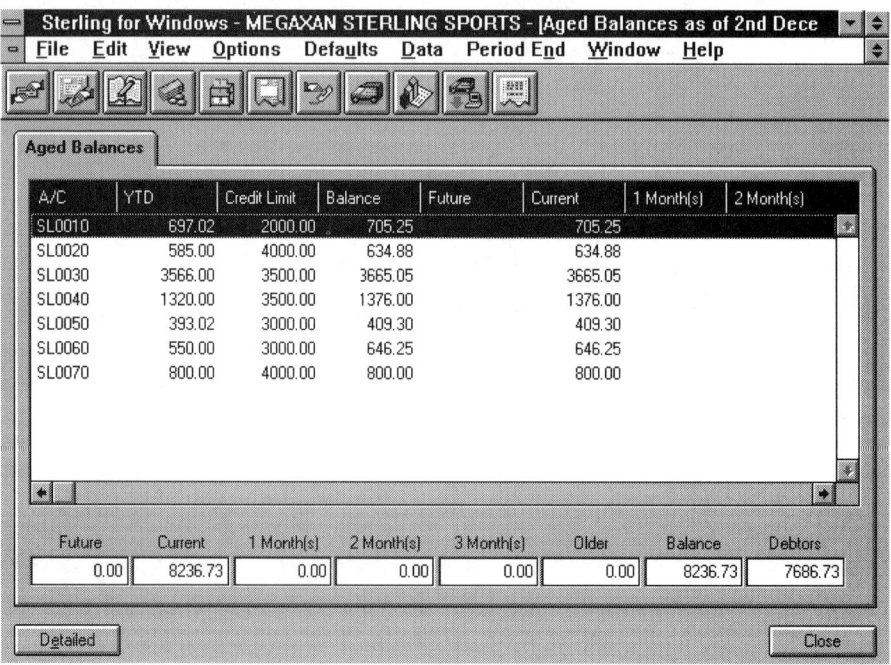

Fig. 2.17

shown in the previous section. The **Current** column shows the amount that is owed and has been outstanding to the business for less than 30 days. The other columns all show zeros. This is because you have only just set up the system. As time goes by, figures will appear in these columns. The use of such a report can alert a business to a potential problem, in that if a customer allows debt to be outstanding too long, you ought to chase it up.

It will always be in the best interest of a business to have its customers pay as soon as possible. While the debt is outstanding, the business is effectively lending its money to another firm. Such money can earn interest in the business's bank accounts or can be used to reduce its own debt. Furthermore, when a customer leaves a debt too long, there is the danger that the customer is in trouble and will not be able to pay at all. The dilemma many businesses face is that to press their customers too hard to settle early payment may result in the loss of trade with them.

Customer statements

Customer statements are reports which are normally sent monthly to customers when a business has undergone large amounts of transactions on a credit-term basis. When the package is first installed, three report files are included, each one assuming you are using preprinted stationery available from Sage.

To create a statement, click on the **Statements** icon from the main Customers menu. You will now have a choice of three statement types. Unless you have the preprinted stationery, there is little point in printing them at this stage. To get an appreciation of what is possible, however, select one of the statement types and set the output to **Preview**; then click on **Run**.

The statement will include a list of all recent transactions along with details of any outstanding invoices. This will allow customers to check your records against theirs and, if any discrepancies do occur, they can be put right. Along with such details, a statement will include a remittance section. This allows customers to send this back with a payment, making it easier for them to pay you and, when a cheque does come back, for you to more easily identify the customer who is paying you.

DISCOUNTS

It was mentioned earlier that it is not in the best interests of a business to allow customers to settle accounts too far into the future. Rather than issue threatening letters or impolite inferences on invoices, many businesses offer settlement discounts to their customers if they settle early.

In the event of discounts being offered under such circumstances, you would enter these amounts when you record a sales receipt. When you examine purchases in Chapter 3, you will see further how this works.

It is worth noting at this stage that allowing cash discounts in this fashion is quite distinct from offering a trade discount. A trade discount is normally offered to another firm in the trade which buys large quantities. Such trade discounts will result in the invoice amount being lower in the first instance. Consequently, you should enter the amounts of settlement discounts into the computer *after* the trade discounts have been allowed for. This is important as the invoice amount (with VAT) is an indication of what is owed by the customer.

EXITING SAGE

To exit from the package, you can perform one of three actions:

- Click on the **Exit** icon that appears on the top of the screen.
- Hold down the **Alt** key and press function key **F4**.
- From the menu bar, click on **File**, then **Exit**.

Whichever one is used, Sage offers you the chance to **Backup**. This will copy all your company data onto a floppy disk for safe keeping. In the event of loss of data, you can later restore the data. For now, click on **No** to exit Sage and return to Windows. Backing up will be discussed in greater detail in Chapter 3.

EXERCISES

As a way of gaining practice, you should try the following tasks:

1. Create at least 12 new customer accounts.
2. Generate for each customer at least two invoices.
3. Generate for four of your customers a credit note each.
4. Receive a payment from five of your customers.
5. Produce activity reports on two of the accounts.
6. Produce an aged debtors report.
7. Determine the outstanding debtors total.

It is not essential to produce printer listings of these, but simply to be able to access such information. Printed output will be covered in greater detail in Chapter 3.

CHAPTER 3

The supplier accounts

INTRODUCTION

Having worked with the customer accounts, you will find that working with suppliers is fairly similar with a common set of keystrokes. All supplier accounts will be organised into what is commonly called the Purchase Ledger. The purpose of the Purchase Ledger, therefore, is to record and help manage all transactions with suppliers.

With the Sales Ledger, you were only concerned with trading sales, namely your customers. You will need to use the Purchase Ledger for all purchases made on a credit-term basis.

The Purchase Ledger can be used just as effectively for services acquired as it can for goods bought (or a combination of both). As depicted in Fig. 3.1, facilities offered by a Purchase Ledger must include allowing a user to create, delete or amend a supplier's details on the ledger as well as to record all transactions between the business and supplier. Good reporting on the Purchase Ledger would also be important to ensure the business is keeping within defined budgets and is not building up too much expensive debt. Controlling expenditure will always be an important part of business management and, although an efficient Purchase Ledger will not by itself control expenditure, the system should be capable of reporting any problems quickly so they can be rectified. Another important requirement of the Purchase Ledger to many businesses is to assist them in offering information on VAT paid out to their suppliers.

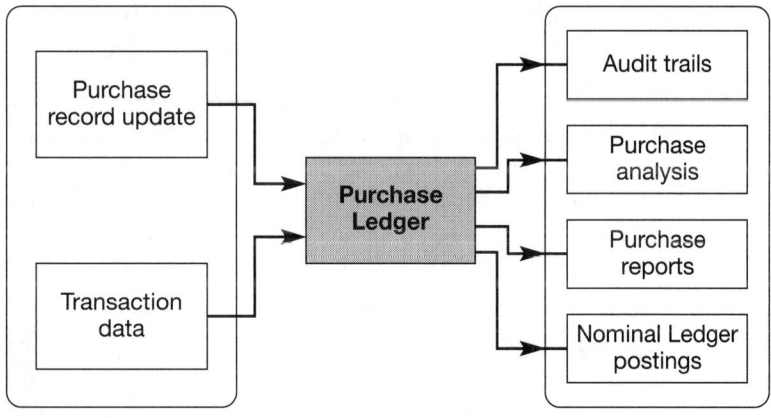

Fig. 3.1

In general, purchases can fall into one of three categories:

- *Purchases for trading*, such as the purchase of raw materials that will go into stock for future manufacturing purposes, or purchases of stock for later resale.
- *Purchases related to business expenses*, such as stationery, computer accessories and general office supplies. Such purchases will make up the overhead expenses of running a business.
- *Capital equipment purchases* such as new machinery, delivery vans or the purchase of fixtures and fittings.

Other categories may also be identified, dependent on the particular type of business. Regardless of the type or nature of purchases, the Purchase Ledger will treat them all exactly the same way. The category of goods or services purchased will have to be considered when invoice details are entered in the Purchase Ledger, and when purchase details are recorded in the Nominal Ledger. When dealing with sales earlier, all sales figures, for the sake of convenience, were posted to a single sales account (4000 Sales Type A) in the Sales Ledger – a convenience that cannot be afforded with the Purchase Ledger.

The Purchase Ledger, in many ways, is the inverted function to that of the Sales Ledger in that its function is almost the same as the Sales Ledger, but goods and services enter the business while payments for these goods and services result in money leaving the business bank account. The effect will be that the nominal accounts that will be used to record the purchases coming into the business, will be *debited* by the purchases while the Purchase Ledger accounts of the suppliers will be *credited* by the purchase value. When sales were made, it was the customer accounts in the Sales Ledger that were debited while the nominal accounts were credited.

Most of the activities carried out within the Purchase Ledger are similar to those of the Sales Ledger. The invoice details that are entered into the Purchase Ledger will be a recording of basic details on the invoices sent by the suppliers. As with sales, it is often a good idea to *batch process* the invoices – that is, entering a series of invoices at one time rather than entering them on an *ad hoc* basis or when they arrive.

At the end of each accounting period (normally each month) there will be an end-of-period summarising activity. Such an activity is carried out on both the customers and suppliers. The result of this will be to remove any invoices that have been completely settled. This will be necessary to ensure that the data held in accounts do not become unnecessarily large as well as supplying important information needed by the business, such as details about VAT receipts and payments for the month.

As an important point, do not destroy or dispose of any supplier's invoices or credit notes. Once their details have been entered on to the computer, such documents should be filed in a safe place in case they are required for future reference – as a good number of them will be.

As a final point in this introduction, you will not be required to enter any cash purchases into the Purchase Ledger. It will work in much the same way as the Sales Ledger in that cash purchases will be entered through the Cash Transactions part of the Sage package (covered in some length in Chapter 4). Consequently, you will only be dealing with suppliers from whom you buy on a credit-term basis.

CREATING SUPPLIERS

Before you can process any transactions with suppliers, you will need to enter the details of your suppliers. Such details will be used to build up a database of suppliers against which various transactions can be associated. To get started, you will need to make sure you are at the main window that shows a set of icons where the icon labelled **Suppliers** is second from the left (this window appears after you have entered your password).

Now click on the **Suppliers** icon to reveal the Suppliers window. Figure 3.2 shows the Suppliers window with Customers placed underneath it in order to show the difference between the two windows.

As you will observe, they are virtually the same. There are only two differences between them. The first difference is that the title bars reflect what they deal with and the Customers window has a **Statement** icon that does not

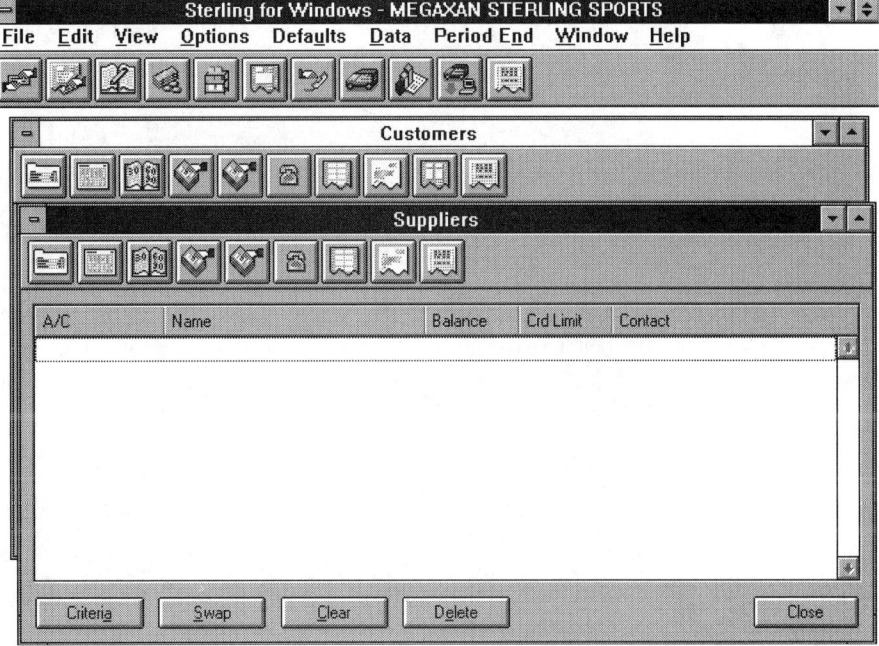

Fig. 3.2

appear on the row of Supplier icons. This is because the business may wish to send its customers statements of their account, while the suppliers will not receive such statements but will often send them.

Now you are able to begin creating some suppliers. From the Suppliers window click on the **Record** icon to reveal a blank Supplier Record form. The details, once entered through this form, will be stored as a supplier record, and give the *standing* (or *static*) details of a supplier – in other words, details about a supplier that only change infrequently such as the address. This compares with the *non-standing* (or *dynamic*) transactions data on each activity, which are entered and amended on a regular basis.

The fields that make up a supplier record are similar to those of the customer records set up in the Sales Ledger. The field that holds the supplier account number (**A/C**) is a *key field* in that it is the key that identifies the supplier. It may be possible that a supplier to a business is also a customer. In this event, an account in each ledger is required.

Account numbers in the Purchase Ledger can be the same as those in the Sales Ledger. However, this is unwise as it could cause some confusion at a later stage.

Figure 3.3 shows a completed Details form for a supplier.

The supplier account number (**A/C**) is prefixed with 'PL' to illustrate that letters and numbers can be combined to create supplier record references. In this

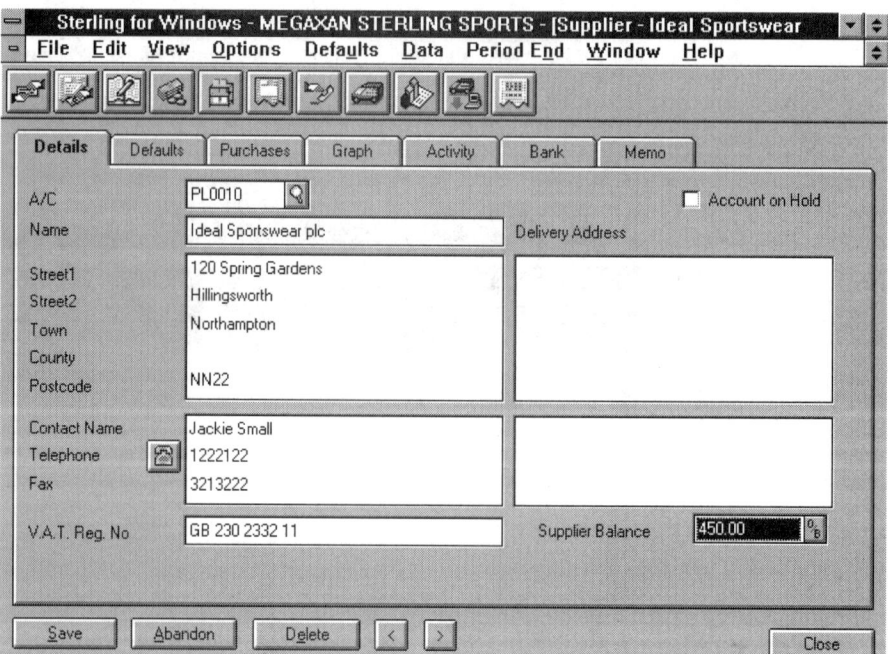

Fig. 3.3

instance, the 'PL' has been used to indicate that the record belongs to a supplier; when working with the Sales Ledger, all customer records were prefixed 'SL'.

The address, **Contact Name**, **Telephone** number and **Fax** number are entered in exactly the same way as with the customers. The **VAT Registration Number** of a supplier is now required if you are purchasing goods or services from a supplier who is based in a European Union country other than the UK. Such numbers will have to appear on any orders you place with such suppliers. When entering details into cells, you can move from box to box by pressing the **Tab** key on your keyboard rather than using your mouse to click on the relevant box.

The **Supplier Balance** box shows that there is an amount of £450.00 now outstanding with the supplier. To enter this opening balance, you have to click on the **O/B** button that appears in the **Supplier Balance** box. The opening details of any outstanding invoices (or credit notes) are then entered, after saving the record details, in exactly the same way as you did when creating opening balances for your customers.

At this stage, click on the page tab labelled **Defaults**; the resulting dialogue box is shown in Fig. 3.4. The **Credit Limit** is imposed on the business by the supplier and should be known by the business. If no such credit limit exists, then this should be left blank. When the credit limit is reached, it would normally mean that the business is unable to receive more from its supplier until a payment is made to bring the balance to within the credit limit.

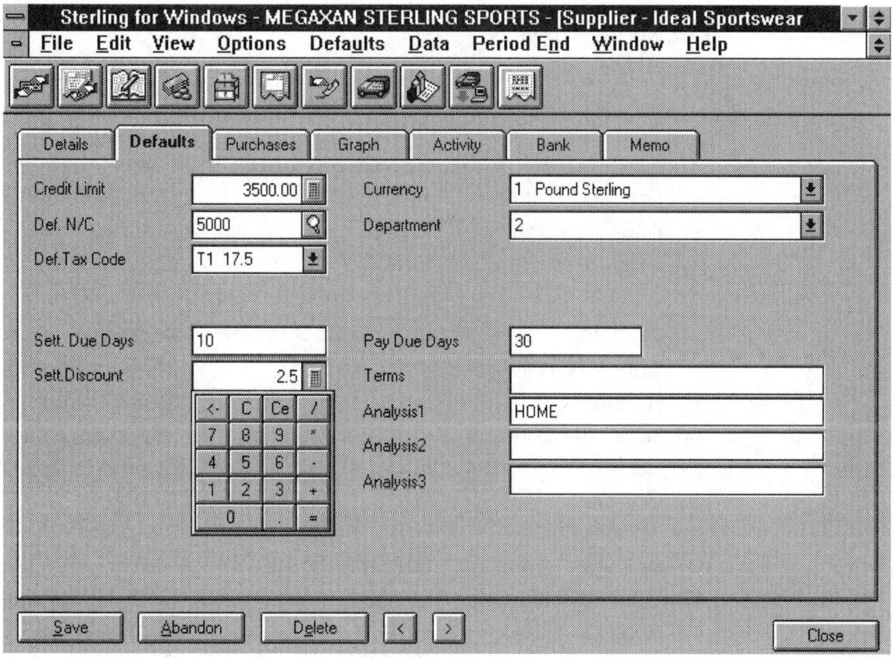

Fig. 3.4

The **Default Nominal Code** of 5000 that appears in Fig. 3.4 is where purchases from this supplier will automatically be posted if an alternative code is not entered. The **Default Tax Code** of 17.5 per cent will assume this is the rate of VAT to be charged. The settlement due days (**Sett. Due Days**) and settlement discount (**Sett. Discount**) indicate that, if payment is made within ten days of the invoice date, you can claim a 2.5 per cent discount. To the right of the **Settlement Discount** box appears an icon of a calculator. If you click on this, you will see a small calculator appear on your screen. This can be used just like a calculator, using your mouse, in that you click on the buttons rather than press them. When you click on the equals sign, the result of the calculation will appear in the box.

The **Currency** and **Department** are set in the same way as for a customer record. The **Terms** show that this supplier expects to be paid within 30 days of an invoice being issued. Finally, the **Analysis** lines are all used for reference to be determined by the business in what ever way it wishes.

PRACTICE

At this stage, you should enter some supplier records so that you have something constructive to work with. The list shown here gives some suggestions but you should feel free to add a few of your own as well.

PL0010
Ideal Sportswear plc
120 Spring Gardens
Hillingsworth
Northampton
NN22
Contact: Jackie Small
Telephone: 1222122
Fax: 3213222
Opening balance: £450
Analysis code: HOME
Credit limit: £3500

PL0020
James & Nichols plc
1 French Avenue
Stevenage
Herts
SG2 9AA
Contact: David
Telephone: 01438 5252411
Fax: 01438 0100201
Opening balance: £2100
Analysis code: HOME
Credit limit: £4000

PL0030
Sports Supplies Inc
Runners Square
New York 2000
USA
Contact: Bill
Telephone: 010 299299101
Fax: 010 299230000
Opening balance: £2150
Analysis code: USA
Credit limit: £4500

PL0040
Minerva Football Club Ltd
Metro Centre
St Albans Road
St Albans AL5 0BY
Contact: John or Richard
Telephone: 29991
Fax: 28182
Opening balance: £650
Analysis code: HOME
Credit limit: £2000

The supplier accounts

PL0050		PL0060	
Odessa Sports		Crazy Sporting World	
3 Town Square		Eastern House	
The Hyde		Main Square	
Adelaide		Calcutta	
South Australia		India	
Contact:	Andy	Contact:	Satinder
Telephone:	010 209 3000111	Telephone:	010 9292992
Fax:	010 209 3111000	Fax:	010 9292883
Opening balance:	£1250	Opening balance:	£1850
Analysis code:	AUSTRALIA	Analysis code:	INDIA
Credit limit:	£4000.	Credit limit:	£3000.

When you have entered these suppliers, return to the main Suppliers window by clicking on the **Close** button in the Suppliers Record window, ensuring that you have saved the last record *and* you have a blank record form.

Help windows

Before you start entering transaction data, it is worth obtaining from the computer a list of supplier details. From the main Supplier window, click on the **Report** icon. A new dialogue box will appear listing the reports that are available. Before requesting any reports, press function key **F1** on your keyboard to reveal a Help window similar to that shown in Fig. 3.5.

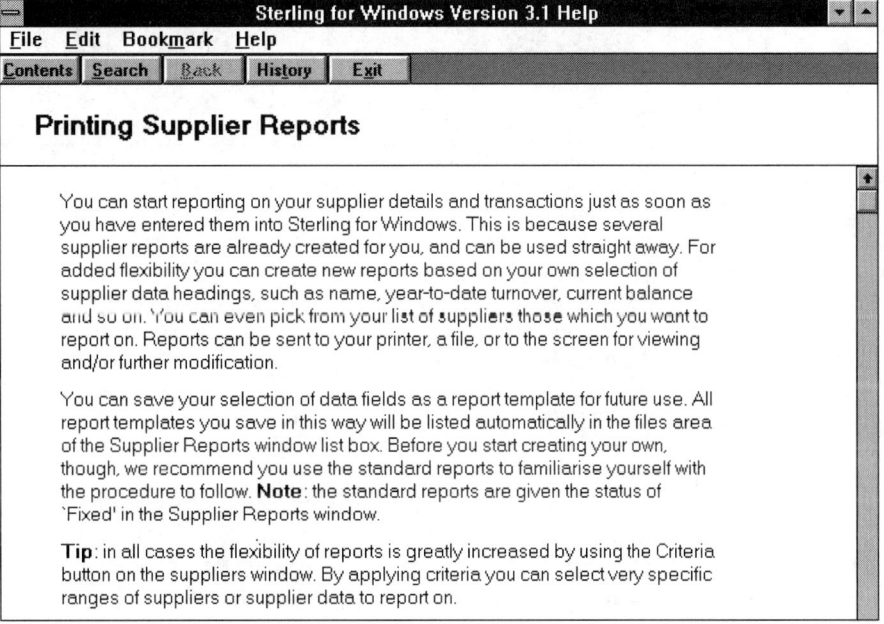

Fig. 3.5

The **Help** windows will give you some details about what to do at any stage and will serve as a useful memory jogger if you have forgotten how to perform a certain task. There are different Help windows according to where you are in the package. In this example, you are given an introductory Help window on customer and supplier reports. The Help window also presents you with a small set of contents allowing you to get further help on more specific topics. To activate any of these, you should move the mouse pointer over the topic (a small hand appears) and click on the topic of your choice. When you have finished with Help, you can return to your Suppliers window by clicking on the E**x**it button. An alternative way to exit from a window of this type is to hold down the **Ctrl** key and press function key **F4** once.

The Reports dialogue box should show a list of reports (*see* Fig. 3.6). These reports will have come with your Sage software. The number of reports can be added to by creating your own or reduced by deleting those that are no longer wanted. To select the supplier list, simply click on the report described as **Supplier List**. To the right of the list of reports is the **Output** panel offering you three options: **Printer** to print, **Preview** to see the report on your screen as it would appear on paper from your printer, and **File** to send the information to a file for future processing. Click on the **Printer** option to set output to print. Once the options have been set, you need to click on one of the buttons at the bottom of the Supplier Reports dialogue box. For now, click on the **R**un button. If a filter screen appears, then click on **OK** to accept any defaults offered to you. A Print dialogue box will

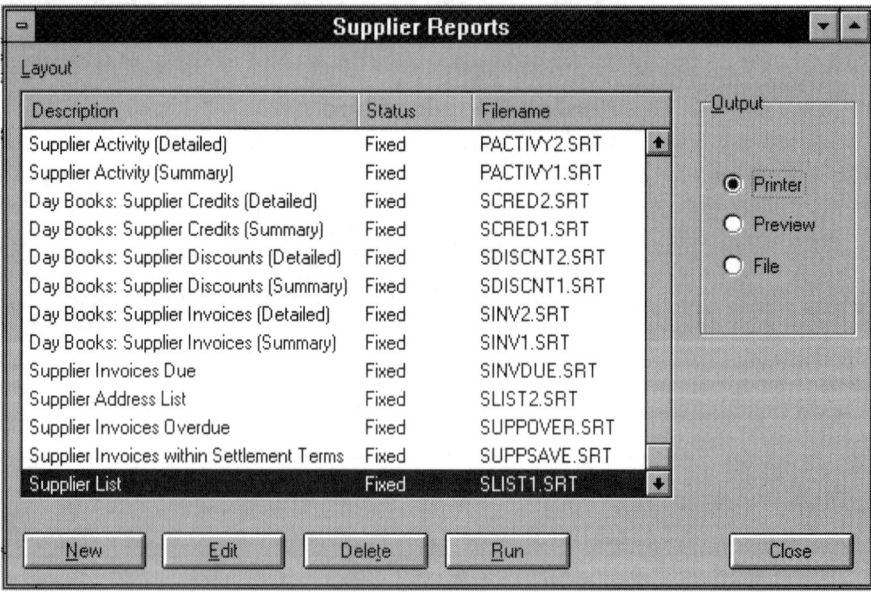

Fig. 3.6

appear, varying according to how your Windows has been set up. Check that you have a printer connected and click on the **OK** button to start printing. The result should be a report listing your suppliers with their contact names, telephone numbers and fax numbers. When you have finished with the Supplier Reports, click on the **Close** button to return to the main Suppliers window.

SUPPLIER INVOICES AND CREDIT NOTES

In this section you will be required to enter details of invoices and credit notes that have been received from suppliers. Before you can enter such details, you will need to make sure that the system is aware of the rates of VAT. As this was set up when you worked in the Sales Ledger, there will be no need to enter these details again. If a business is registered for VAT then it is obliged to charge its customers VAT and later pass this on to HM Customs & Excise. With respect to purchasing, the business will be paying out VAT. In this event, the business can claim this VAT back from HM Customs & Excise.

Activities of this nature will involve entering a whole series of transactions. Each transaction will be stored in the computer as a transactions record. As with the transactions carried out with customers, a transaction record with a supplier will have its own record structure and will be stored as such. From these records, you will be able to extract various activity reports.

Entering invoices

Now you are in a position to enter invoice details against suppliers. In practice, you would be entering invoice details from those sent to you from suppliers. If invoices were being batch processed, then you would have a pile of these ready to be entered. From the main Suppliers window click on the **Batch Invoices** icon. The next stage will be to determine against which supplier you want to set an invoice. A small **Finder** icon appears next to the **A/C** box. Click on this **Finder** icon to reveal a list of supplier accounts.

Now click on the supplier required – say, PL0040 Minerva Football Club – in the list and then click on **OK** to start the processing. The main Supplier Invoice window requires summary details about the invoice as shown in Fig. 3.7.

Once the **A/C** box has had an account number entered in it, the **Account Name** will automatically be shown. The **Date** will default to that of the computer system, but you should enter the date shown on the supplier's invoice if this is different. The **Ref** box is for an invoice reference, usually the invoice number.

The invoice lines then appear below beginning with the **N/C** column. Each line can represent a different product. The **N/C** column refers to a *nominal code*. These nominal codes refer to an account that has been set up in the Nominal Ledger (covered in depth in Chapter 5). The code 5000 that appears

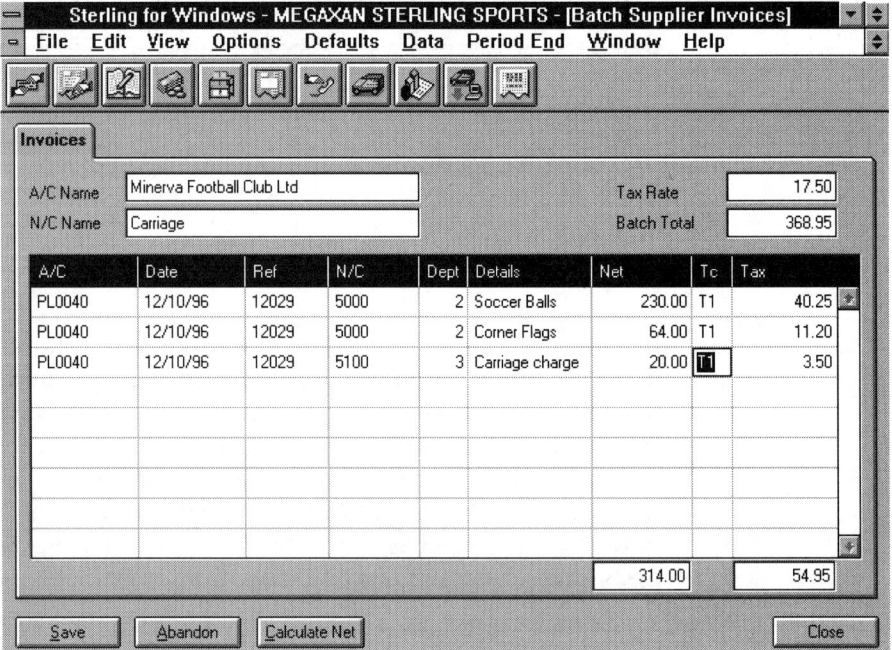

Fig. 3.7

in Fig. 3.7 is an account code that will be used to record purchase figures net of VAT. Irrespective of the suppliers who have sent the invoices, purchase information can be stored in this way. There are other purchase accounts available, but it may well be the case that none of these reflect, in their titles, the kind of goods that are being purchased. Such account names can be changed and new accounts created in the Nominal Ledger. For now, we will use Accounts 5000 (Material purchases) and 5001 (Imported materials) for the purchase of goods. Figure 3.7 also shows the use of a nominal code 5100 for the carriage cost. These nominal account names can be changed, as you will see later in this chapter.

The **Details** column is for your own use and is there for future reference so that you have a better idea about what you have purchased. The **Amount** is again entered and is an amount exclusive of VAT. The VAT is then calculated for you based on the rate that was set earlier against the code placed in column **Tc**.

If you have the gross amount but have not calculated the VAT, then Sage has the facility to calculate the VAT for you. To do this, enter the total invoice amount in the **Net** box and then click on the **Calculate Net** button that appears at the bottom of the screen. The effect will be to calculate VAT and deduct this from the total invoice amount which you entered.

As each line is entered, the totals of Net and VAT are calculated for you. When you have completed the invoice details, click on the **Save** button to record the invoice details and update how much you now owe the supplier. The result of this transaction, therefore, is to:

- increase the amount that is owed to the supplier – by the gross figure for each invoice;
- record the VAT that will be paid out;
- record the amount of purchases (this figure not including VAT);
- update the audit trail (*see* Chapter 10).

The VAT that appears on the invoices represents the VAT that has to be paid by the business to the supplier, in much the same way as VAT has to be paid by customers to the business. VAT, however, is a tax on consumer expenditure rather than on business expenditure. Consequently, the business will be able to claim this VAT back from HM Customs & Excise. In practice, the amount of VAT the business has to pay out will be deducted from the VAT it collects, with the balance then being due. In order for this to work properly, it is vital that the business keeps all documents stating the VAT to be paid if any VAT is to be reclaimed.

PRACTICE

Enter the list of invoice details in Table 3.1 as invoices against the suppliers, adding a few of your own, through the Invoices options from the Supplier Records.

Table 3.1

A/c	Date	Ref	N/C	Details	Net (£)	VAT (£)
PL0010	0080296	2100	5000	Shirts	500.00	87.50
PL0020	0080296	544152	5000	Tennis rackets	320.00	56.00
	0080296	544152	5000	Tennis balls	30.00	5.25
	0080296	544152	5000	Arm bands	25.00	4.38
PL0030	0080296	302/99	5001	Sports bags	250.00	
	0080296	302/99	5001	Sports shoes	330.00	
PL0040	0080296	12029	5000	Soccer balls	230.00	40.25
	0080296	12029	5100	Corner flags	22.00	3.85
PL0050	0080296	221112	5000	Football kits (clothing)	940.00	
	0080296	221112	5000	Rugby kits (clothing)	235.00	
PL0060	0080296	233112	5001	Squash rackets & balls	400.00	
	0080296	233112	5001	White socks & tie ups	180.00	
	0080296	233112	5101	Accessories	70.00	

When you have finished entering invoices, click on the **Close** button at the bottom of the Supplier Invoice window to return to the main Suppliers window.

Entering credit notes

Entering credit notes that have been received from your suppliers will have the effect of reducing the amount outstanding to them. A credit note often comes about because you have returned goods to the supplier for some reason. In entering credit note details, you will also have the opportunity of adding a new nominal account in order to record goods returned back to suppliers – to be called Returns Outward.

The effect of the credit note will be to *debit* the supplier's account while at the same time *crediting* the nominal account that will be created. This compares with the invoice that had the effect of crediting the supplier's account while debiting one of the nominal accounts that would record such purchase details.

A credit note will also have the effect of reducing the amount of VAT that can be claimed back from Customs & Excise. This is because, once the goods have been returned (or some other reason), the amount of the credit note will no longer be paid to the supplier, inclusive of the VAT.

From the main Suppliers window, click on the **Batch Credits** icon to reveal the Supplier Credit Note window. Entering the credit note details will be the same as that for invoices and as you did when entering credit notes for customers. Once the **A/C**, **Date** and **Ref** have been entered, click on the **Finder** icon next to **N/C** to select the nominal account. Instead of selecting a nominal code from the list, click on the **New** button. Figure 3.8 illustrates the kind of window that appears and the entry that can be made.

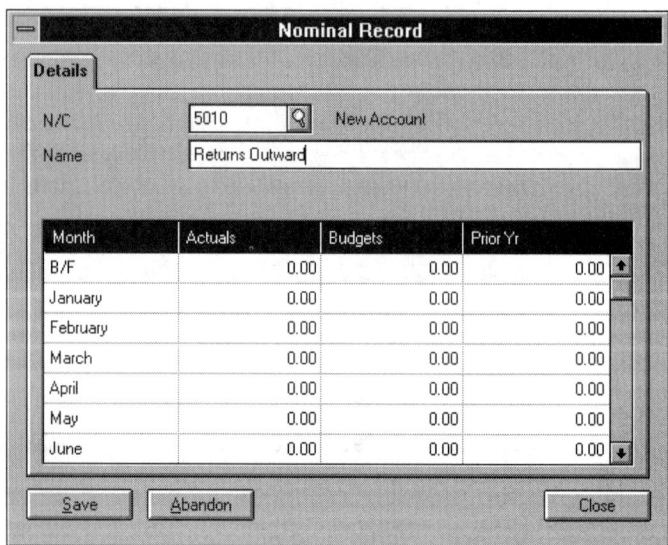

Fig. 3.8

The supplier accounts **49**

The only two entries that are needed are the **Nominal Code** and **Account Name**. In Fig. 3.8 the code 5010 has been given and the name Returns Outward to indicate that the goods are being taken out of stock to go back to the supplier. When adding new nominal accounts like this, you need to be sure that no other account has the same code.

When this has been done, click on the **Save** button to add the new account to the list, then click on the **OK** button so that credit details are posted to this new account via the Credit Note. From the Credit Note window, complete the credit set of details and click on the **Save** button to record the details.

PRACTICE Enter two more credit note details before moving on.

When you have finished entering credit notes, click on the **Close** button to return to the main Suppliers window.

Printing labels

Sage offers the facility of printing labels for all your suppliers and customers.

Make sure you are in the main Suppliers window and click on the **Labels** icon. The result of this is that a small dialogue box will appear on top of the Suppliers window. From Fig. 3.9 you will see that the dialogue box is on top but is probably in a different location on the screen to your own. If you are

Fig. 3.9

unable to see the window behind the Supplier Labels dialogue box, click on the **Normalise** button to the right of the title bar that contains the title Supplier Labels.

The dialogue box is a window in its own right and can be moved around the screen. Place your mouse on the title bar of this window (where it says Supplier Labels) and hold down the left button on your mouse without letting go. Now move the mouse slowly (again, not letting go) to the right and observe how the whole window moves. When you have moved the dialogue box to the right, let go of your mouse button and observe how the box has repositioned itself on the screen.

This ability to move windows about is a common feature of Windows applications such as this and is often referred to as *drag and drop*. Sage also allows you to have more than one window displayed at the same time.

Click on either of the file types in the **Description** box – each one representing a different file that prints labels for different types of stationery. Then click on the space to the left of **Preview** in the **Output** panel of the Suppliers Labels dialogue box to set output to Preview. Now click on the **Run** button to see on the screen what you will get if you print the labels. This offers you a list of names and addresses of your suppliers which, provided you have the stationery, can be printed on sticky-backed labels. If you want these printed, then click on the **Print** button at the bottom of the window. The other features of this will be investigated later.

To close this window, click on the **Close** button at the bottom of the window. An alternative way to close this window is to use the key stroke used before of holding down the **Ctrl** key and pressing the function key **F4**. This will return you to the Supplier Labels dialogue box. Exactly the same label printing facility is available in the Customers part of the package. As before, to close the dialogue box, you can either pull down the small menu from the left of the title bar of this window and click on **Exit** or hold down the **Ctrl** key and press function key **F4**.

Manipulating Windows

In order to gain appreciation of other parts of the package, click on the **Nominal** icon that appears on the top row of icons.. This will create another window that will appear on top of the Suppliers window. To obtain a better nominal name for your purchases, click on the **Record** icon from this Nominal window and enter 5000 as the nominal code (**N/C**). Now change the name to Goods Purchased for Stock as appears in Fig. 3.10.

Now click on the **Save** button. Once this is done, the nominal name will change permanently. All the transactions relating to that account name will stay unaltered. It is the account reference that matters as far as Sage is concerned, rather than what it is called. From Fig. 3.10 you will see that there is a

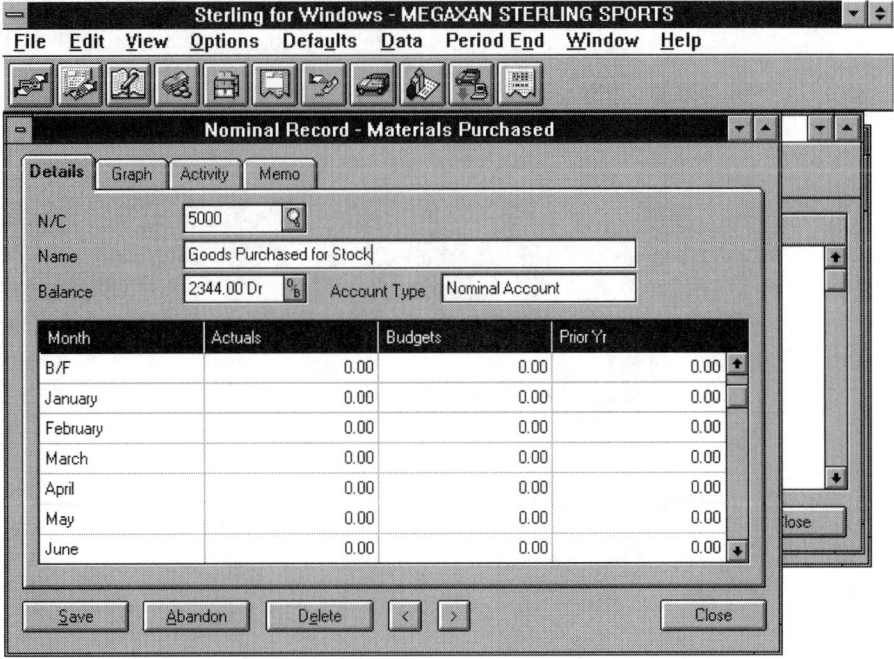

Fig. 3.10

balance figure of 2344 Dr, indicating that total purchases of £2344 (net of VAT) have been posted to this account. Click on the **Close** button to return to the main Nominal window.

Next you will see how to open and shut windows and access more than one window at a time. First, close the Nominal Ledger window by clicking on the small **Minimise** button that appears to the right of the Nominal title bar. Rather than closing the window, Sage minimises the window by creating a small icon for it and placing it near the bottom of your screen.

The main Suppliers window should now appear on your screen. Without closing this window, click on the **Customers** icon that appears in the row of icons above the Suppliers window. Having done this, click on the **Bank Accounts** icon. At this stage, you will have *four* windows active. One has been minimised (Nominal), and the others are stacked above each other, with Bank Accounts at the top, simply because Bank Accounts was the last to be opened.

Double click on the **Nominal** icon that you created when you minimised it; this action has the effect of reactivating the window. Now pull down the **Window** menu that appears on the menu bar near the top of your screen. From this menu click on **Cascade** to see the effect. You should have something similar to that shown in Fig. 3.11.

The Cascade effect will show the four windows appearing on top of each other. To move to any of these windows, click on the title bar of the window

Fig. 3.11

of your choice. The advantage of this is that you can jump between windows quickly by using a single click stroke rather than closing one window before you can move on to another.

For a further demonstration of the effect of Windows, click on the **Maximise** button on *one* of the three windows in turn. The **Maximise** buttons appear to the far right of the respective title bars. The effect of this is to cause the window to occupy the whole working area of the screen. The **Maximise** button will now be replaced with a **Normalise** one. Now click on the **Minimise** button. Repeat clicking on the **Minimise** buttons until all the windows have been minimised and you see a blank working area with a collection of icons representing each part of the Sage package you have minimised.

Figure 3.12 shows an example of the icons. The difference may be that the icons are positioned in different places on the screen. To move an icon, point your mouse pointer over an icon and then hold down the left button on your mouse without letting go. Now slowly move the mouse and you will see the icon move along the screen. When the icon is in the position of your choice, let go of the mouse button and the icon will re-appear in the new location. This is a further example of drag and drop. To activate the icon and restore it to the screen, simply double click on the icon of the function required.

Manipulating windows in this way will serve a useful purpose later in the book, as it gives you practice at moving things around to suit your circum-

The supplier accounts 53

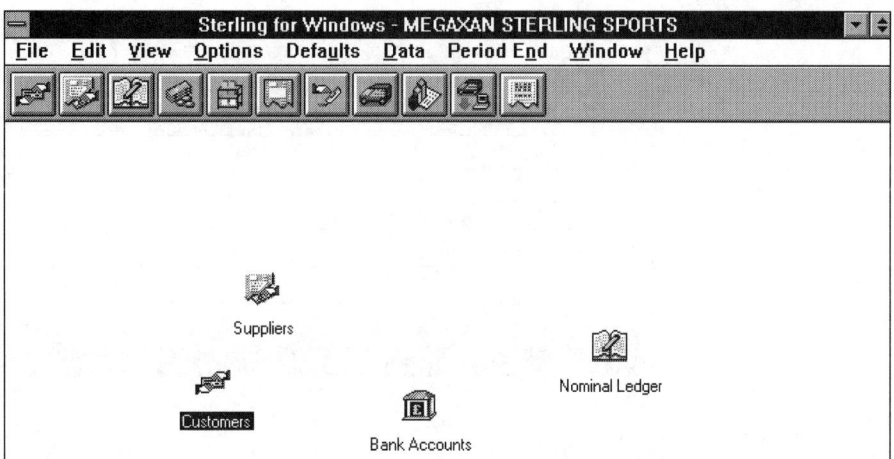

Fig. 3.12

stances. Before moving on, experiment with this. When you are ready to move to the next section, make sure you have the Suppliers window displayed.

Paying suppliers

When paying suppliers for goods and services received, you will need to bear in mind any discounts offered for prompt payment as well as the terms under which the purchases were made. For most businesses, good relations with their suppliers can be as important as good relations with customers. This is particularly so when dealing with suppliers who are specialists in their field or who offer generous discounts and/or credit terms. It may also be true for many manufacturing firms who work with low stocks of materials and rely for continuous production on efficient and reliable deliveries from their suppliers.

When making payments to suppliers against their accounts, you are settling outstanding invoices with the suppliers. The effect will be to *debit* supplier accounts and *credit* the bank account of your business with the payments.

At this stage, you should have either two rows of icons or icons dotted around the screen because they have been minimised. Click on the **Bank Accounts** icon to reveal the set of icons that are related to banking transactions. The Bank Accounts window should now be displayed. Maximise this window using the **Maximise** button to the right of the Bank Accounts title bar.

In order to enter details about paying a supplier, you will need to click on the **Supplier Payment** icon from the set of banking icons. This will reveal a new dialogue box that must be completed in a similar way to that shown in Fig. 3.13

Before you can enter details about which invoices are being paid, you must enter the account reference (**Payee**) of the supplier. As before, you can access a list of suppliers by clicking on the **Finder** to the right of **Payee**. When you

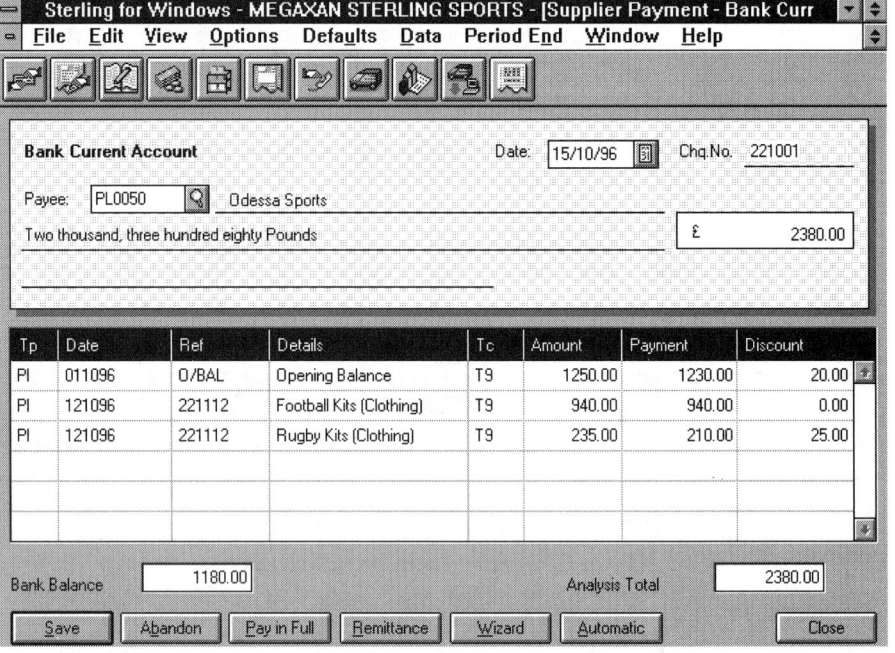

Fig. 3.13

have selected the supplier account reference, click on the **OK** button and a list of all unsettled transactions will appear in the Supplier Payment dialogue box. The **Date** needs to be altered if it is to be different from the system date. The **Chq.No.** box should be filled in with the cheque number so that it can be referred to at a later date if anything goes wrong. The **Amount** will be the amount the cheque has been made out for. You will notice that when the amount in figures has been entered, Sage will produce the amount in words to assist you when actually writing out the cheque.

When the top of the screen has been completed, it is now a matter of determining which invoices the cheque has to cover. In the example shown in Fig. 3.13, the cheque amount is £2380 and is going to settle the account with the supplier. The cheque will clear most of this, with the amount left owing being a cash discount allowed by the supplier. The first line (Opening Balance) has been settled in full – where the sum of the **Payment** and **Discount** equals the **Amount**. To enter these, click on the **Payment** and **Discount** boxes and type in the figures. The total amount paid will have to be equal to the amount the cheque has been made out for.

A quicker way of settling invoices would be to enter discount figures first and, instead of entering the amounts against each invoice, click on the **Automatic** button at the bottom of the screen. When payments have been allocated against invoices, the account balances will have been reduced accordingly. You will also see that Sage lets you know what your Bank Balance is, warning you of a potential problem existing where you may have insufficient funds to pay the supplier.

PRACTICE   Before moving on to the next section, enter a few more payments.

Settling invoices with credit notes

This was covered briefly when you worked with the Sales Ledger, and is now dealt with in greater detail. The purpose here is to use any credit notes to settle invoices – whether customers or suppliers. The principle is simple enough: it means that credit notes will be used to help clear out invoices from your system.

In the example that follows, you will enter a supplier and use a credit note to part-settle an invoice. No money will be paid in this instance, although you could use a combination of both to settle an invoice in full. From Fig. 3.14 you will see that a credit note of £23.50 is being used to reduce the amount owed on the Corner Flags.

Select the supplier required and then, instead of entering any amount on a cheque, click on the **Payment** box where the credit note line appears. The credit note line will have a **Tp** of **PC** (Purchase Credit) in it. Now enter the amount of the credit note. At this point, the **Analysis Total** will show –23.50

Fig. 3.14

(or the amount entered, if different). Now click on the Payment box on the line against which you want the credit note to be offset. You can then enter the amount. When completed, click on the **S**ave button to record the transaction.

In the months to follow, this invoice will remain on the system until it is completely paid off.

Any cash discounts that are subsequently offered to reduce the invoice amount outstanding can also be entered through the Supplier Payments part of the program. This can happen if a tiny amount (a few pence) is left on an account and it is felt wise to clear the amount as a cash discount rather than to try and pay it.

EXTRACTING SUPPLIER REPORTS

In this section you will extract three reports that will give you details about the transactions you have entered against your supplier in much the same way as you did when working with customers. Each of the reports can be extracted through the main Suppliers window. If you are still in the Bank part of the program, you will need to exit from this. If you are a Windows 3.11 or lower user, click on the small icon to the left of the option title bar (in the shape of an = sign) and select E**x**it from this option. If you are a Windows 95 user, then click on the small **X** that appears to the right of the Bank title bar. Alternatively, **Ctrl–F4** has the same effect for all users. Restore the Suppliers window by clicking on its icon.

Supplier account balances

From the main Suppliers window, you will see a list of supplier accounts and a summary of the business undertaken with them. The **Balance** column is the amount the supplier is now owed by the business and *will* include VAT. These balances form part of its *creditors*, which will appear on a balance sheet as a current liability. The list of **Credit Limits** was set when the supplier records were created and represents the maximum amount you are allowed to have outstanding with a supplier.

Although it can be claimed back from HM Customs & Excise, VAT is still owed by the business to the supplier if the invoice has not been settled. With the exception of small firms, the VAT is claimed by the business from HM Customs & Excise when the invoice is issued rather than when the money is actually paid. In terms of the purchase figures, the business will need the amounts net of VAT if it is to eventually determine whether it is making a profit or not.

While in the main Suppliers menu, click on the **Reports** icon to reveal a list of available reports, similar in content to what appeared when you worked with the customers. Now click on the report that is described as **Supplier Activity**

(**Summary**). Now set the Output as either **Print** or **Preview** and then click on the **Run** button. Accept the filter defaults and proceed with the running of the report. When you have the report, either on screen or paper, observe the contents carefully. The report gives a brief summary of all transactions with the suppliers.

Aged creditors reports

Rather than obtaining a simple statement of how much each supplier is owed, you can produce an aged creditors report, giving details of how long your suppliers have had money owing them. Making sure you are still in the Supplier Activity window, click on the **Aged Balances** button that appears at the bottom of this screen.

The first column shows the **Account Number** only. The **Balance** column is the amount owed to the supplier as shown in the previous screen. The **Current** column shows the amount that is owed and has been outstanding to the supplier for less than 30 days. The other columns all show zeros. This is because you have only just set up the system. As time goes by, figures will appear in these columns. The use of such a report can alert a business to a potential problem in that, if suppliers are not paid on time, they may stop supplying. Furthermore this means the loss of potential cash discounts for early payment.

Transaction histories

From the main suppliers window, click on **Activity**, accept the defaults to accept all transactions. A transactions history allows you to examine the transactions undergone with any particular supplier or group of suppliers. Figure 3.15 is an example of such a supplier account history.

The number that appears in the first column (**No**) is the transaction number. Each transaction you have entered will have been given a separate number in the sequence in which the transaction was carried out. This was also the case with the customer transactions. Every transaction – whether customer, bank or supplier – has a different number.

The second column (**Tp**) indicates the transaction type. These types are:

PI	Purchase Invoice
PC	Purchase Credit
PP	Purchase Payment
PD	Purchase Discount

The **Ref** and **Details** columns were entered when the details were originally entered. The **Amount** column shows the value of the transaction. The **O/S** column is the amount outstanding on that particular invoice. The **Debit** column shows transactions that reduce what you owe the supplier, while the **Credit** column shows amounts that will increase what you owe the supplier. In summary, the transaction history shows:

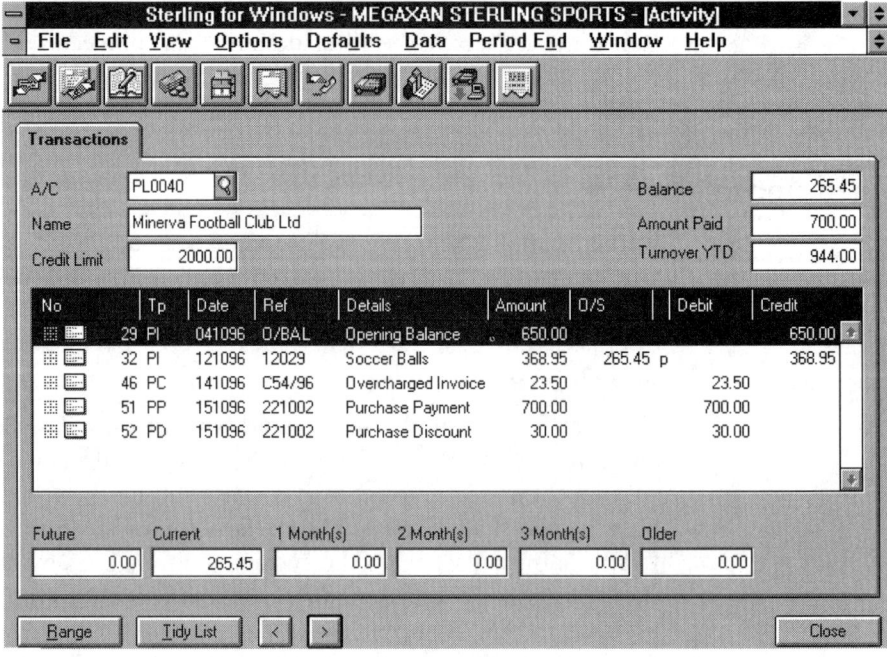

Fig. 3.15

Total credits as :	£1018.95
Total debits as :	£ 753.50
Amount you still owe:	£ 265.45

All of this is outstanding on Transaction 32 – a purchase invoice. As with the customer histories, the following symbols are used:

p to indicate an invoice has been part-paid
*   to indicate nothing on this transaction has been settled.

BACKING UP YOUR DATA

When you leave the Sage package to return to your Microsoft Windows screen, you are asked: Do you wish to Backup your Data? If you answer **Yes** to this question, the data files, where the accounts information for your business is held, are copied onto another disk for safe-keeping. In the event of anything going wrong with the computer system later, the information can be restored to the state it was in when it was backed up.

For a business using a computer fairly regularly, it may be prudent to back up once or even twice daily. How often you need to back up is dependent on the frequency with which the computer is used.

There are four stages to the back-up procedure. Figure 3.16 shows four of the dialogue boxes you will see on your screen when going through the stages.

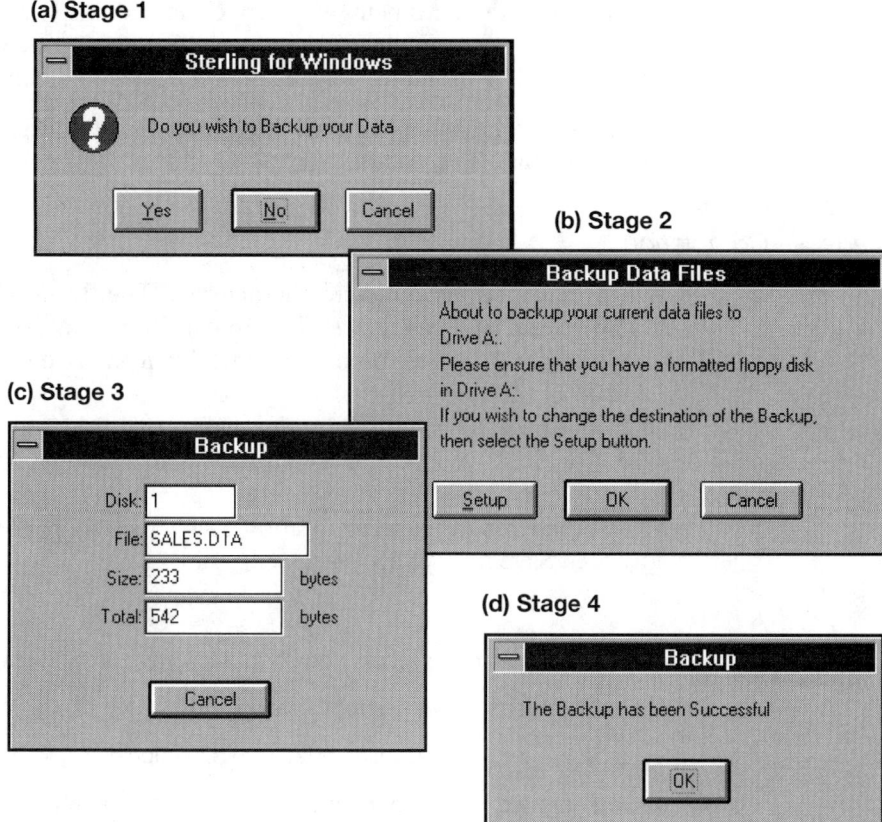

Fig. 3.16

Stage 1 – The question

When you are ready to exit Sage, you should pull down the File menu from the menu bar near the top of your screen and select **Exit**. A dialogue box will appear and ask the question, 'Do you wish to Backup your Data?' as shown in Fig. 3.16(a). Click on the **Yes** button.

Stage 2 – The disk

You must now insert a formatted disk into your drive. If your drive is designated as drive A:, then this is all that is required. If your system is different from this, you will need to click on **Setup** and tell Sage where it is to back up the data. A dialogue box, shown in Fig. 3.16(b), prompts you accordingly.

Once the disk is in the drive, click on **OK** to start the backup.

Stage 3 – Backing up

If there is nothing wrong with the disk, a panel appears on the screen (*see* Fig. 3.16(c)) indicating the disk number, the file being backed up, the size of file and the total bytes being used up for your data. The only important piece of data at this stage is the disk number. If there is not enough room on your disk, you will be prompted to put another disk into the drive.

If the backup fails, then you will be told of this and will need to put in a different disk that is acceptable.

Stage 4 – Completion

When the backup is complete, the message 'The Backup has been successful' should appear in a panel (*see* Fig 3.16(d)). If this has not happened, then you should repeat the whole process with freshly formatted disks.

Once the backup is complete, the disks should be stored in case they are needed again. If you have backed up, then label and date your disks.

More on backing up and restoration is covered in Chapter 10 when the more advanced Sage utilities are discussed.

EXERCISES

As a way of gaining practice, you should try the following tasks:

1 Create at least 12 new supplier accounts.
2 Generate for each supplier at least two invoices.
3 Generate for four of your suppliers a credit note each.
4 Pay five of your suppliers part of the money owed them.
5 Use the credit notes to settle parts of the invoices.
6 Produce transaction histories on two of the accounts.
7 Produce an aged creditors report.
8 Determine the outstanding creditors total.

CHAPTER 4

Bank transactions

INTRODUCTION

This chapter takes a close look at the bank transactions of the business. When you were paying suppliers and receiving payments from customers, you were in fact going through some banking transactions. Consequently, this chapter will be an extension of what has already been covered in some detail. You can, of course, pay suppliers in cash and be paid by customers in cash. Dealing with Cash will be covered in Chapter 5.

For a business to survive it needs to fulfil two main objectives: profitability and liquidity. This chapter will deal mainly with the issue of liquidity. A business must keep a close check on whether it has sufficient funds to pay its immediate bills. For example, if it does not have sufficient funds in its bank account, then it will not be able to pay its suppliers for goods received, the wages of its employees or various expenses. This inability to pay such bills could well result in a business having to cease trading altogether and having to sell its possessions to honour its debts.

Profit can come about by selling goods and services for more than they cost the business in the first place. It does not necessarily hold true, however, that because a business is profitable it is also liquid enough to settle its debts. Both aspects are important when running a business and must be looked at separately.

This chapter will also look at some other aspects of the Sage package. In particular, you will have the chance to investigate in some detail the printing of reports and how to set up your printer to suit your circumstances.

Before you consider bank transactions, however, make sure that the Sage package has been set up correctly for dealing with such transactions. At this stage, re-enter the Sage package.

CONTROL ACCOUNTS

Control accounts are special accounts needed to store data about various transactions to allow them to be recorded in the first instance. For example, when you made payments to your suppliers in Chapter 3, the actual bank payments were recorded in a special bank account which was given the code 1200. This account was held in the Nominal Ledger and, without it, you would have been unable to enter the transaction.

Figure 4.1 shows a Control Accounts entry dialogue box. To activate this, select **Defaults** from the main pull-down menu near the top of your screen. From the list, click on **Control Accounts**. At this stage, you need to follow the settings down the left-hand side; the others will be covered in later chapters.

The **Debtors Control** Account and **Creditors Control** Account appear at the top of the list. These cannot be changed at this stage. This is because once transactions have been carried out with customers and suppliers, the accounts are already active and cannot be changed. The Debtors Control Account will keep a tally of how much your customers owe you. Each time an invoice is issued, this figure will be increased by the appropriate amount, while receipts from customers and credit notes sent to them reduces the amount. The Creditors Control Account has exactly the same type of function in that it keeps a tally of what is owed to suppliers and increases each time an invoice is received and decreases each time payments are made and credit notes are received.

The **Default Bank** (1200) will be used each time a bank payment is made and a receipt comes in – unless you specify otherwise. As you will see later, other bank accounts can be set up and used. When customers made payments in Chapter 2, this account was automatically used to receive this money.

The two **VAT** (2200 and 2201) accounts have already been used to record VAT and are used to post VAT transacted in the Sales and Purchase Ledgers. VAT charged on sales is referred to as *VAT outputs* in that the amounts will have to be paid *out* to HM Customs & Excise. Any VAT paid on purchases is referred

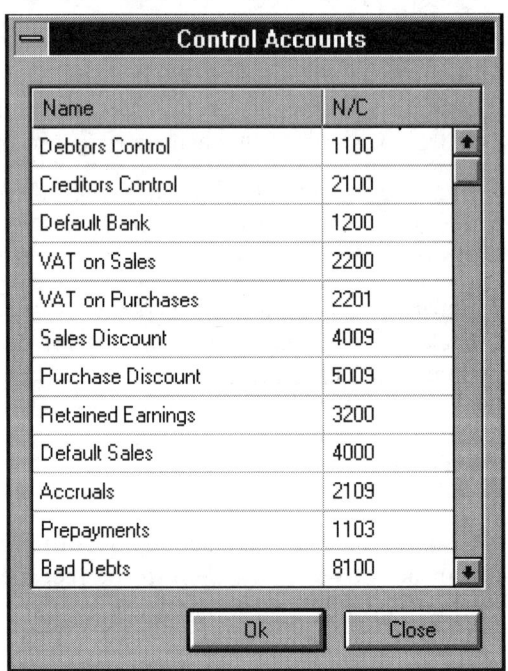

Fig. 4.1

to as *VAT inputs* in that the amounts paid can be claimed back *in* from HM Customs & Excise. Many bank transactions will also have to make use of these accounts. Both of these account numbers will appear in a lighter shade because they cannot be altered at this late stage.

The **Sales Discount** (4009) and **Purchase Discount** (5009) accounts are to record any discounts allowed to customers and discounts received from suppliers respectively. The remaining five accounts (Retained Earnings – Bad Debts) are needed by other parts of the Sage program and will be covered in Chapter 6.

At this stage, there is no need to alter any of the account numbers. These were set when the package was installed. In practice, the accounts need to be set prior to any transactions being entered. This activity should be carried out as part of the planning stage. The problem faced is that a fairly good knowledge of both Sage and accounting is needed to get this right first time.

From the Control Accounts dialogue box, click on **Cancel** so that you return to the main screen without any changes being recorded.

CREATING BANK ACCOUNTS

Click on the **Bank** icon to reveal all the icons relating to bank transactions. From Chapters 2 and 3, you will have already used both the **Customers** and **Suppliers** icons in order to record receipts from customers and make payments to suppliers. At this initial stage, you will see a list of the bank accounts, as set up when the package was installed, and their respective balances. These balances would have been generated when you processed banking transactions with customers and suppliers.

These bank accounts are all held in the Nominal Ledger and can be added to. To demonstrate this aspect of the package, you will begin by creating a new bank account with an opening balance of £5000. The purpose of this extra bank account is to record actual transactions with the business's bank. Each time a receipt comes from a customer, the amount is entered in the Default Account. In practice, however, a business may take a whole batch of cheques to the bank in one go. The purpose of this new account is to try and reflect as closely as possible what is actually happening with respect to banking. In practice there is no reason why you cannot operate the business with one single bank account.

Click on the **Bank Record** icon – the far left icon on the row of Bank icons. The window will appear showing the Default Bank Account as 1200. Enter 1205 into the N/C box to indicate that the new bank account will have Nominal Code 1205 and click on the **Nominal Name** box (or press your **Tab** key). The text 'New Account' will appear to the right of the account number to confirm a new account is about to be created. Figure 4.2 shows an example of a complete record.

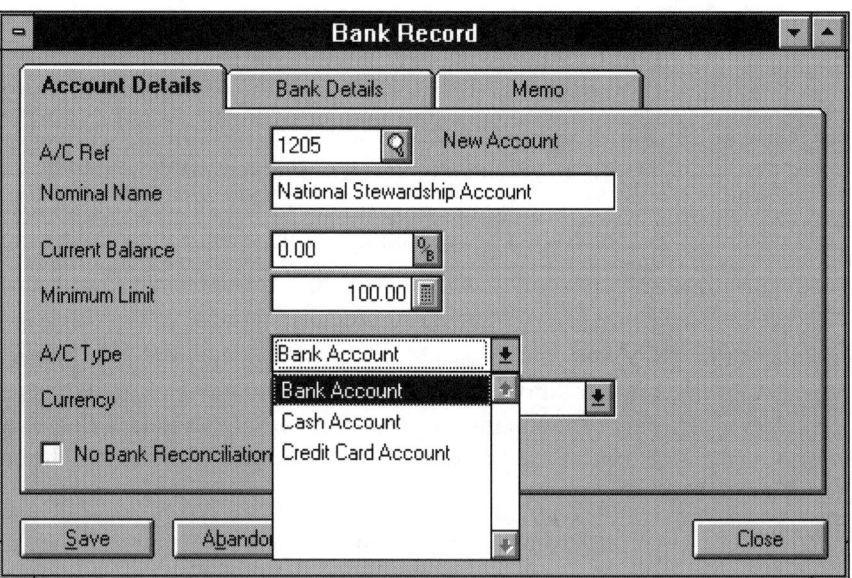

Fig. 4.2

The record will contain all the details that will normally appear on a cheque book or single cheque. The **Minimum Limit** of 100 indicates that you do not want the account to fall below this amount. Figure 4.2 also shows that if you click the small icon next to the **A/C Type** box, you will be given a choice of three accounts. When you have completed the record details, do not save at this point, but click on the **O/B** button that appears alongside the **Current Balance** amount. You will use this feature to enter the opening balance of £5000. Before you can enter the amount, Sage will ask you to save the record details; click on **Yes** to do this.

An Opening Balance Setup dialogue box will show the **Ref** to be **O/BAL** to indicate that it is an opening balance you are entering. The **Date** is the computer system date. Figure 4.3 shows that if you click on the **Calendar** icon, beside the **Date** box, a small calendar appears from which you can select a date.

The current month will be displayed by default, but you can move between months and years by clicking on the following buttons on the calendar:

>   To move to the next month
>>   To move forward one year
<   To move to the previous month
<<   To move backwards one year

You will now be required to enter the amount in the **Receipt** box. If you were to enter an opening overdraft, then you would enter the overdraft amount in the payment box. When you have done this, click on the **Save** button to store the information. A bar will fill up to indicate that the data is now being written

Fig. 4.3

to the record – referred to as *posting*. When you are back at the Bank Record dialogue box, click on the **S**ave button to return to the main Bank window.

NOMINAL BANK PAYMENTS AND RECEIPTS

The new account should now appear on your list of bank accounts with the £5000 balance. The next stage will be to record some cash sales in this new bank account. When doing this, it is important to distinguish those receipts collected for VAT from those for net cash sales. The VAT collected from sales revenue will have to be recorded as such and eventually passed on to HM Customs & Excise.

From the main Bank menu, click on the line that shows the new bank account. This should highlight the bank account where you wish to deposit the money. Now click on the **R**eceipt icon. Although you are processing cash receipts from your customers, you should not choose **Customers** from the list of banking options because you are not receiving money from any particular customer who owes you money. This transaction will record cash taken *over the counter* in the chosen bank account. The **Ref** box would normally hold the paying-in slip number or some other reference number that would identify the transaction at a later date.

You now need to select the Nominal Account (**N/C**) in which you wish to have the receipt recorded. In Fig. 4.4 Account 4000 has been chosen (Sales Type A) as happened when an invoice was issued to a customer. The **Net** figure should represent the total amount *net of VAT* deposited with the bank, while the **Tax** figure is the *VAT amount* being deposited. Both figures are then added together to give the total **Amount** being deposited at the bank. The new total in the bank will appear in the **Bank Balance** box. The

Fig. 4.4

Analysis Total shows the amount deposited for this transaction. When you have completed the form, click on **Save** to post the transaction. This transaction will have its own unique transaction number along with all the others now undertaken.

Money banked in this way will not only represent sales income. Money could, for example, be received from other sources, such as a commission received (4902). Again, all that is required is to identify the nominal account number and enter the amount being deposited for this category of income.

PRACTICE Before moving on, add a couple of deposits for commission received to the bank account.

Making payments from the bank works in exactly the same way. Return to the main Bank window by clicking on the **Close** button in the Receipts window. Make sure that the Bank Account (1205) is highlighted in the window and then click on the **Payments** icon (*see* Fig. 4.5 for resulting window). When entering the payment details, you will have the opportunity to learn a few more short-cuts which can be used in many other activities in Sage.

The first box that needs to be completed is **Payee**. This can be ignored by pressing the **Tab** key on your keyboard or clicking the next box to be completed. The **Date** needs to be altered, if different, with the use of the calendar visual aid. The **Chq.No.** can also be left blank by pressing the **Tab** key. You

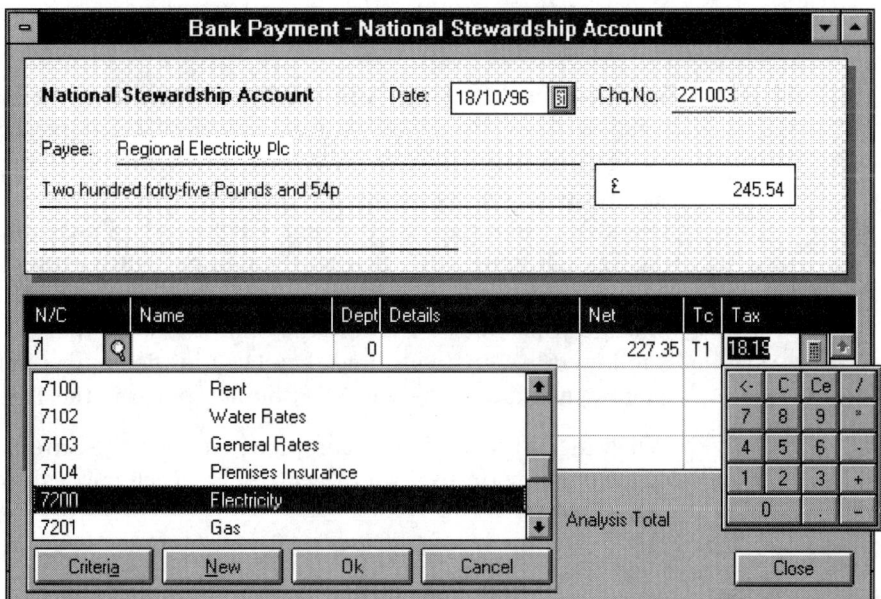

Fig. 4.5

can also leave the £ amount box blank and allow Sage to work it out for you as you enter the payment details.

The next stages cannot be left blank as they are the details of what you are paying for. In this example, you will be paying an electricity bill. The bill will amount to £245.54, of which £18.19 is VAT. Click on the small **Finder** icon in the **N/C** column to reveal a panel containing a list of account numbers. Figure 4.5 shows such a panel and has highlighted the position of the *scroll bar*. You will also notice that a 7 has been entered in the **N/C** box. This was done to speed up the location of the account that will be debited. If you know that the account starts with a 7, Sage will begin its search with the accounts that start with that number.

The list of accounts available in the Nominal Ledger is too large to fit into this panel. Consequently, the scroll bar will allow you to *scroll* through the names of accounts to seek out the one for which you are looking. The small square box on the bar (to the right of the list) can be used to move rapidly through the names. Place your mouse pointer on the small box and, holding down the left button on your mouse, move it up and down the bar to see the effect. If you want to move more slowly through the list, then move the mouse pointer to either the down arrow key above the scroll bar or the up arrow key below the scroll bar, and press the left button on your mouse. If you keep the button depressed, you will move through the account names in the direction requested.

When the account name appears in the panel (7200 Electricity), click on the **Account Name** and then click on the **OK** button in the window. The

Nominal Code and **Account Name** will then appear automatically in the Bank Payments window.

You now need to enter both the **Net** amount and the **VAT**. Remember, the **Analysis Total** must equal the total bill. In this example, enter the Net amount of 227.35 and click on the **Tax** box. From Fig. 4.5 you will see that an on-screen calculator appears as another visual aid. You will now use your mouse to add VAT at a rate of 8 per cent. Click on the **Calculator** icon to the right of the **Tax** amount. Now click on the number buttons on the calculator so that 227.35 appears on the calculator. Now click on the * (asterisk) button to indicate you want to multiply the number by another number. Then click on **8** followed by **/** to divide, and then click in the number **100**. Now click on the **equal** sign and the number 18.19 should appear in the **Tax** column.

When the entry window is complete, click on the **Save** button at the bottom of the window (in Fig. 4.5 the button has been covered by the pull-down dialogue box).

PRACTICE Enter a few more such payments of expenses in order to gain the practice needed.

You can also pay for the purchase of stock in the same way, except you need to make sure it is a Stock Purchases Account you use rather than one of the expense accounts. Once you have entered a few more payments, click on the **Close** button to return to the main Bank window.

TRANSFERRING FUNDS BETWEEN ACCOUNTS

You have now created a bank account with an opening balance and added money to this account by receiving money against sales and any other sources of income. You have also reduced the amount of money in the account by paying a number of bills or buying stock.

Now you will transfer some money from the Default Bank Account (1200) to the newly created one (1205). The purpose of the Default Bank Account was to allow an account for automatic posting of bank transactions between customers and suppliers. Now we will assume that £1300 of cheques collected from our customers are to be banked. In this case, you need to remove £1300 from the Default Account and pay it into the new account.

From the main Bank window, click on the **Transfer** icon and Sage will present you with an entry window which begins by asking you from which account and to which account you want to transfer the money. Figure 4.6 shows an example of a completed entry form.

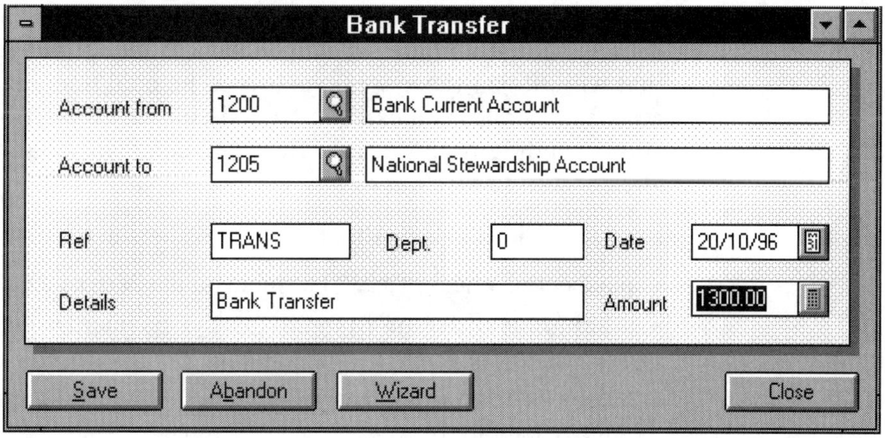

Fig. 4.6

In this instance the transfer is **from** 1200 **to** 1205. The **Ref** box contains the words TRANS by default, to indicate a transfer, but this can be altered to suit any differing circumstances. The **Details** box holds information about why the transfer has taken place. Once the **Amount** has been entered, you should click on the **Save** button and the transfer will take place. Having saved this transaction, click on the **Close** button to return to the main Bank window.

The chances are, you now have a negative figure on the Default Bank Account (1200), signified by a minus sign in front of the **Amount**. If this is not the case, then transfer more money into the bank account until you do have a negative amount.

We will now assume that the negative amount on the Default Account has come about because payments have been made to suppliers, but the money has not yet appeared on our proper bank account. To perform this task, click on the **Transfer** icon again and transfer the amount from the newly created account (1205) to the Default Account (1200). This should leave the Default Account with a zero balance.

As a final act in this section, transfer £1000 to the Deposit Account (1210) and £2000 to the Building Society Account (1220). This should leave three accounts showing balances and the Default Account showing a zero balance.

RECURRING BANK ENTRIES

This facility allows you to set up recurring bank payments and receipts. For example, if you have a number of standing orders or direct debits, then setting them up within the program allows you to update your bank account automatically rather than having to enter these details every month. The principle is fairly straightforward. First, you have to set up the recurring entry details that will inform the system what is to be paid and against which nominal account. Second, you can run an activity that will perform these entries for you depending on both the date they have been set and whether they have already been carried out or not.

In order to demonstrate this, set up the following recurring entries:

- payment of wages of £2300 payable on the 28th of each month;
- a standing order of £176,25 for the payment of insurance premiums payable on the 4th of each month;
- a debit of £200 to be received for the renting of a garage receivable on the 8th of each month.

The first two will be Bank Payments and the third one will be a Bank Receipt. The dates are different for the sake of demonstration.

From the main Bank window, click on the **Recurring Entries** icon to reveal the entry window required. Each line represents a recurring entry that can be entered. For now, you will be entering two of the four types of entries available:

BP for Bank Payment
BR for Bank Receipt

At this stage you will be presented with a Recurring Entries dialogue box that will be blank. Click on the **Add** button at the bottom of this dialogue box. From Fig. 4.7 you will see how one of the three entries listed above has been entered.

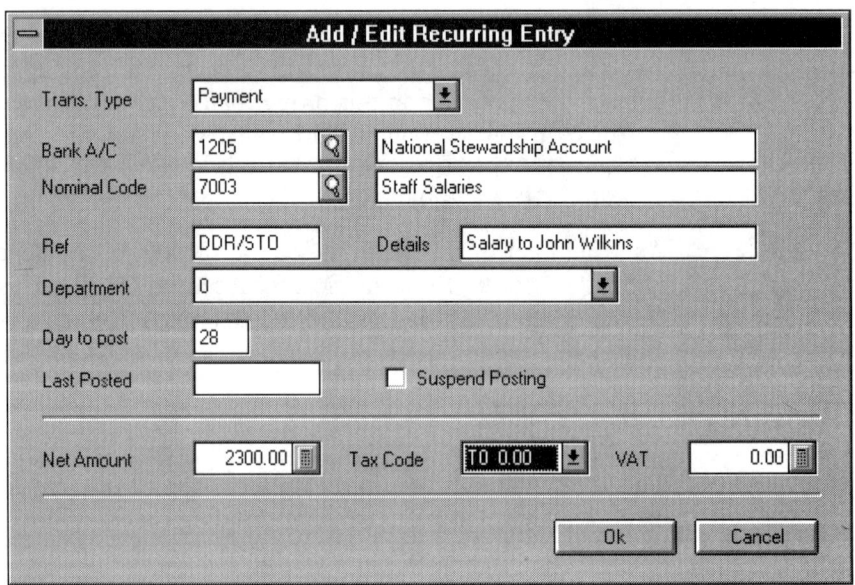

Fig. 4.7

Completing this dialogue box will set up the recurring entry. In the example shown in Fig. 4.7, you will see the **Transaction Type** is a payment. It will be made from the new bank account (1205) and will pay staff salaries. The **Ref** and **Details** boxes give more information on this. The **Day to post** is set at 28, indicating that it is to be paid on the 28th day of each month. As you will also see, VAT can also be set, if applicable. When this is complete, click on the **OK** button to add this to the list of recurring entries. Fig. 4.8 shows that the other recurring entries mentioned above have now been added to the list.

The first box (**Tp**) indicates the first two entries are Bank Payments and the third a Bank Receipt. The **Ref, Details** and **Amount** columns are as you would have entered them when you added the line to the list. The **Next Posting** column will indicate whether or not it is time to process the recurring entry. To process any recurring entries now due, simply click on the **Process** button.

Once the entries have been made, you can keep returning to this window and click on **Process** as many times as you wish, as well as adding new recurring entries. Once the recurring entry has been processed, it will not be processed again. However, each entry must be processed at least once a month.

Entries can be altered by highlighting the entry and clicking the **Edit** button. Quite often the amounts will change over time. You may also feel the reference and details information may need to be altered. To delete a recurring entry, simply highlight any required line and click on the **Delete** button. Such recurring entries can, therefore, be added to or subtracted from as often as you wish and at any time during a month. Each time you amend this window, remember to click on **Save** in the Add/Delete Recurring Entry dialogue box.

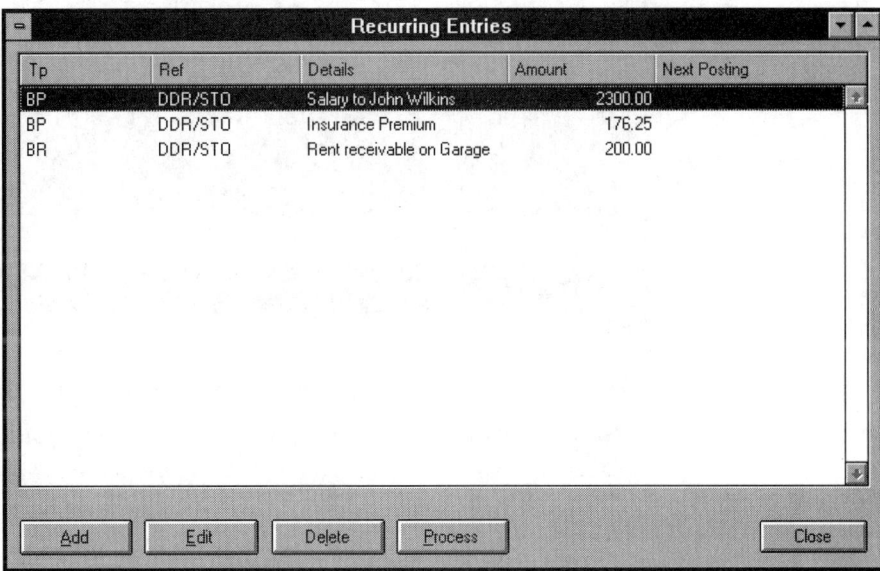

Fig. 4.8

BANK RECONCILIATION

Sage allows a facility whereby you can compare your nominal bank statement with that sent by your bank. You can mark each entry in your bank statement that agrees with that of the bank records and then make any additions and alterations. It is inevitable that the two may disagree for some of the following reasons:

- Some cheques sent out will not have cleared and will not appear on the bank statement.
- Some cheques received may not have been taken to the bank.
- Bank charges may appear on the bank statement, but will not have been entered in the nominal bank account.
- Standing orders, direct debits and credit transfers may not have been entered. The recurring entries should have taken care of this, however. It may be a simple matter of your not having processed them.
- An entry mistake may have been made on someone's part.

It is necessary to check the bank statement against your own records and ensure that all the above circumstances have been taken care of.

From the main Bank window, click on the new bank account from the list of accounts (1205). Now click on the **Reconcile** icon. The window that appears

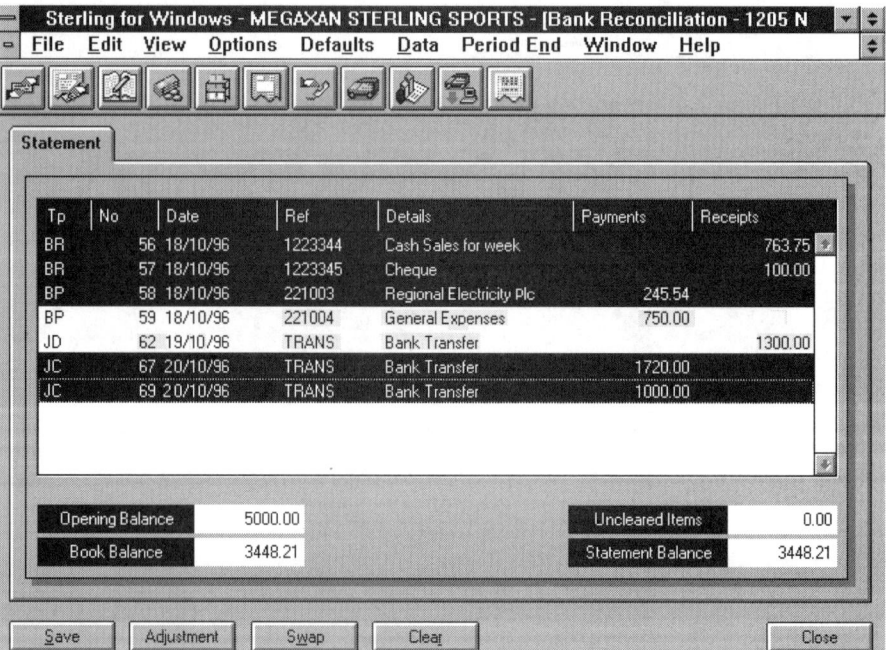

Fig. 4.9

will contain the transactions entered. Figure 4.9 shows such a window with all lines high-lighted.

Lines are highlighted by clicking on each line in turn. Highlight most lines on your window now, leaving a couple clear, indicating that you have reconciled these highlighted transactions with your bank statement. In other words, they all agree with the bank statement. When you click on **Save**, the **Uncleared Items** figure at the bottom right of the screen will alter. The **Uncleared Items** figure indicates how much of the nominal bank account amount is yet to be reconciled while the **Statement Balance** figure shows what should be on the bank statement sent by the bank when everything has been reconciled and brought up to date.

You are aiming to have zero in the **Uncleared Item** box and a bank statement amount that is accurate. The **Book Balance** figure is the amount that appears from all the payments and receipts entered so far. If any amounts have been left off the bank statement, then this figure too will need to be adjusted. The **Opening Balance** is the amount you either entered as the opening balance when you created the account or the amount at the close of the last month.

When the lines you want reconciled are highlighted, click on the **Save** icon. Sage asks you to confirm this action and requires you to click on the **Yes** button. This will put you back to the main Bank window. Now click on **Reconcile** again to see the effect. The only lines that will appear in this window are those still to be reconciled. This now allows you a much clearer idea of what is still to be done.

As mentioned earlier, you may need to make some adjustments to the bank account. Suppose now that bank charges of £32 have to be included. From the Reconcile window click on the **Adjustment** icon near the bottom of the window. A dialogue box will appear similar to that shown in Fig. 4.10.

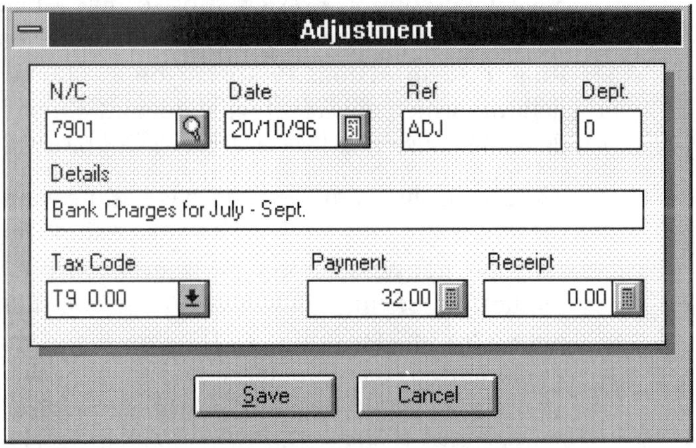

Fig. 4.10

As with entering banking transactions, you will need to enter the Nominal Code (**N/C**) and **Date**. The **Details** box is for you to enter those details you want to appear on the statement. Again, the VAT (Tax Code) must be specified if appropriate. If money is to be charged against the bank statement, then enter the amount in the payment box; otherwise, enter the amount in the receipt box. Now you need to click on **S**ave and the amount will be immediately entered onto the bank statement *awaiting reconciliation*.

If you need to adjust an item already entered, then this is a good place to enter the details. If, for example, a cheque has been paid out but the figure entered is too high, then use the Adjustment dialogue box to enter exactly the same **Nominal Code** as before and then enter the *difference* as a receipt. When you have finished this, you can then highlight the rest of the transactions and click on **S**ave from the Reconciliation window.

PRACTICE Complete the reconciliation for the other bank accounts in the same way and experiment by making various adjustments.

BANK STATEMENTS

You have now entered quite a few transactions through the bank which ought to be checked. The inspection of a bank statement will also give you the opportunity to see the status of the account. It is important to note that, until you have gone through the reconciliation processes, nothing will appear on the statements. Consequently, the bank statement is a statement of reconciled banking transactions.

From the main Bank window click on the **Statements** icon. You will now see a small dialogue box asking you in which form of output you wish the report. You will first **Preview** the statement to consider and work on other aspects of Sage. Click on the **Preview** spot so that a black dot appears inside it. Now click on **OK**. The next dialogue box allows you to determine parameters limiting the transactions to appear on a statement. Click on **OK** to accept the defaults which will create a statement showing all transactions between all dates. The resulting Preview screen will be similar to that shown in Fig. 4.11.

The screen shown in Fig. 4.11 has had its window maximised so that more of the statement can be seen. The page appears to the left of screen and it is probably not possible to read it, even when maximised. The **Z**oom button at the bottom of this window allows you to take a closer look at the page. To obtain an image similar to the one that appears in Fig. 4.11, click on the **Z**oom button, then on **200%**, and then on the **OK** button. This will give you an image twice the size of the original preview image and enable you to get a closer look at what is on the statement. The individual pages show how the statement would look if printed.

Bank transactions 75

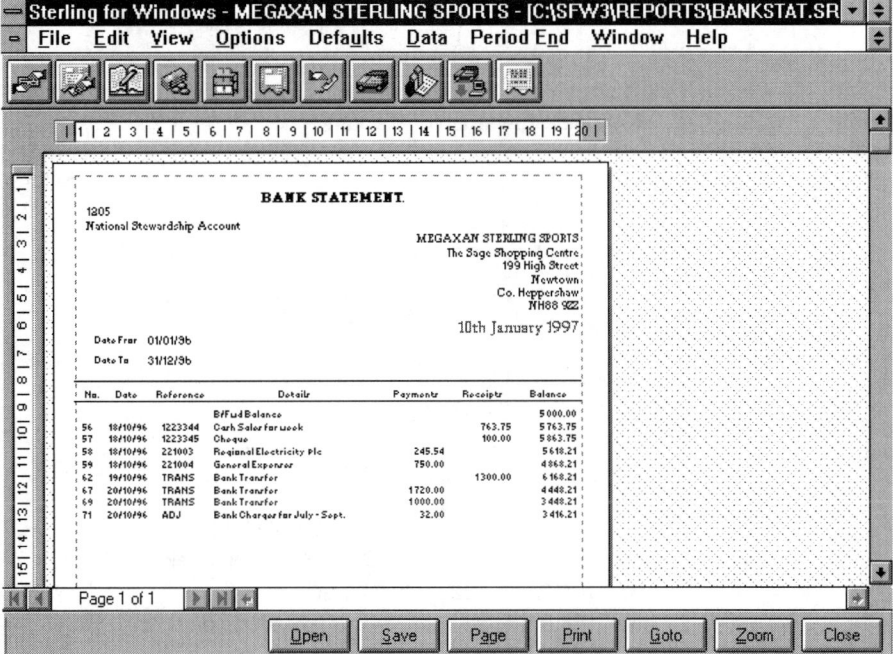

Fig. 4.11

To zoom out, you simply click on the **Zoom** button and select a smaller figure such as **50%** or **Full Page**. Figure 4.12 represents the bank statement that appears in Fig. 4.11. This will obviously differ from your own if you have entered different banking transactions.

The bank statement shows the reconciled transactions details and should agree with the bank statement that you receive from your bank. The balances down the right of the statement show the balances left in the bank at the end of each transaction, which may well appear in a different order to the bank statement issued by the bank.

To get a printout of this, you begin by determining how you want the statement printed. To do this, click on the **Page** button at the bottom of the Preview dialogue window to reveal a new dialogue box, similar to that shown in Fig. 4.13(a).

This allows you to set up your margins – left, right, top and bottom. The dialogue box also has two other tabs: one to determine the **Paper Size** in your printer and the other the **Paper Source**. Many of these facilities will vary in use according to the type of printer you have. When you have made the required settings, click on the **OK** button to return to the Statement Preview dialogue box.

Click on the **Print** button to activate the Print dialogue box. A dialogue box similar to the one in Fig. 4.13(b) will now be displayed. The default **Printer**

```
                          BANK STATEMENT

1205
National Stewardship Account
                                          MEGAXAN STERLING SPORTS
                                             The Sage Shopping Centre
                                                       199 High Street
                                                              Newtown
                                                        Co. Heppershaw
                                                             NH88 9ZZ

Date From:  01/01/96                              10th January 1997
Date To:    31/12/96

No.  Date      Reference  Details              Payments  Receipts  Balance
                          B/Fwd Balance                             5000.00
56   18/10/96  1223344    Cash Sales for week             763.75   5763.75
57   18/10/96  1223345    Cheque                          100.00   5863.75
58   18/10/96  221003     Regional Electricity plc  245.54         5618.21
59   18/10/96  221004     General Expenses        750.00            4868.21
62   19/10/96  TRANS      Bank Transfer                  1300.00   6168.21
67   20/10/96  TRANS      Bank Transfer          1720.00            4448.21
69   20/10/96  TRANS      Bank Transfer          1000.00            3448.21
71   20/10/96  ADJ        Bank Charges July–Sept.  32.00            3416.21
```

Fig. 4.12

Name installed on your computer will be displayed. If you have more than one printer to choose from, then click on the **Printer** button to make the selection of printer. The **Print Range** will allow you to print either **All** pages making up the statement or a selected range of pages. For example, if you only wanted pages 2 and 3, then you would click on the **Range** dot to indicate that you are selecting pages and, enter 2 as the **From** value and 3 as the **To** value.

The **Print Quality** allows you to choose from:

- High
- Medium
- Low
- Draft

The higher the quality you choose, then the better the quality you obtain. Higher quality is more likely to take full advantage of any fonts and special layouts you have chosen. It will also take longer to print. A good policy is to make do with draft if you are only using the information to check things over and then select a higher quality print when you are ready to print the final version.

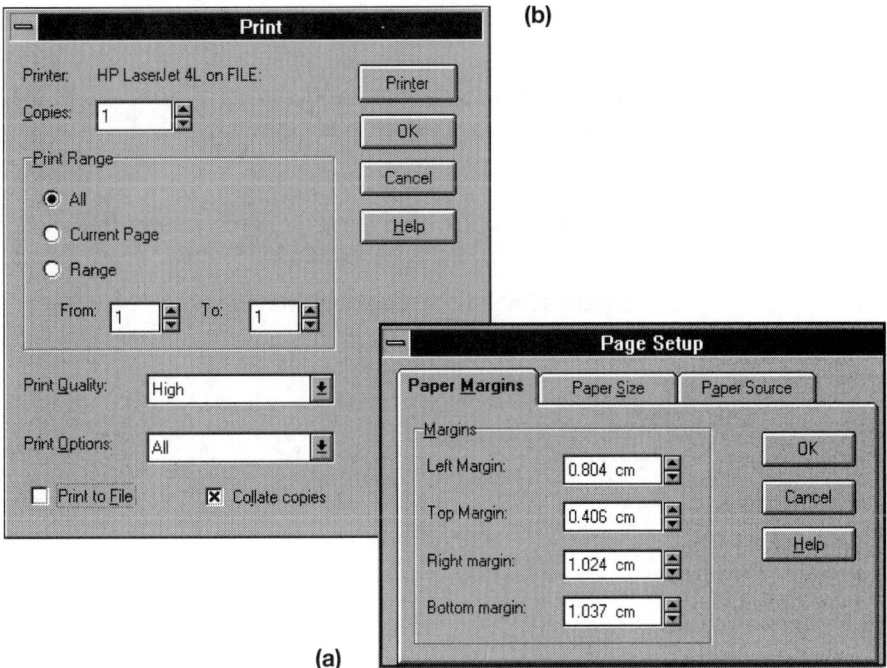

Fig. 4.13

The **Print Options** box will give you the choice of whether to print the lines and quality of text that appears in the Preview screen. By selecting **All**, you should get a printout similar to the one that appears on your Preview. Again, a lot of this depends on the type and quality of printer you are using.

If you click on the **Print to File** option, output will be printed to file for later printing or inspection. Chapter 10 will deal with this aspect in some detail.

The **Collate copies** option will ensure that, if you choose to print multiple copies, they will be printed in page sequence, one set at a time, rather than all the first pages followed by all the second pages and so on.

Click on **OK** when you are ready. As the printing is under way, a bar across the screen will fill up. When the printing image has been created, it will be sent to the printer for printing.

EXERCISES To gain practice, you should try the following tasks:

1 Generate four transactions where customers pay part or all of their accounts. The receipts will be posted to the Default Bank Control Account.

2 Generate four transactions where suppliers are paid part or all of their accounts. Again, the payments will be posted to the Default Bank Control Account.

3 Now transfer both amounts to the main bank account created.

4 Generate five payments of various expenses via your main bank account.

5 Create another three recurring entries and cancel one that has been previously created. Make sure that the dates on at least two of them are earlier than the current date on your computer system.

6 Process the recurring entries.

7 Use the Reconciliation feature to reconcile all transactions and include some bank charges via the Reconciliation feature.

8 Extract a final reconciled bank statement.

CHAPTER 5

The Nominal Ledger

INTRODUCTION

The Nominal Ledger is used to record all dealings involving, on the one side, assets of the firm such as buildings, stock and work in progress and, on the other side, how these assets have been financed. The financing of a business will be undertaken either by its creditors or by those who own it – referred to as the liabilities of the business. Apart from the recording of assets and liabilities, the Nominal Ledger will also be used to record all the overheads of the business and income generated. In addition to this, the Nominal Ledger will be used to indicate the status of various accounts, as well as to produce statements of profit, assets, liabilities and liquidity. In essence, the Nominal Ledger records in some form all financial transactions, many of which you have already come across. Figure 5.1 gives an overview of the main function of a Nominal Ledger.

In Chapters 2 and 3 you worked with customers and suppliers, and in so doing you have already posted a considerable amount to the Nominal Ledger. This was supplemented further when you entered more banking transactions

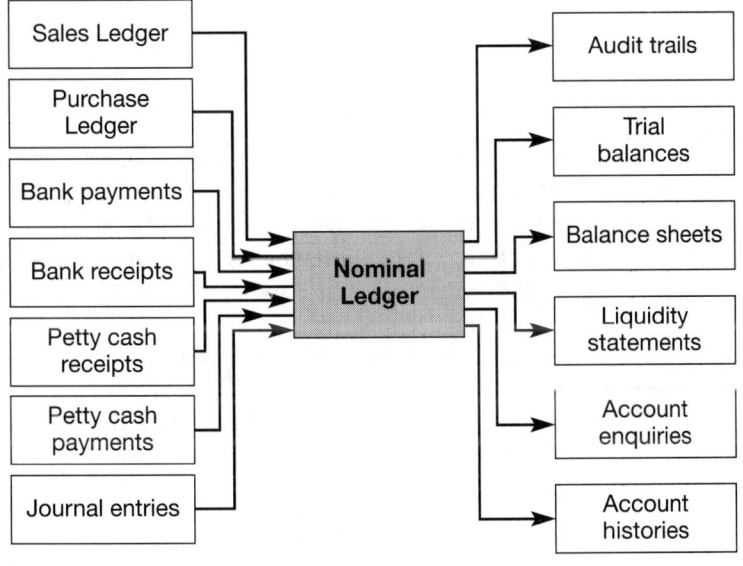

Fig. 5.1

in Chapter 4. For example, each time a sale was recorded, an amount was entered into one of the sales accounts in the Nominal Ledger as goods being sold. Similarly, when a payment was received, the bank account in the Nominal Ledger was updated to record this fact.

The Nominal Ledger, by its nature, is the cornerstone of an accounting system as all business transactions, in varying forms, will pass through it. It is worth noting that not all business transactions necessarily involve money, as we have already seen. The Nominal Ledger uses the *principle of double entry* – a process whereby any transaction entered to the nominal accounts must have both a source account and a destination account (credit and debit). As you work through this chapter and the remaining ones, it is hoped you will gain a good understanding of this principle.

LOOKING AT DOUBLE ENTRY

To gain an understanding of the principle of double entry in practical terms, you can examine the entries made into the Nominal Ledger from the work you have undertaken in Chapters 2, 3 and 4. Start off by entering the Nominal Ledger by clicking on the **Nominal** icon from the main Sage window. A list of accounts should now appear with account balances, where appropriate.

One of the first nominal accounts that can be checked is the Bank Account. From the list of accounts in the **Nominal** window, scroll down until you find the account you created in Chapter 4 – N/C 1205. Click on this line to highlight the account name.

Now click on the **Activity** icon, and then accept the defaults given by clicking on **OK**. A list of the transactions that have gone through this account will appear. You should have something similar in style to that shown in Fig. 5.2. If there are too many transactions to fit on the screen, then you can scroll through the transactions in the same way as you can scroll through the list of accounts.

The window in Fig. 5.2 has been maximised to show as much as possible. The **No** column is the transaction number while the **Tp** column shows how the transaction was entered. At this stage it is worth getting to grips with which figures were entered into the **Debit** column and which into the **Credit** column. Any payments made are entered into the **Credit** column, while receipts (money coming into the business) go into the **Debit** column. When a supplier is paid by cheque, for example, the Bank Account is credited while the Supplier Account is debited. When the bank sends us a statement of banking transactions, then the credits and debits will appear the other way round because we then see the account from the bank's perspective rather than our own.

This example of double entry typifies how transactions are handled in accounts. As a rule, all asset accounts will be debited when assets are entering the business and credited when they are leaving the business. These accounts

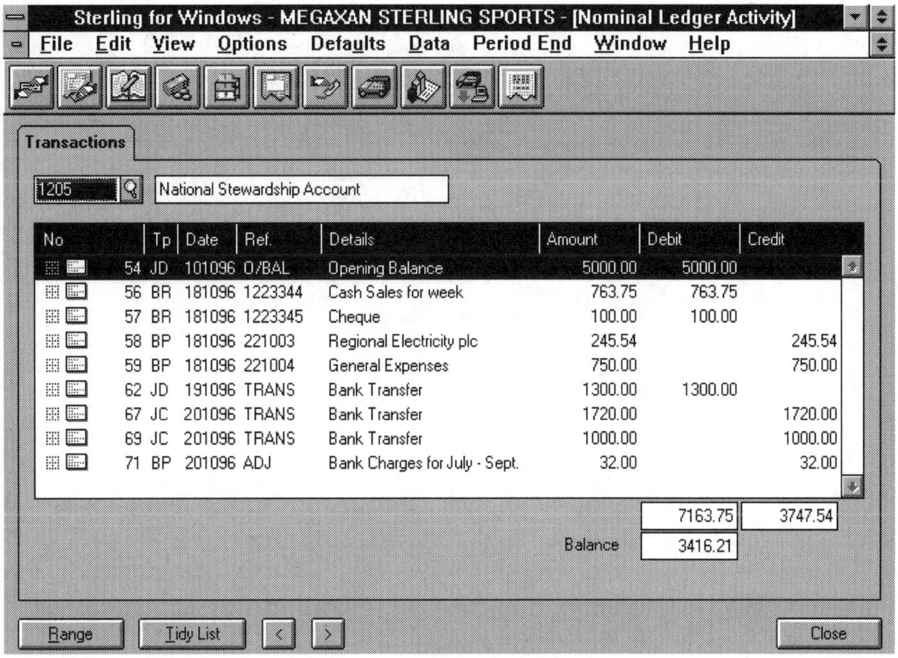

[Figure 5.2 screenshot of Sterling for Windows - MEGAXAN STERLING SPORTS - Nominal Ledger Activity window showing account 1205 National Stewardship Account with transactions:]

No	Tp	Date	Ref.	Details	Amount	Debit	Credit
54	JD	101096	O/BAL	Opening Balance	5000.00	5000.00	
56	BR	181096	1223344	Cash Sales for week	763.75	763.75	
57	BR	181096	1223345	Cheque	100.00	100.00	
58	BP	181096	221003	Regional Electricity plc	245.54		245.54
59	BP	181096	221004	General Expenses	750.00		750.00
62	JD	191096	TRANS	Bank Transfer	1300.00	1300.00	
67	JC	201096	TRANS	Bank Transfer	1720.00		1720.00
69	JC	201096	TRANS	Bank Transfer	1000.00		1000.00
71	BP	201096	ADJ	Bank Charges for July - Sept.	32.00		32.00

Totals: 7163.75 / 3747.54 Balance: 3416.21

Fig. 5.2

'nominally' belong to the asset and not the business. The totals that appear in the panel at the bottom of the screen show the total for **Debits** (receipts) and **Credits** (payments) with the **Balance** being the amount of money in the account. To move on, click on the **Close** button to return to the Activity window and **Close** again to get to the main Nominal window.

VAT control accounts

The Sales Tax Control Account and the Purchase Tax Control Account are also an important pair of VAT control accounts. Figure 5.3 shows the Purchase Tax Control Account. From the main Nominal window, begin by clicking on the **Clear** button at the bottom of the window. This has the effect of removing the highlighted bank account line. When you have done this, you can then highlight the *two* tax control accounts in the same way as you highlighted the bank account line. When you have done this, click on the **Activity** icon again and accept the defaults by clicking on the **OK** button.

You will begin with the transactions history for the Sales Tax Control Account, as this was first in the list of accounts you highlighted. To obtain the Purchase Tax Control Account, as shown in Fig. 5.3, click on the **>** (greater than) button at the bottom of the Transactions window. To get back to the Purchase Tax Account from the Sales Tax Account, you would need to click on the **<** (less than) button.

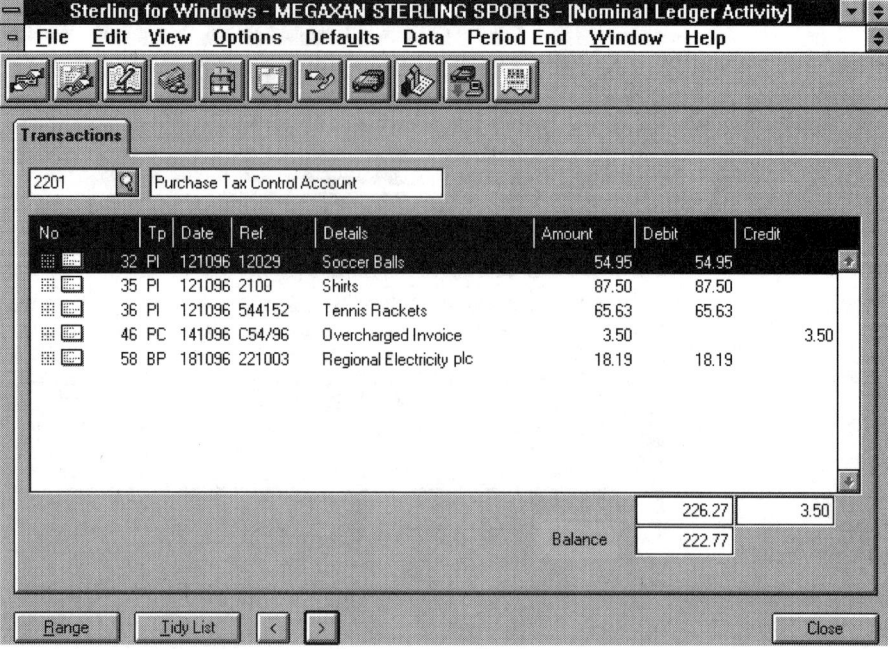

Fig. 5.3

The tax control accounts are used to record all VAT payments and receipts that pass through the Sales and Purchase Ledgers plus those that are recorded when making banking transactions. When a customer is invoiced for goods sent, the Sales Account in the Nominal Ledger is credited by the net amount. The VAT has to be credited to the Sales Tax Control Account. The gross (net plus VAT) amount is then debited to the customer who is in receipt of the goods and now owes that amount to the business (i.e. is a debtor). Alternatively, when goods are purchased with VAT on them, the nominal account that records the purchase is debited by the net amount, with the VAT being debited to the Purchase Tax Control Account.

The two tax control accounts show, in transaction order, all VAT collected by the business in the **Credit** column (to be passed on to HM Customs & Excise). The VAT paid by the business is shown in the **Debit** column (can be claimed from HM Customs & Excise). From Fig. 5.3 you will see that the amount that can be claimed is £226.27. You collected £3.50 in VAT and so you will have to pass this on. In practice, most businesses will collect far more VAT than they pay out and will, as a result, need to pay HM Customs & Excise the difference. Sage has a special facility for helping you settle VAT which will be covered in Chapter 6.

Debtors Control Account

This can be examined in the same way as the other nominal accounts in that if you look at the transaction history, you will see the details of transactions carried out with customers. Return to the main Nominal window and click on the **Clear** button at the bottom of the window. Locate the Debtors Control Account (1100) and Creditors Control Account (2100) in the list of nominal accounts and highlight them by clicking on them. Click on the **Activity** icon and accept the defaults. The transaction history for the Debtors Control Account will appear first.

The Debtors Control Account is used with the Nominal Ledger to record the totals of advances made to customers. The account shows, therefore, the total amount owing to the firm. This preserves the double entry system because, when a sale is made the Sales Account is credited while the Debtors Control Account is debited.

When the customer makes a payment, the Debtors Control Account will be credited (so the debt outstanding is lowered), while the Bank Account is debited (the money being paid to the business).

The use of the Debtors Control Account means that all double entry transactions concerned with selling goods and services are confined only to the operation of the Nominal Ledger.

Creditors Control Account

From the Debtors Control Account, click on the > (greater than) button to move to the Creditors Control Account transaction history.

When a business receives goods from a supplier on a credit-term basis, the Purchase Account or some other account in the Nominal Ledger has to be debited by the value of the goods while the Suppliers Account in the Purchase Ledger is credited. The Creditors Control Account is used with the Nominal Ledger system to record the total of advances received from its suppliers. The account shows, therefore, the total amount owing by the business to its creditors. This also preserves the double entry system because, when credit purchases are made, an asset account is debited while the Creditors Control Account is credited.

When the business makes a payment to its suppliers, the Creditors Control Account will be debited (so the amount outstanding to creditors is lowered) while the Bank Account is credited by the money being paid out by the business.

The use of the Creditors Control Account means that all double entry transactions regarding purchases are confined to the operation of the Nominal Ledger.

Non-control accounts

The control accounts have been used by the Purchase and Sales Ledger to summarise the transactions that have gone through them. Later in this chapter, you will see how these control accounts are used for further analysis of the finances of the business.

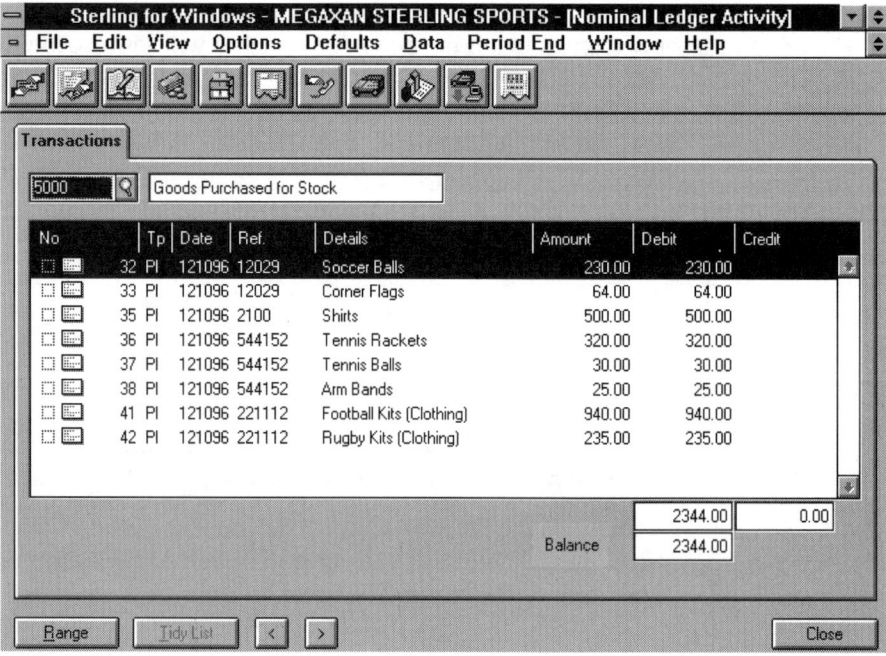

Fig. 5.4

The Nominal Ledger holds many other accounts, many of which you have already used. In Fig. 5.4 the nominal account 5000 was used to save many of the purchases of stock. To view this, you need to return to the main Nominal menu, **Clear** the control accounts from being highlighted and then, as before, highlight what accounts you wish to analyse and click on the **Activity** icon.

Figure 5.4 shows the balance of the nominal account in the Activity window as being £2344 in the **Debit** column and shows how this figure was arrived at. The significance of this is that the purchases for this account totalled £2344 net of VAT. The VAT relating to these purchases would have been debited to the VAT Control Account. You will observe that there are no credit entries in the account. Any credit amount would be treated as the opposite to a purchase and would only come about if, for example, a purchase was reversed because of an entry error.

The trial balance

We shall now deal with a trial balance. This is a report that can be extracted using a different part of the Sage program. The top row of icons includes a **Financials** icon (third from the right). Click on this and you will see another row of icons.

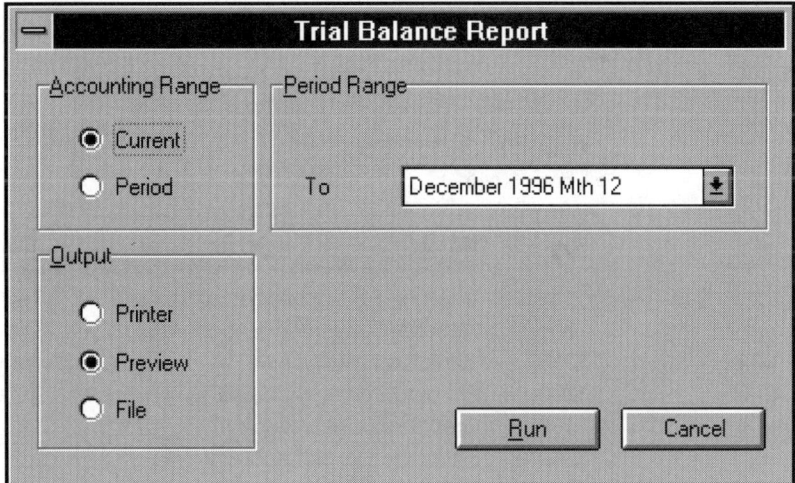

Fig. 5.5

The **Trial Balance** option from the set will produce a trial balance on the screen. Click on this **Trial Balance** icon to reveal a dialogue box as shown in Fig. 5.5. The **Accounting Range** will default at **Current**, which will represent a report for the current month. Setting this as **Period** will allow you to specify a period to the month-end as specified in the **Period Range** where you can select the month using the drop-down list box next to **To**.

Set the accounting period as **Current** and the output to the **Printer** or **Preview**; then click on **Run**. If you choose to print out your trial balance, it will look something like Fig. 5.6. Your trial balance will probably show a set of figures different from the one in Fig. 5.6, but the principle of what appears will be the same.

The significance of the figures is important as they represent, for each account, the net balance. In the Bank Account (1205), for example, we can see at a glance that the debits have exceeded the credits by 3416.21, indicating a bank balance of £3416.21. The other accounts can be read in exactly the same way.

When the figures in the **Debit** and **Credit** columns are added up they will be equal amounts. If each entry has been credited and debited in the Nominal Ledger, then all the debits must add up to all the credits and so must the net difference shown in the trial balances. A Suspense Account exists to ensure that the two sides add up to the same figure. These particular suspense figures came about when opening balances on customer and supplier accounts were entered at the time they were first created. Clearing suspense accounts will be an important topic covered in Chapter 6.

MEGAXAN STERLING SPORTS

TRIAL BALANCE

Date: 17/12/96
Time: 10:18
Page: 1

N/C	Name	Debit	Credit
1100	Debtors Control Account	3 536.73	
1205	National Stewardship Account	3 416.21	
1210	Bank Deposit Account	1 000.00	
1220	Building Society Account	2 000.00	
2100	Creditors Control Account		9 058.58
2200	Sales Tax Control Account		439.44
2201	Purchase Tax Control Account	222.77	
4000	Sales Type A		2 533.04
4009	Discounts Allowed	40.00	
4010	Sales Returns	22.00	
4902	Commissions Received		100.00
5000	Goods Purchased for Stock	2 344.00	
5001	Materials Imported	1 230.00	
5009	Discounts Taken		75.00
5010	Returns Outward		35.00
5100	Carriage	20.00	
7000	Gross Wages	750.00	
7200	Electricity	227.35	
7901	Bank Charges	32.00	
9998	Suspense Account		2 600.00
	Totals:	14 841.06	14 841.06

Fig. 5.6

NOMINAL LEDGER ORGANISATION

The Nominal Ledger function, as has already been seen, is very different from the Sales and Purchase Ledgers. It does, however, require a good deal of information from them. The focal point in the Nominal Ledger function is the actual nominal accounts organisation. Each nominal account has a name given to it which is determined by the business which uses the system. Account names will vary considerably, depending on the type of business using the system. Sage allows a default setup which creates a series of accounts organised into a number of groups. If you have followed the guidelines set out in this book, you will already have this setup with the defaults given by Sage. For most businesses, this setup will probably suffice, perhaps with some small alterations and additions.

Given this layout, or any other, accounts have to be placed into a category. These categories are important when it comes to extracting various reports. The accounts are broken into two main groups: profit and loss and balance sheet.

Profit and loss

These include all accounts relating to transactions that contribute to making a profit or a loss. Such accounts fall into the following subcategories:

- *Sales.* Accounts relating to selling goods or services. Such accounts will also include any goods returned to the business by its customers.
- *Purchases.* Accounts relating to buying stock or the cost of finished goods manufactured for stock. Such accounts will also include any goods returned to the supplier or back into manufacturing.
- *Direct expenses.* Accounts needed by manufacturers to work out total production costs that can then be carried forward to the trading part of the business. Such accounts will include direct material costs, labour costs and various factory overheads.
- *Overhead expenses.* Accounts that refer to the expenses incurred generally in the running of the business, such as electricity, wages and rent.
- *Revenues.* Accounts that are used to record income coming into a business such as income from clients for services carried out.

Balance sheet

- *Financed by.* Accounts used to hold transactions regarding the long-term financing of the business, such as share capital, mortgages, long-term loans and retained profits.
- *Current liabilities.* Accounts referring to those debts owed by the business that will need to be repaid in the near future. An obvious example of this will be the sums owing to trade creditors as recorded in the Purchase Ledger. Another example would be a bank overdraft or any short-term loans arranged.
- *Fixed assets.* Accounts recording transactions relating to the permanent assets of the business such as land, buildings, machinery, furniture, fixtures, fittings and motor vehicles. Also included with these accounts will be any depreciation on such assets which will come about as a result of wear and tear, obsolescence or, in the case of leaseholds, expiry date.
- *Current assets.* Accounts holding transactions regarding those assets of the business that will be required to be used in its operations, and so will have a more temporary nature to the fixed assets. Examples are stocks, trade debtors, cash and money held in a bank current account.

Most accounts will fall into their respective categories quite easily. With the exceptions, experience will be required to ensure they fall into the correct category. In practice, an accountant will be involved in the process of setting up the structure of the nominal accounts system. If you are in any doubt where an account should fall, then *ask* – do not attempt to guess.

Nominal account layout

To illustrate how to create an account and how to place it into the correct category, this section will take you through the following processes:

- Create an account called Computer Software & Support.
- Give the account a budget.
- Create a nominal group of accounts called Computer Software.
- Place the Computer Software group of accounts into the Overheads.

Make sure you are at the main Nominal screen and click on the **Record** icon. You should now have a window that allows you to add a new nominal account to the system or amend an existing one. Figure 5.7 shows a window completed with the details that follow. Enter as the Nominal Account (**N/C**) number 8010. This will create a new account. Enter as the **Account Name** Computer Software & Support.

If there is already an opening balance, then you can enter this either as a figure in first line of the **Actuals** column, or by clicking on the **O/B** icon beside **Balance** and entering the amount as a **Debit** item. Entering the details in the **Actuals** column will require you to have a breakdown of the costs as an amount per month.

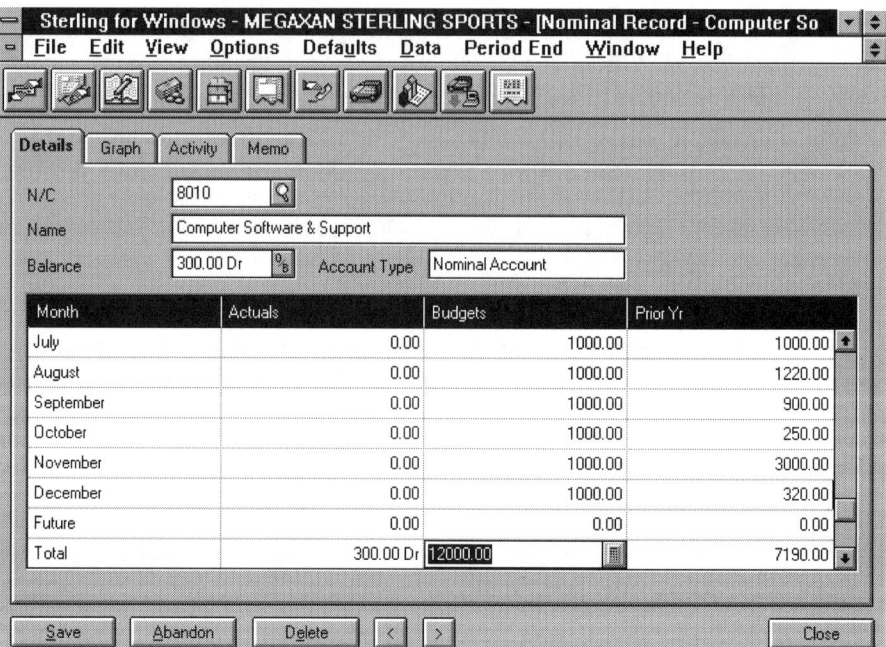

Fig. 5.7

This window also shows a panel where you can enter **Budget** details. The yearly budget allows you to enter a figure that you believe should not be exceeded over the year. There is little point in placing a **Budget** figure for either trading purchases or sales, because you will aim to maximise sales in most cases, which will require a high amount of purchasing if sales demand proves to be high. A **Budget** figure placed on these accounts will tend to be used as a target figure rather than as an attempt to control costs.

If you scroll down the panel to where the **Totals** are, and then enter a single figure for the whole year, Sage will automatically allocate an equal amount to each month. Alternatively, instead of entering the total like this, you could enter the figure for each month separately and then the total would be calculated for you. The other analysis columns are for the actual spending (**Actuals**) and the spending of the previous year (**Prior Yr**). As spending takes place, the **Actuals** column will show figures so that you can compare the actual figures against the budget. Consequently, you cannot enter the actual figures for all months of the year through this window – only those that have passed. The previous year's figures can be entered for the sake of comparison.

When you have completed this window, click on the **Save** icon to allow the new account to become a permanent part of your system. Click on the **Close** button to return to the main Nominal window. The next stage will be to place the account in the nominal system so that the amount can be included in future reports for future extraction.

From the main set of icons near the top of your screen, click on the **Financials** icon. This is the part of the system you used to extract a trial balance. Now click on the **Chart of Accounts** icon that now appears. You will now be presented with a list of layouts, of which only **Default Layout of Accounts** will appear. Click on this to reveal how the accounts have been grouped. On the left of the screen you will see the list of categories in which accounts will appear. Click on **Overheads** to see the list of accounts in this group appear in the panel to the right. Figure 5.8 shows the dialogue box where Overheads appear.

Each account group will have its own name and set of accounts. You will enter the account Computer Software & Support (8010) into a group to be called Computer Software. First, click on the **High** figure that appears on the **Depreciation** row and alter it to 8005. This will prevent your new account appearing in two groups. Now click on the first blank line and enter the details showing Overheads to have the heading Computer Software & Support and the **Low** value as 8010 with the **High** at 8099 – all accounts between (and including) these numbers will be a part of this category. Figure 5.8 illustrates the required entry. Category **A**ccount will be the heading used for the group. When you have done this, click on **OK**. In future, you will be able to add more accounts to this group because you have provided for additional account numbers – i.e. 8011 to 8099 inclusive.

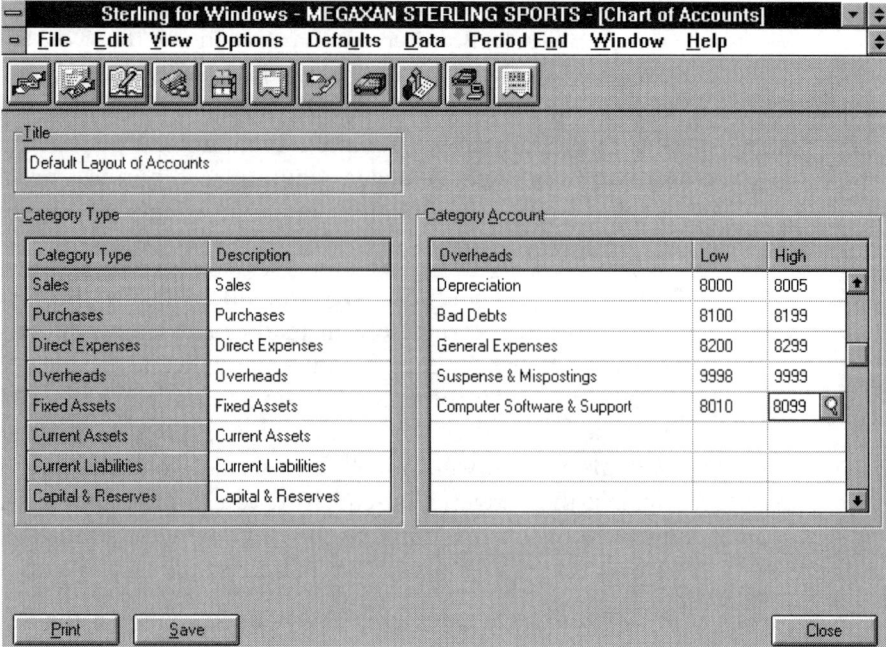

Fig. 5.8

To see how the accounts have been placed in their respective categories, look at the panel to see the inclusion; you may have to scroll up or down to see it. When you have done this, click on the **Print** button below to examine how this fits into the nominal structure.

Fig. 5.9 shows the dialogue box that will appear, offering three print options. If you select **Print Chart of Accounts** you get:

- a list of profit and loss accounts categories and these, in turn, are broken down into groups of accounts – Sales, Purchases, Direct Expenses and Overheads;
- a list of balance sheet categories and these, in turn, are broken down into groups of accounts – Fixed Assets, Current Assets, Current Liabilities and Capital & Reserves.

Print Missing Accounts will print those accounts that appear in no category and, consequently, will not appear in a final set of accounts. **Print Duplicate Accounts** will print those accounts that appear in two categories. Experiment with the printouts. For each one, you have the option of **Preview** rather than printing on paper each time.

Keep clicking on the **Close** buttons until you are at the main Nominal window.

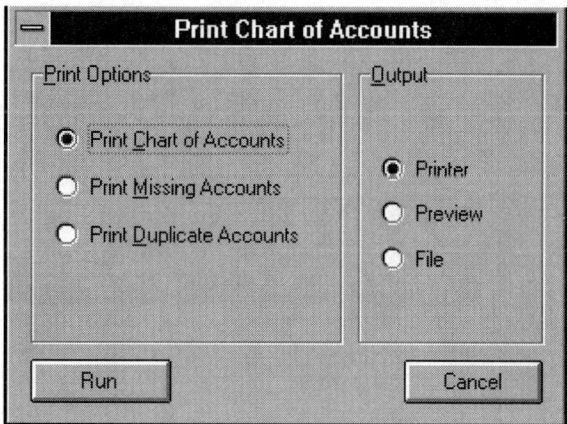

Fig. 5.9

DOUBLE ENTRY SUMMARISED

Throughout this chapter, you have been made aware of the principle of double entry. An understanding of this is important to be able to get the best out of the reports available and to be able to correct any errors. It is also needed if you are to make effective use of the journal entries. As an exercise, you should enter some details about the fixed assets of a business. Assume that the fixed assets are as described in Table 5.1.

Table 5.1

Fixed asset	Cost	Nominal account
Office equipment	£60 000	0030
Fixtures and fittings	£18 000	0040
Motor vehicles	£24 000	0050

These fixed assets are all going to be financed by the capital of the business whose details are entered in Account 3000 (Ordinary Shares). To finance these fixed assets – totalling £102 000 – the capital will have to equal that amount. Figure 5.10 shows how this has been entered.

To enter this click on the **Journal Entry** icon from the main Nominal window. Now enter the details. Try and vary the figures from those that appear in Fig. 5.10. To post a journal entry with Sage, *all the debit figures must add up*

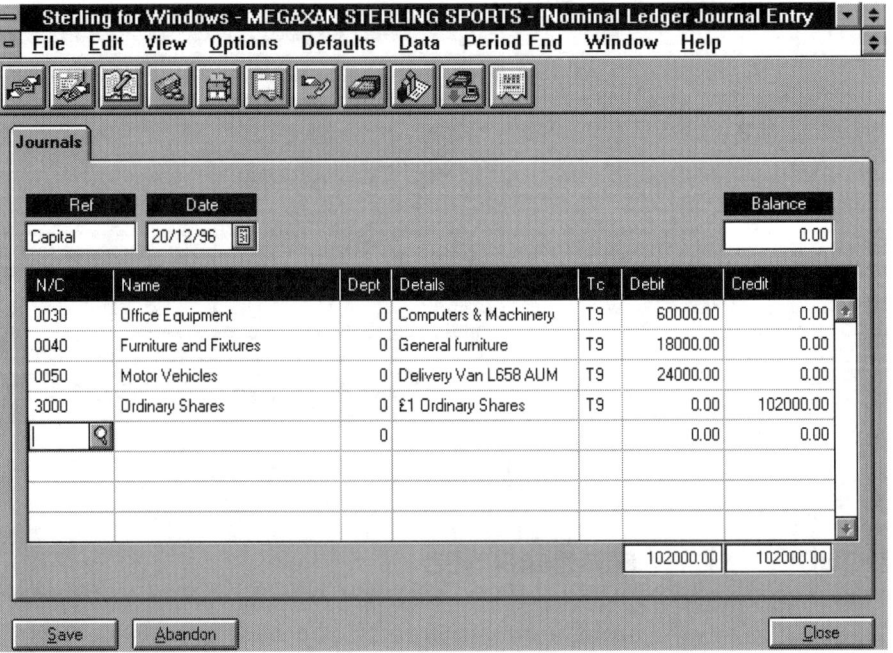

Fig. 5.10

to the credit figures. In fact, this will be shown in the **Balance** box (top right) which will have to be zero when the Journal Entry window has been completed. When the journal is complete, you should click on **Save**. If the balance is not zero, then Sage will not post the entries.

Figure 5.11 shows a further example of how the Journal Entry window is used to make double entries to the nominal accounts. The first two entries are used to make a provision for depreciation on motor vehicles owned by the business. The effect of depreciation is to create a valuation of fixed assets below what was paid for them. This is an attempt to give a true asset valuation of the business. To do this, you have to credit accounts that are especially set up for the assets in question. The asset that has to be debited is an expense which, in this case, has been called simply Depreciation. Chapter 6 will return to the issue of depreciation.

Another type of transaction that can be entered through the journal, and is also illustrated in Fig. 5.11, is when a business purchases fixed assets on a credit-term basis. The example shows that a new computer was purchased for the office at a cost of £2300. As the business did not pay by cheque or cash for it, you cannot enter the transaction as though it were a bank payment. If it had, it would have credited the bank and debited the Office Equipment (Fixed Asset) Account. Instead of crediting the bank, the journal entry has allowed you to credit the business that has supplied the computer (Q-Tek Computer Systems). At a later date, when you are ready to pay Q-Tek for the

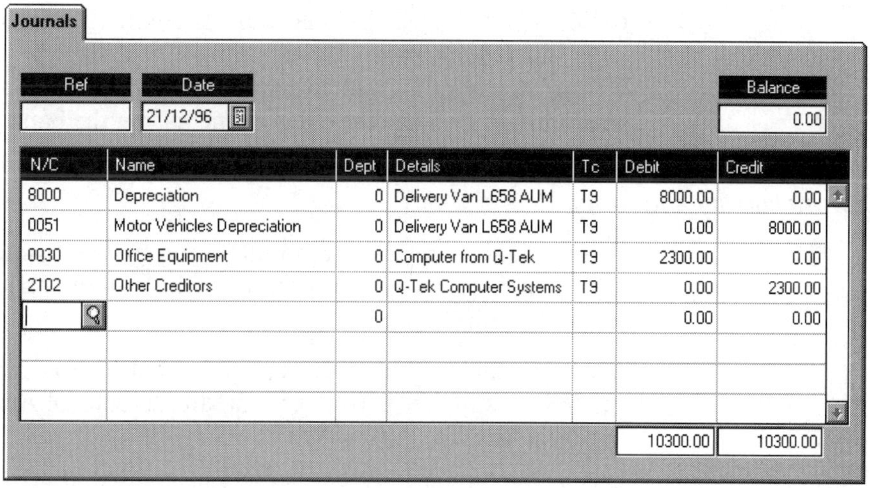

N/C	Name	Dept	Details	Tc	Debit	Credit
8000	Depreciation	0	Delivery Van L658 AUM	T9	8000.00	0.00
0051	Motor Vehicles Depreciation	0	Delivery Van L658 AUM	T9	0.00	8000.00
0030	Office Equipment	0	Computer from Q-Tek	T9	2300.00	0.00
2102	Other Creditors	0	Q-Tek Computer Systems	T9	0.00	2300.00
		0			0.00	0.00
					10300.00	10300.00

Fig. 5.11

computer, you will enter the payment as a bank payment and Sage will debit the Q-Tek account and credit the bank account.

The journal allows you to enter any Nominal Ledger transaction that cannot be done through the Sales Ledger, Purchase Ledger, Banking transaction or Cash transaction. To use the journal effectively, you have to be clear about when to debit or credit. The rules listed in the following section may help you in future.

The balance sheet

Fixed asset accounts

- *Debit.* These accounts are debited when more of a fixed asset is purchased. As you debit such accounts, so the value of fixed assets on the balance sheet increases.
- *Credit.* When an asset is disposed of, these accounts are credited by the amount paid for such assets. Most fixed assets also have a Provision for Depreciation Account relating to them which is credited each time this provision is increased. It has the effect of reducing the value of fixed assets on the balance sheet.

Current assets accounts

- *Debit.* These accounts are debited when more of a current asset is acquired. Current assets are largely made up of stock, debtors, bank (other than an overdraft) and cash. Each time they are debited, they are added to. The use of the word 'current' would indicate that they do not form as permanent a feature of the business as do fixed assets.

- *Credit.* Each time such an account is credited, it falls in value on the balance sheet. For example, every time a customer pays a bill, the Debtors Control Account is credited reducing the value of debtors. Where a debtor pays a bill, it also has the effect of increasing the bank balance.

Current liability accounts

A current liability refers to amounts owed by the business normally payable within the next few weeks or months, such as an outstanding bill to a supplier or a bank overdraft.

- *Debit.* As such accounts are debited, what is owed will be reduced. If, for example, a supplier is paid, the Creditors Control Account will be debited to reflect this.
- *Credit.* Each time a current liability is credited, it adds to the amount owed by the business. Hence, if goods are purchased from a supplier, then the Creditors Control Account is credited.

Financed by

- *Debit.* This reduces the amount that is financing the business. If, for example, the business settles a long-term loan, then the loan account is debited while the Bank Account (if the settlement is by cheque) is credited.
- *Credit.* This increases the finance to the business and can either be in the form of the owners' (or shareholders') interest or the form of long-term loans. If, for example, new shares are issued and taken up, the Shareholders Accounts are credited with the amount while the Bank Account (or wherever the money is deposited) is debited.

Profit & loss accounts

Manufacturing

Manufacturing accounts that are debited represent additional costs of manufacturing. Typically, they might include such accounts as Direct Labour, Direct Materials, Factory Overheads, Depreciation of Manufacturing Equipment. There will be fewer occasions when such accounts are credited but an example of this would be if the stock of raw materials or work in progress had to be taken off this year's manufacturing costs and carried over to next year.

Trading

These accounts are needed to help determine gross profit – the difference between sales income and the cost of goods sold. The accounts in this section are required for businesses who trade in stock.

- *Credit.* Trading accounts that are credited result in stock leaving the business. The accounts that normally constitute this part are those of Sales, Returns Outwards and the Closing Stock.
- *Debit.* Such accounts are debited when they represent stock coming into the business. The accounts that normally constitute this part are those of Purchases, Returns Inwards, Carriage on Purchases and Opening Stock.

When all the debits are taken away from the sum of the credits you will arrive at the *gross profit*.

Expense and revenue

Expenses

- *Debit.* Whenever an expense is incurred, the respective expense account will be debited. All such debits will have the effect of reducing profit.
- *Credit.* Expense accounts will not be credited too often as such an effect is to reverse an expense. This may occur if something, such as rates, is rebated or an expense is found to have been paid in advance at the end of a year.

Revenues

Revenues represent income to a business and debiting such an account has the effect of reducing income.

- *Debit.* Few occasions should occur when this happens. Refunding a client some money previously paid could be such an occasion.
- *Credit.* Whenever such income is received, the respective revenue account will be credited. All such credits will have the effect of increasing profit.

PETTY CASH TRANSACTIONS

This was left until now as it will help you develop a better understanding of how to use the journal entries, as well as understand double entry. Start off with some money held as a cash float. You can achieve this in two ways: either make a journal entry to credit the Bank Account and debit the Petty Cash Account, or perform a bank transfer. Fig. 5.12 shows both methods being used where a transfer of £400 from the Bank Account into Petty Cash is being made.

Method 1 – Journal entry

From the main Nominal menu, click on the **Journal Entry** icon and then, as shown in Fig. 5.12(a), debit Petty Cash by the £400 and credit the Bank Account by the same amount.

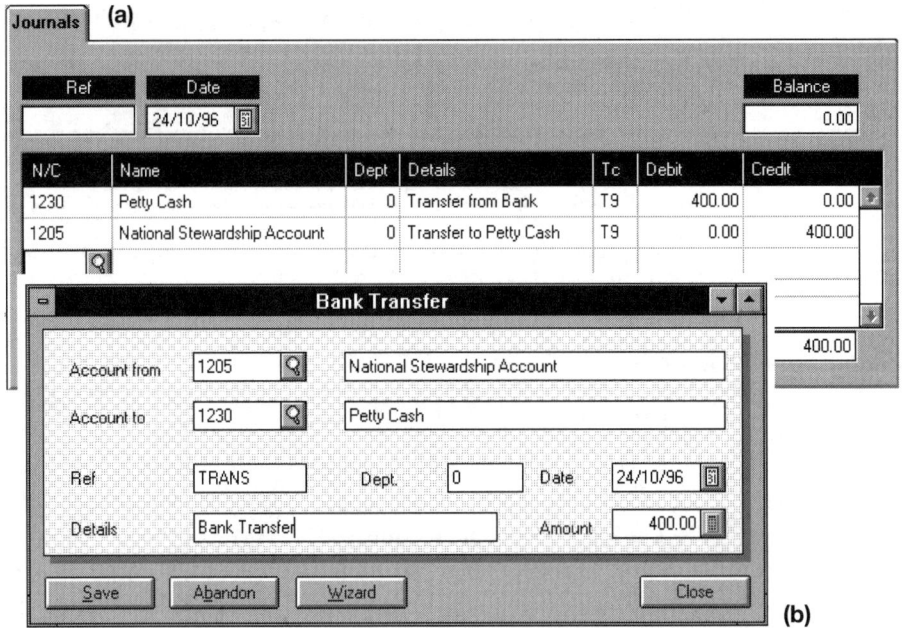

Fig. 5.12

Method 2 – Bank transfer

This is really the preferred method as it does not require much double entry knowledge. To do this, click on the **Bank Transfer** icon from the main Bank window. Then, as shown in Fig. 5.12(b), transfer £400 **from** Account 1205 (Bank Account) **to** Account 1230 (the Petty Cash Account).

Use *one* of these methods now. Do not do both as this would create twice the amount in Petty Cash. Now that you have something in the way of a cash float, you can begin to show some petty cash spending.

Although the vast bulk of business spending will be by cheque and, consequently, will generate a banking transaction, some spending will be by petty cash for convenience sake. In the next example, you will use some of the petty cash to purchase tea and coffee (£10 plus £1.75 VAT) and some to purchase petrol (£18 plus £3.15 VAT). As a principle, there is no need to create a single nominal account for every conceivable type of expenditure. As has already been seen with the purchase of a computer earlier, some generic heading that covers a range of expenditure types will suffice. It will be up to a business and its accountant to apply a degree of common sense.

To enter a cash transaction, return to the main Sage window by closing the Journal window and then closing the Nominal window. Now click on the **Bank** icon from the main set of icons. Highlight Account 1230. This has been set up as a cash account. When this is highlighted, click on the **Payment** icon and you will see a dialogue box confirming that you are about to record payments from a cash account.

The Nominal Ledger 97

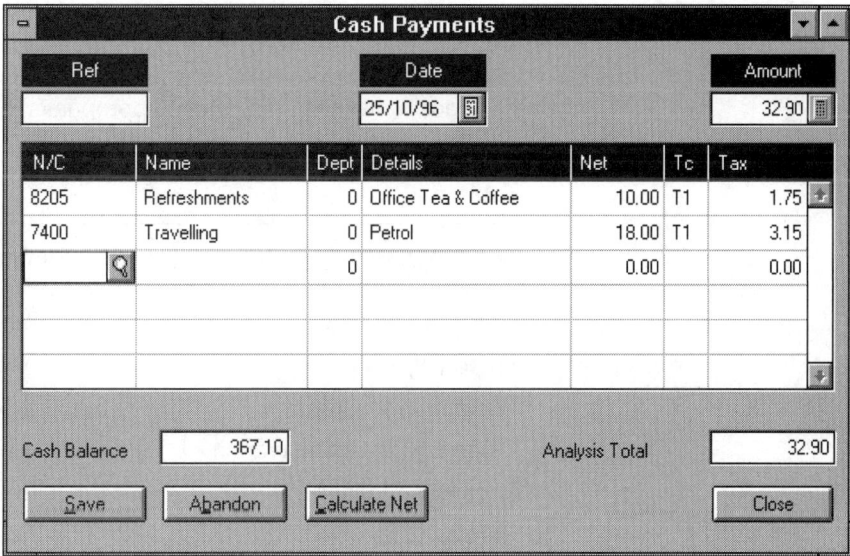

Fig. 5.13

Figure 5.13 shows the two petty cash payments being recorded. As you will see, this entry window is similar to that of the Banking Payments entry window. The result of this transaction, when saved, will be to debit the two expense accounts and credit the Petty Cash Account. When the petty cash amount either reaches or passes zero, you will need to repeat the process of transferring money from a bank account to the Petty Cash Account.

As with a bank account, you can create new cash accounts. It is done in exactly the same way as you created a bank account in Chapter 4. When creating such an account, you need to set its type of account as Cash. In a practical situation, more than one petty cash float may be needed if, for example, you have many departments in a business, each needing its own petty cash.

EXERCISES

As a way of gaining a greater knowledge of the Nominal Ledger, try the following questions. If you have already set up the Nominal Ledger as you worked through this chapter, then some of the tasks should be missed out.

1 Extract an accounts list in order to determine where your control accounts are.

2 (a) Determine the grouping of accounts being used for the fixed assets and current assets.
  (b) Create the following fixed asset accounts:
    – Warehouse Leasehold
    – Warehouse Fixtures & Fittings
    – Office Machinery
    – Company Delivery Van.

3 (a) Determine the grouping of accounts being used for the expenses and revenues.
   (b) Create the expense accounts listed in Table 5.2, placing a budget figure against the accounts indicated, where appropriate:

Table 5.2

Account name	Budget needed?
Carriage & Postage	Yes
Entertainment	Yes
Warehouse Insurance	No
Office Equipment Insurance	No
Printing & Stationery	Yes
Rent on Garages	Yes
Telephone	Yes
Travel	Yes
Office Wages & Salaries	Yes
Warehouse Wages & Salaries	Yes
Water Rates	Yes

Note: Some of the expense accounts that already exist can have their account names altered to suit this list rather than you creating new account numbers.

   (c) Create or amend for the following revenue accounts:
   – Client Consultancy Receipts
   – Interest received on Bank Deposit Account.

4 Create or amend for the following financed by accounts:
   – Shareholders' equity
   – Long-term bank loan.

5 Enter, via a journal entry, an opening trial balance for the following:

	£	£
Shareholders' equity		50 000
Long-term bank loan		20 000
Client consultancy receipts		2 400
Interest received on bank deposit account		600
Bank deposit	11 000	
Electricity	400	
Warehouse wages and salaries	18 000	
Warehouse leasehold	20 000	
Fixtures and fittings	18 000	

Entertainment	750	
Office equipment insurance	1 200	
Rent on garages	2 000	
Telephone	650	
Water rates	1 000	
	73 000	73 000

6 Transfer £300 from the bank to petty cash and then enter some cash transactions for the following:

Payments
- An electricity bill
- Milk and sugar for the office
- Postage stamps

Receipts
- Cash received from an employee for a telephone call made
- Cash received for a sale

Transfer all petty cash to the bank leaving £100 as a float.

7 Make a journal entry to reduce the value of motor vehicles by crediting the relevant depreciation account for the fixed asset and debiting the Depreciation Expense Account.

8 Extract a trial balance.

9 Extract the following reports as a way of examining the effects of the tasks undertaken:
- a trial balance
- control account histories
- history of all other active accounts
- a balance sheet.

CHAPTER 6

Advanced ledger work

INTRODUCTION

This chapter takes you through a number of important features required in most businesses. You will deal with ending a year of trading and clearing out many balance sheet accounts, leaving only balances brought down from the previous year in the new accounts and opening completely fresh profit and loss accounts. You will need to address the problem of accounts becoming too large as the year progresses, and find a way of streamlining the accounts so that they are manageable while not losing their completeness and accuracy.

This chapter will start by examining some of the more advanced features of managing the ledgers more effectively. One of the more important uses of a computer is to manage accounts efficiently, especially when they become large in number. An important requirement later in this chapter will be to make alterations to your accounts in the Nominal Ledger so that the final accounts produced at the end of any year truly reflect the performance of the business. This was touched upon in Chapter 5 when you accounted for depreciation on fixed assets. This chapter will take this a stage further as well as showing you how to adjust expenses and revenues to reflect the true overheads and income of the business in a trading period.

MANAGING THE SALES LEDGER

Opening customer balances

When a business starts a Sales Ledger for the first time, it must set up all its customer accounts *and* enter their opening balances before the Sales Ledger can be used on a day-to-day basis. This was done in Chapter 2 when you created some customers. You will now investigate what actually happened a little further.

When customer details were entered for the first time, you were offered the option of entering an opening balance. When you did so, Sage asked you for the opening balance by requesting the amount – as an invoice if the customer owed you money, or as a credit note if the customer had a credit balance. When the amount was entered, the account was duly debited or credited with the amount. Assuming the amount was a debit balance, the following would have happened:

1 The Customer Account would have been debited by the amount on the invoices outstanding and would have been given the reference O/BAL.
2 The Debtors Control Account in the Nominal Ledger would have been debited by the same amount to indicate that this is a current asset to the business.
3 The Suspense Account, which Sage sets up as Nominal Account 9998, would have been credited to allow a double entry to be made.

The purpose of the Suspense Account in this instance is to allow the transaction to proceed without hindrance and for you to make the necessary adjustments later so that the trial balance correctly reflects the state of affairs of the business at a specific point in time. What matters at this stage is that all customer details are on the computer showing an accurate account of what is owed. Later in this chapter you will examine the role of the Suspense Account and what you have to do about the transactions in it. For now, we will proceed with dealing with Sales Ledger transactions.

Returned cheques

This refers to the situation where a cheque that has been received by a customer has been returned by the bank after it has been deposited. When the cheque was first received, you will have debited the Bank Account and credited the Debtors Control Account in the Nominal Ledger, and credited the Customer Account in the Sales Ledger. When the cheque is returned by the bank, you will need to get Sage to reverse this process completely.

Sage allows you to do this automatically via the Features part of the program. Begin by making sure you are not in either the Sales or Purchase Ledgers (Customers or Suppliers main windows). Now click on the **Data** option from the main pull-down menu. This will reveal a sub-menu from which you need to click on **Write off, refund, return Wizard**. Figure 6.1(a) shows the resulting dialogue box.

Sage uses its Wizard to guide you through each of the stages involved. You need to start by selecting which of the ledgers you wish to work with. Click on the **Sales Ledger** option, which is the top one. When this is done, click on the **Next** button to move to the second stage. The next dialogue box is shown in Fig. 6.1(b). Select the second entry in this list, **Customer Cheque Returns**, by highlighting this option and clicking on the **Next** button.

As shown in Fig. 6.1(c), you must now choose the customer. Highlight any customer and then click on the **Next** button. A list of cheque receipts for that customer will appear, as shown in Fig. 6.2(a). If you do not have any cheques against a chosen customer, then return to the previous dialogue box by clicking on the **Back** button.

Click on the line that contains the necessary cheque details, thus highlighting it (*see* Fig. 6.2(a)). Now click on the **Next** button to record the cheque

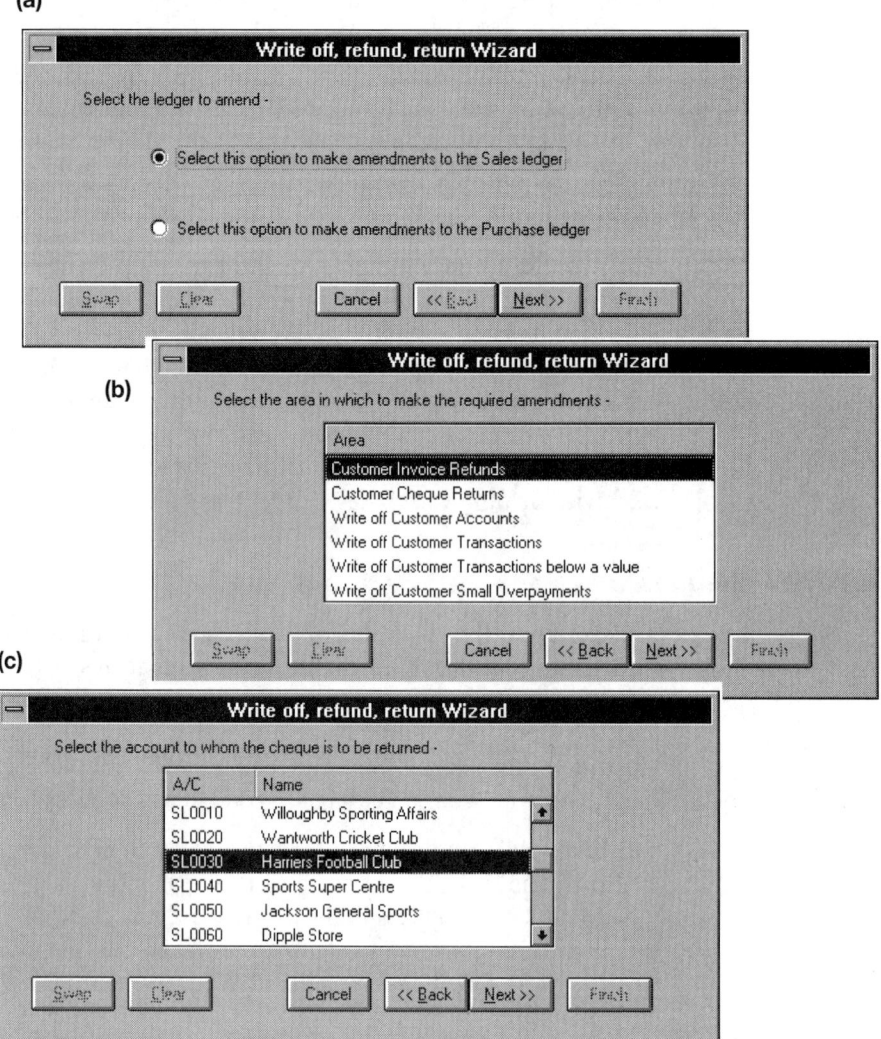

Fig. 6.1

return. You will now be asked to confirm that you want this transaction to go ahead, as shown in Fig. 6.2(b). Click on **Finish** to confirm. If you did not want this cheque cancelled, then click on **Cancel** to abort the whole transaction or click on **Back** to repeat the last process. This window will automatically close after this transaction and will cause the following entries to occur:

- The customer record will show a void cheque payment and will have its account debited to record the fact that the money is still owing.
- The Debtors Control Account will be debited by the amount.
- The Mispostings Account will be credited.

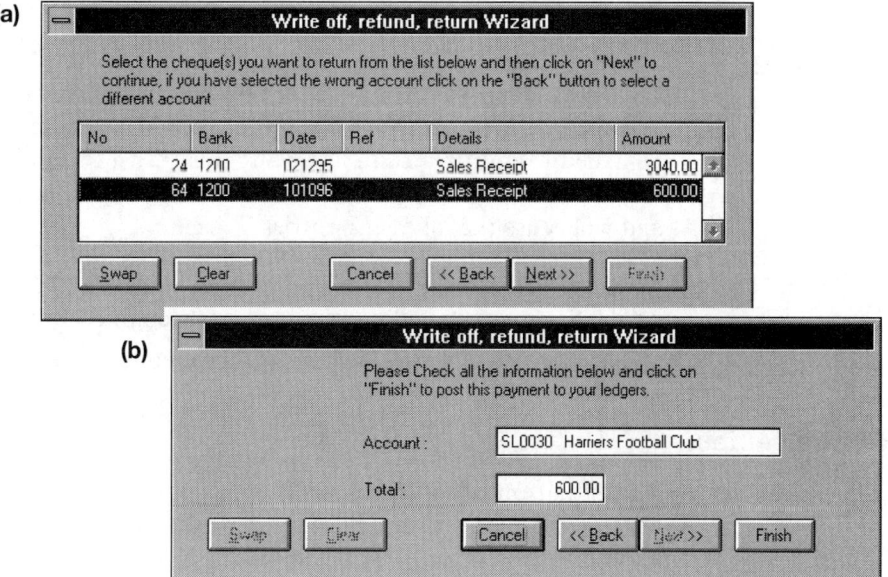

Fig. 6.2

To complete the transaction, Sage will then carry out a journal entry to:

- debit the Mispostings Account;
- credit the Default Bank Account.

It may still be necessary for you to transfer the money from another bank account to the default one if the cheque is to be abandoned.

Cancelling invoices

If an invoice has been sent to a customer in error or, because of the existence of too many errors, you wish to cancel an invoice and issue another one, Sage has a facility for doing this which is referred to as a *customer invoice refund*.

For whatever reason, the effect is similar to processing a cheque that has been received from a customer. On the Nominal Ledger, you will need to credit the Debtors Control Account (reduce what is owing) by the complete invoice amount and debit the Nominal Sales Accounts that were previously credited (lower the sales value). On the Sales Ledger, you will need to credit the Customer Account as though the invoice had been settled.

The steps here are almost identical to that of entering a returned cheque. Click on the **Data** option from the main pull-down menu. This will reveal a sub-menu from which you need to click on **Write off, refund, return Wizard.** Now click on the **Customer Invoice Refund** option from the available list and click on **Next**.

You must now choose the customer. Highlight any customer and then click on the **Next** button. A list of invoices for that customer will appear.

Click on the line that contains the required invoice details, thus highlighting it and then click on the **Next** button to record the cheque return. You will now be asked to confirm that you want this transaction to go ahead. Click on **Finish** to confirm. This window will automatically close after this transaction and will cause the following entries to occur:

- The invoice amount will be credited to the Customer Account.
- The Sales accounts that were previously credited will now be debited.
- The Debtors Control Account will be credited.

Contra entries

This situation often arises when a business deals with another business as both a supplier and a customer. In other words, a business both sells to another business and buys from it. In this instance an arrangement may be made where, instead of paying for all your supplies from this business and then invoicing it for all that is owing, you simply settle the difference between you. Entering a transaction that cancels an amount owing by you with an amount owing to you is called a *contra entry*. Before you attempt this, it is important to understand the stages involved.

Let us suppose that a firm is both a customer and a supplier to the business. To make a contra entry using a method involving both sides paying cheques, you would first pay the amount owing to the supplier in the normal way through Bank Payments to a supplier. Second, through the Bank Receipts as a customer, you would record the receipt of the cheque from the customer. Sage allows you to do the whole transaction in a single step.

Before you can start, you will have to ensure similar accounts exist in both the Sales and Purchase Ledgers. In the example shown here, Minerva Football Club Ltd, which existed in the Sales Ledger, is added to the Purchase Ledger. Create such an account now and generate a purchase invoice so that you have a debt outstanding with which to process a contra entry. Ensure you have at least one sales invoice outstanding.

Now click on the **Data** option from the main pull-down menu and, from the sub-menu which appears, click on **Contra**. The resulting dialogue box will begin by requesting the account references of both a customer and supplier. When these are entered, two boxes will list the invoices outstanding for the Sales Ledger on the left and Purchase Ledger on the right, as shown in Fig. 6.3.

In the example shown, there is a sales invoice outstanding of £117.50 and a set of purchase invoices outstanding amounting to £265.45. Minerva Football, therefore, owes £117.50 but is also owed £265.45. The contra entry should clear the £117.50 they owe us on the Sales Ledger and leave us still owing them £147.95 on the Purchase Ledger. Now click on the sales invoice that contains

Advanced ledger work **105**

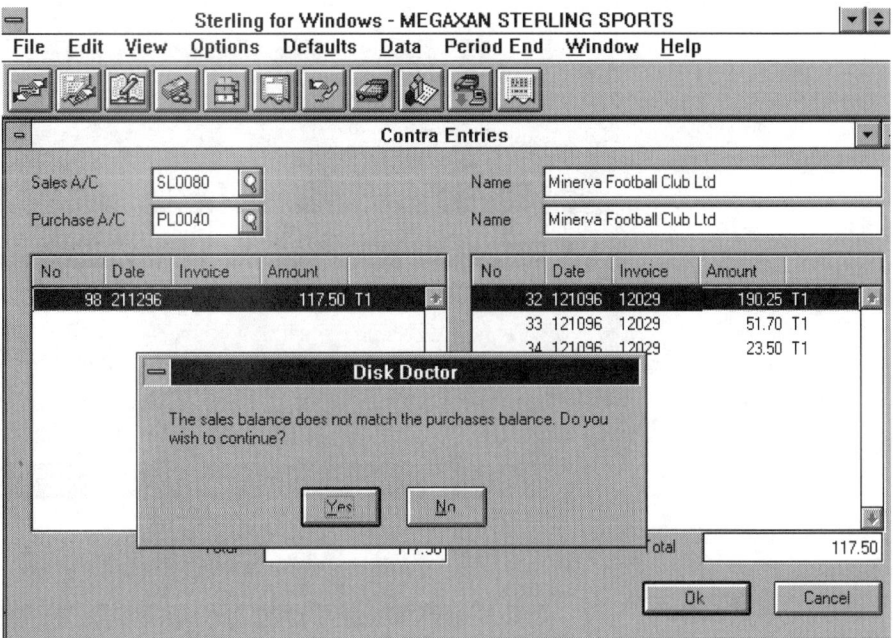

Fig. 6.3

the invoice amount and on any purchase invoice line that can be settled with this amount. If it is more than the sales invoice, then do not highlight any other lines. If it is less, then highlight more lines until it reaches the figure.

When this is done, click on **OK** to perform the contra entry. If the amounts do not balance, then a message will come up to this effect, as shown in Fig. 6.3. Click on **Yes** in answer to this message to part-pay the purchase invoice(s) with the sales invoice.

The effect, in this case, will be to settle the sales invoice and pay £117.50 towards the purchase invoices. Sage will work out the fact that there is insufficient to settle the amount completely. In this example, the double entry on the Nominal Ledger will be to:

- credit the Debtors Control Account by £400;
- debit the Creditors Control Account by £400.

From Fig. 6.4, you will see that both the sales activity and purchase activity histories each show the contra entries and how they have affected the balances now outstanding on their respective accounts.

Bad debts

A bad debt occurs when your business decides no longer to pursue money owing by a customer and shows in its accounts that this debt is no longer regarded as an asset to the business. The effect of a bad debt is to add to the

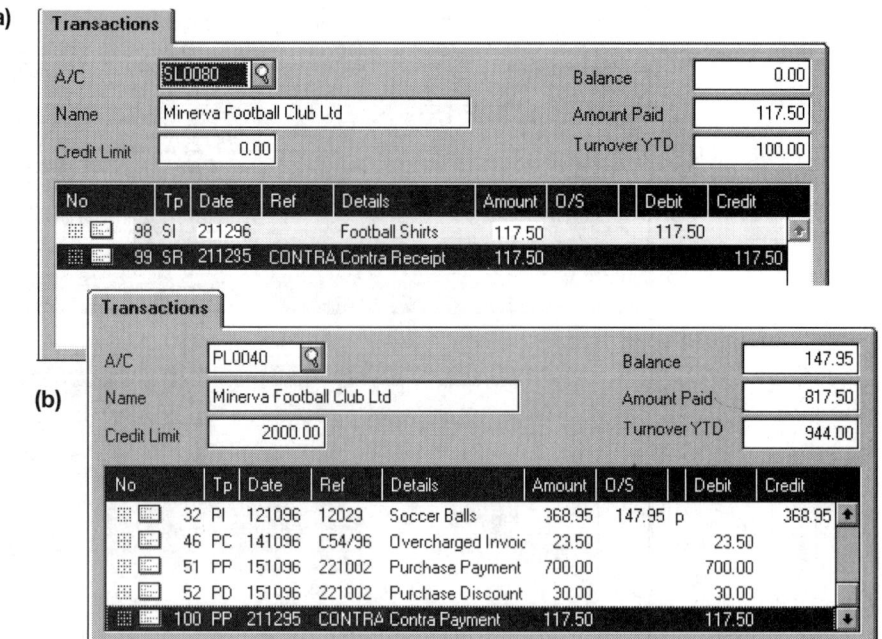

Fig. 6.4

expense of a business. What is effectively being done, is that the business is paying the debt for the customer. The result is to credit the account of the customer and debit an expense account called bad debt write off.

This facility within Sage is again done via the **Data** pull-down menu. Pull down this menu and then click on **Write off, refund, return Wizard**. Now click on the **Write Off Customer Accounts** option from the available list and click on **Next**. As before, you must now choose the customer. Highlight any customer and then click on the **Next** button. A list of customer accounts will appear. Click on the customer to write off and then click on the **Next** button. Sage will ask you to confirm this action and then, when you click on **Finish**, will perform the operation and return you to the main Sage window. The following transaction will have occurred:

- The Debtors Control Account is credited by the amount.
- The Bad Debt Write Off (Expense) Account is debited.
- The Customer Account is cleared of money owing, but not deleted from the list of customer accounts.

Note that no adjustment is made to the VAT amount. If you want the VAT to be cancelled as well, so that you avoid having to pass it on to HM Customs & Excise, you will have to make a separate entry where you would credit the Bad Debt Write Off Account and debit the Sales VAT Account.

Sage also has the facility for writing off single or sets of transactions across accounts without writing off a whole account. The situation may arise where it makes sense to clear all transactions below a certain amount. For example, it may be felt that all transactions with a value below £2.00 are simply not worth recording and then later chasing up. To perform this, pull down the **Data** menu and click on **Write off, refund, return Wizard**. Now click on the **Write Off Customer Transactions Below a Value** option from the available list and click on **Next**. Figure 6.5 shows the three dialogue boxes that represent the remaining stages.

In Fig. 6.5(a) the amount of £10 has been entered in order to demonstrate what Sage does. In practice, this figure will probably be too high. Sage will now search through all customer transactions to find transaction amounts equal to and below this amount. These will then be listed in a new dialogue box, as shown in Fig. 6.5(b). The list will indicate the customer accounts that generated the transactions, the nominal accounts which have been credited, the date of the transaction, a description of the transaction and the amounts. Any transactions that have been settled will not be included in the list of transactions.

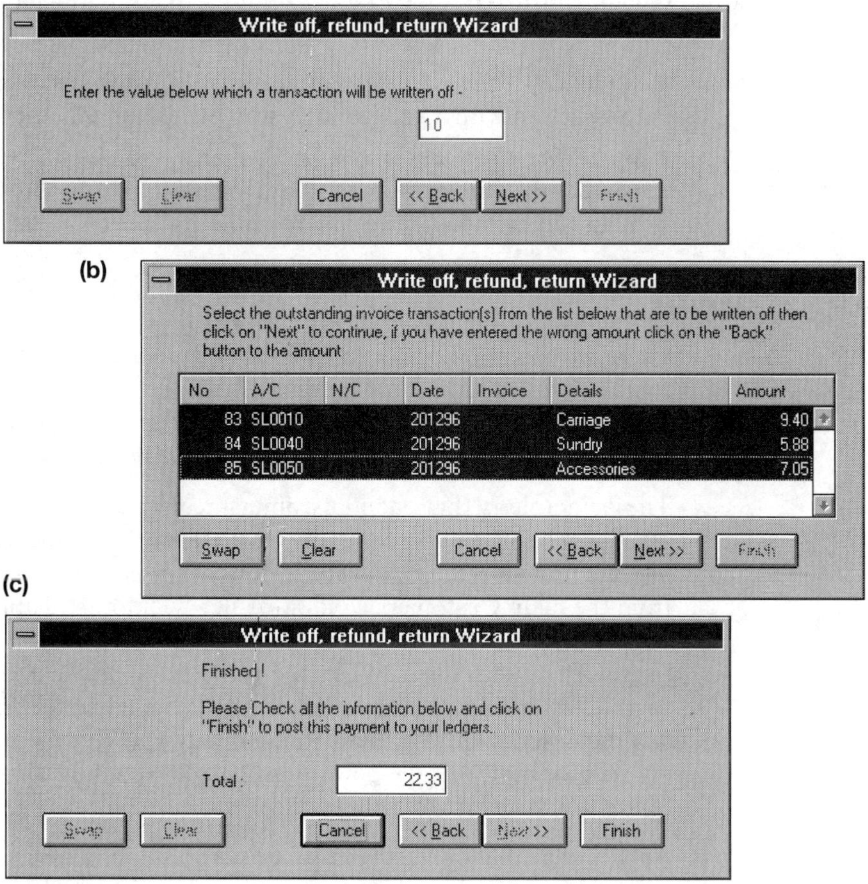

Fig. 6.5

To write off transactions, you need to first highlight those transactions you want written off by clicking on them. The two buttons below the list allow you to either **Clear** what you have highlighted or **Swap** all the highlighted lines with those not highlighted. When you have highlighted those transactions that are to be written off, click on the **Next** button to carry out the transaction.

The third dialogue box, as shown in Fig. 6.5(c), will add up the amounts to be written off and give you the chance to cancel the operation, to go back a stage or to finish the operation. After clicking on **Finish**, the following entries are then made:

- The Debtors Control Account is credited by each amount.
- The Bad Debt Write Off Account is debited by each amount.
- The customer accounts are credited by the respective amounts.

As with the Complete Account Write Off, the VAT Account is not adjusted and so will need a separate journal entry if it is to be adjusted.

When you select **Data** from the pull-down menu, and then click on **Write off, refund, return Wizard**, two other options are also available and accessed in the same way as the others:

- *Write Off Customer Transactions*. This allows you to write off a single transaction with a particular customer, leaving all other transactions intact.
- *Write Off Customer Small Overpayments*. This will remove all such overpayments. This can come about because of rounding errors and would incur too big a handling cost to reimburse the customer.

Mailing customers

There are going to be many occasions when a business wishes to mail all its customers. This section will examine the way in which Sage allows you to send personalised letters to all customers, or a selected range of customers. Figure 6.6 is an example of a letter customers will receive if their accounts fall overdue.

The principle is that each customer receives such a letter but with details altered to apply to that company only, such as its name and address – a technique often referred to as Mail Merge. To see how it works, select **Letters** from the main Customers window. A new window will appear on your screen. Sage allows a number of these standard letters to be created to suit a whole range of circumstances. When the package is installed, Sage has some standard letters already available. Click on the file name **REMIND1C.SLT**, which has the description 'Payment Reminder (v.1) (With Contact)' and then click on the **Edit** button at the bottom of this dialogue box. Figure 6.7 shows a part of the window that you will now see.

At this stage the top left-hand part of the letter contains a few odd lines. Click on the **Maximise** button to make this letter fill the whole screen. In Chapter 10 you will examine the creation and amendment of such documents in

Advanced ledger work **109**

MEGAXAN STERLING SPORTS
The Sage Shopping Centre
199 High Street, Newtown
Co. Heppershaw, NH88 9ZZ

Willoughby Sporting Affairs
23 The Oval
Baker Street
Watford
Herts   21 December 1996

Dear Don Beckerstuff

Your account with us is overdue. Please arrange for full and immediate settlement by first class mail.

Yours sincerely

Fig. 6.6

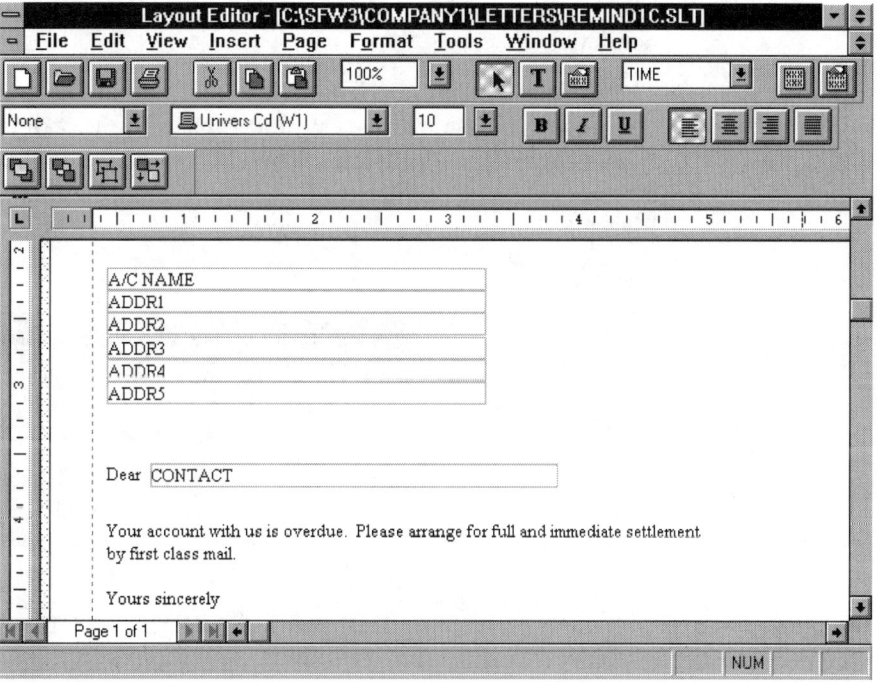

Fig. 6.7

greater detail. However, an examination at this stage will help you understand what Sage will attempt to do for you.

The data inside the dotted lines are *field names* that will be extracted from the customer records inside the Sales Ledger. Sage will print each letter replacing these brackets with details from the customers. For example, the line that reads:

Dear [CONTACT................]

is replaced with

Dear Don Beckerstuff

in the sample letter that appeared in Fig. 6.6. Consequently, Sage will produce a series of such letters unique to each customer. You will also observe that a new pull-down menu will appear which is unique to this part of Sage. If you are already experienced with a word processing package, then the features here will already be familiar to you. At this stage, you can change the wording of the letter as you please. In so doing, leave the data contained in the rectangles alone.

When you have finished with this, click on the **File** option on the pull-down menu. Now click on **Exit** to return to the Customer Letters window.

To gain a quick idea of what these letters are, click on **New** from the main Letters window. Sage will present you with a small Layout Wizard dialogue box, as shown in Fig. 6.8. Click on the **Finish** icon to proceed with creating a new letter.

The principle of these documents is that you are able to insert two types of *objects* into a document: *text* or *variable*. The text object contains any text that is common to all letters. The variable object will be collected from the customer records, such as the CONTACT name used in the previous example. Figure 6.9 gives an idea of the two objects that can be created.

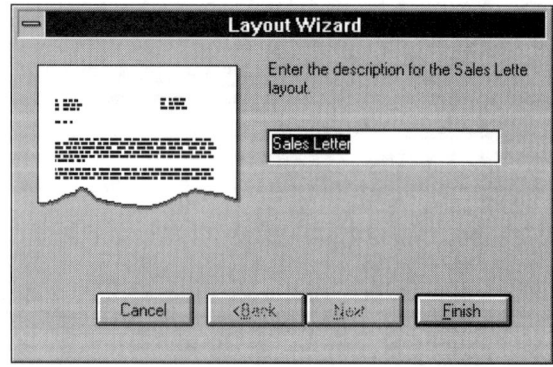

Fig. 6.8

To insert an object, you need to click on the **Insert** option from the pull-down menu and click on your choice. For the text objects, you need to use your mouse to draw an object big enough to contain the text. You can do this by dragging out a rectangular shape. When you have a rectangle of some size, type the text in. When you later click over the text, the object appears with blocks around it. This allows you to subsequently reshape the object or drag and drop it elsewhere.

From Fig. 6.9 you will see a drop-down panel of field names in the top right-hand part of the screen. This allows you to select the field names to be inserted into your letter. These too can be moved around your letter using the drag and drop technique.

Once you have objects in place, you can format them by clicking on the object and then using the options available in the **Format** pull-down menu. Other aspects of this part of the Sage will be dealt with in Chapter 10.

At this stage, experiment a little and, when finished, exit from this window (**File** and **Exit** or **Ctrl–F4**) and try and print one of the letters available with Sage. From the Letters window, you need to either direct the output to the printer or preview it first. In practice, you may wish to print these letters on letter-headed paper belonging to the company or you can purchase special stationery from Sage.

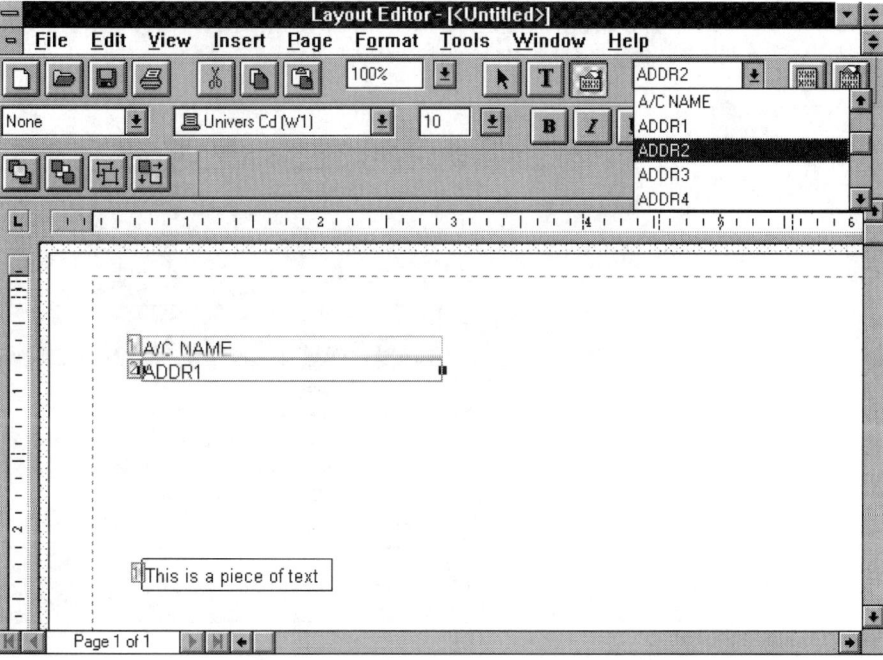

Fig. 6.9

MANAGING THE PURCHASE LEDGER

Many of the more advanced facilities for the Purchase Ledger are exactly the same as for the Sales Ledger and will require little explanation. The **Data** option that applied to the Sales Ledger, and is accessed using the pull-down menu, also allows you the same facilities as that for the Purchase Ledger. Figure 6.10 shows the dialogue box which appears when you select from the **Data** pull-down menu, **Write off, refund, return Wizard** followed by selecting the **Purchase Ledger**.

Opening balances

As with opening the customer accounts for the first time, the Purchase Ledger will need to be set up with all supplier details and their opening balances before you can carry out the day-to-day business with your suppliers.

The reason for this is that, if opening balances are not placed into these accounts, they will not accurately reflect what a business owes its suppliers. Entering the opening balances can be done when the account is created. Alternatively, if the account exists and the opening balance has not been entered, then this can be done by selecting the **Records** option from the main Suppliers window. After selecting the supplier, you then have a button that appears allowing you to enter the opening balance.

If you owe the customer money, then the opening balance is entered as an invoice amount with the reference O/BAL. If you have a supplier where there is a credit balance in your favour, then the opening balance is entered as a credit note, also with O/BAL as the reference.

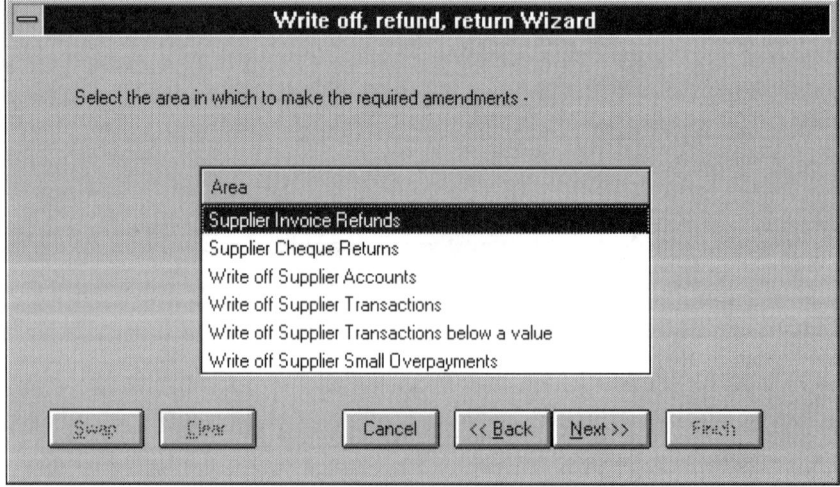

Fig. 6.10

When the amount is entered, the Creditors Control Account is updated to reflect the amounts now outstanding. In order to carry out the double entry, Sage will place the balancing figure into the Suspense Account (9998), as it did when creating opening balances for the customers.

Remittance advice notes

Many businesses may decide that they wish to send a remittance advice note with their payments. The information on the advice note assumes that you are using preprinted stationery available from Sage. The facility prints out details of what the business owes the supplier and creates a detailed account of what invoices have been received and what the business is settling with the supplier.

Many businesses will not use this option at all because they often receive statements of account from their suppliers and such documents sent with payments serve no useful purpose.

To create a remittance advice note, click on the **Bank** icon from the main Sage window and then click on **Supplier Payment**. The top part of this window needs to have the account number (**Payee**), **Cheque Number** and **Amount** entered. You then need to enter into the **Paid** column the items you wish to have paid. When the entry window is completed, click on the **Remittance** button to reveal another window similar to that shown in Fig. 6.11.

The principle here is the same as that for mailing customers. Sage has two files on the disk: one for A4 paper and one for 11-inch paper. These files can be edited in the same way as the overdue letter could. If you select **Edit**, you will get a screen with the document appearing in it allowing the alterations to be made. For example, you may wish to enter additional details to avoid having to use special stationery.

Click on the **Preview** spot in the **Output** panel to direct output to the screen prior to printing and then click on the **Run** button when done. Figure 6.12

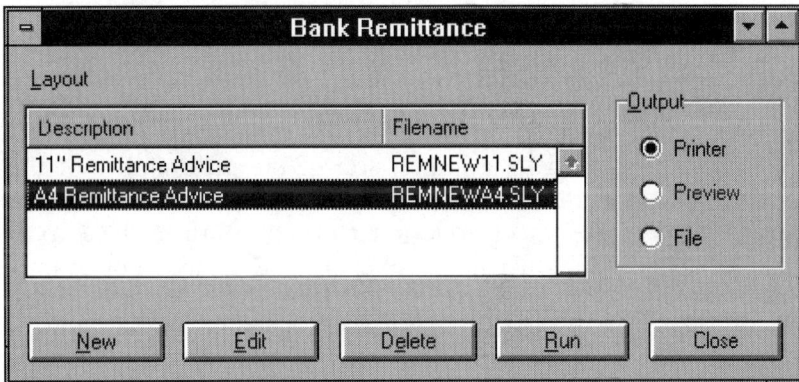

Fig. 6.11

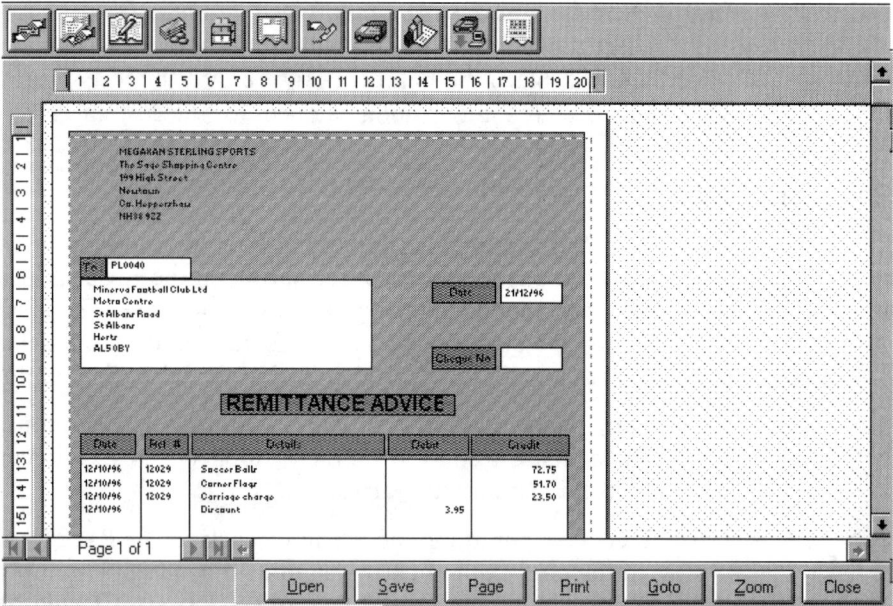

Fig. 6.12

shows the top part of the remittance advice note and gives you an idea of what it would look like on preprinted stationery.

The image in Fig. 6.12 has been zoomed outwards by 50 per cent using the **Zoom** facility. If you do not wish to have the remittance advice note, then click on the **Close** button; otherwise, click on **Print**.

MANAGING THE NOMINAL LEDGER

Prepayments

Many expenses that are paid for in any given month are not necessarily incurred in that month. For example, water rates may be paid twice yearly in advance. The effect on the accounts would be to suggest that water rates expenses were all incurred in the month in which they were paid. This would give a false impression of the profitability of the business for any given month. To get around this, Sage allows you to record only the actual part of the expense relevant to that month in the Expense Account, placing the remainder in a Prepayments Account. For example, if water rates costing £150 were paid in April for the next six months and the month is now June, then we would want the accounts to read as in Table 6.1.

The Water Rates Account is an expense and the Prepayment Account is a current asset. It is important to understand that when the bill is actually paid, the Expense Account is debited and the Bank Account credited.

Table 6.1

Account	Time period	Dr	Cr
Water Rates Account	Apr–Jun	£75	
Prepayment Account	Jul–Sep	£75	
Bank Account			£150

To set up a prepayment, click on the **Prepayments** icon from the Nominal main window. Figure 6.13 is an example of a prepayment setup as described.

The Nominal Account Code (**N/C**) in Fig. 6.13 is for the water rates and the **Details** column explains that the water rates actually paid are for the *next* three months rather than the current one. As the total amount is £75 and is spread over three months, Sage has entered the net amount per month as being £25.

When a period end occurs (as explained later) the following will occur:

- The Water Rates Account will be debited.
- The Prepayments Account will be credited.

The end result, therefore, is to spread the costs to match the months in which they are actually incurred. Many more can be set up using the Entry screen. Other examples might include insurance, stock of office supplies, etc.

When the Entry screen is complete, you need to click on **Save**. Sage will remind you that the actual processing of this transaction will occur at month or year end.

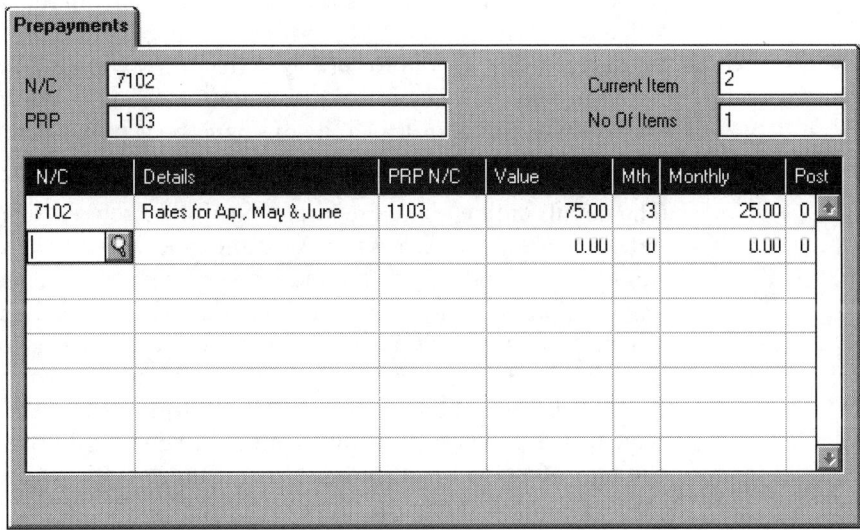

Fig. 6.13

Accruals

Accruals work in almost exactly the same way as prepayments. Many expenses are not paid for when they are actually accrued. For example, electricity consumption is not actually paid for until a bill is received, which could be several weeks after much of it has been consumed. To get a better impression of what expenses are actually being accrued, you should set up the details in the same way as you set up prepayments. There are many differences to prepayments, however.

One main difference is that an accrual will show an expense that has not actually been paid for. Hence, as each month passes, the Expense Account has to be debited to the value of the accrual and an Accrued Expenses Account credited to show the money is owed. The Accrual Account forms a current liability on the balance sheet of the business. When the bill actually arrives, you will need to pay it to the Accrual Account rather than the Expense Account again. In other words, you credit the Bank Account in the usual way and debit the Accrual Account. If the bill is more than has been allowed for, then only the excess must be debited to the Expense Account.

To set up an accrual, click on the **Accrual** icon from the Nominal menu and an Entry window will appear similar to the Prepayment one. Entries are then carried out in the same way as for prepayments.

Depreciation

Depreciation has already been mentioned in Chapter 5, but now you will deal with it in more detail as Sage has a useful way of helping you to both set up fixed assets and then subsequently depreciate them at the end of each month.

To set up depreciation, click on the **Assets** icon from the main window. As you will have set up no assets using this method, Sage will present you with a list of no assets. Click on the **Record** icon from this window. You will need to enter data via two dialogue boxes – a *Details* one and a *Posting* one. Figure 6.14 shows an example of a Details dialogue box, where details about a van have been entered.

The details entered here are largely for future reference. You will need to have entered the basic Fixed Asset Account using **Bank** (when purchased) or via a nominal journal entry if the final accounts are to make any sense. Remember, what you are entering here are details about how to depreciate accounts and where to post the details. You will notice from Fig. 6.14 that a **Supplier Account** (PL300) has been created for this purpose. To enter the depreciation details, click on the **Posting** tab. The Posting details are needed in order for Sage to store the assets in the Nominal Ledger and hold details needed when the end-of-period routines are run. Figure 6.15 shows a completed set of Postings for the van.

Figure 6.15 shows the depreciation of an asset (a delivery van) which is depreciated at 25 per cent per annum. Each time this asset is depreciated, the

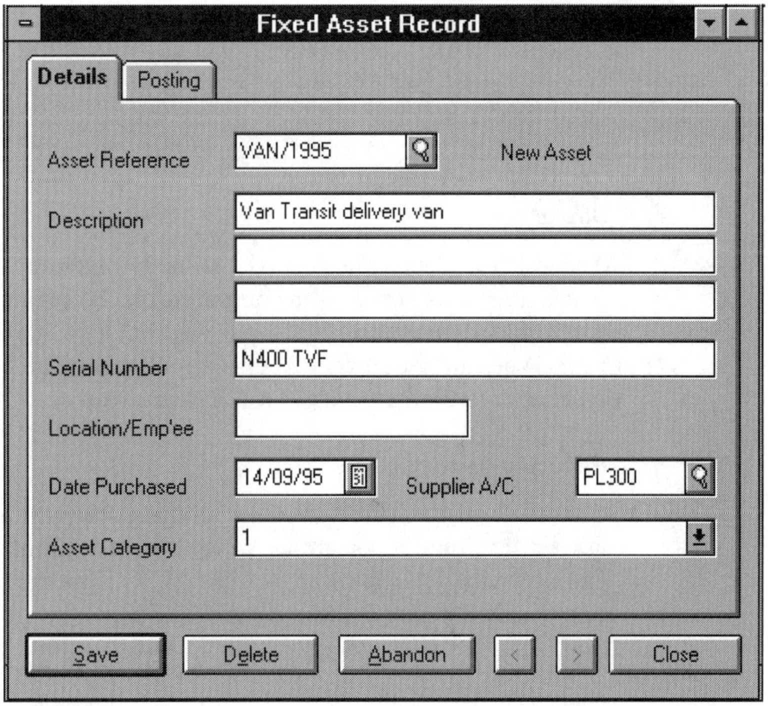

Fig. 6.14

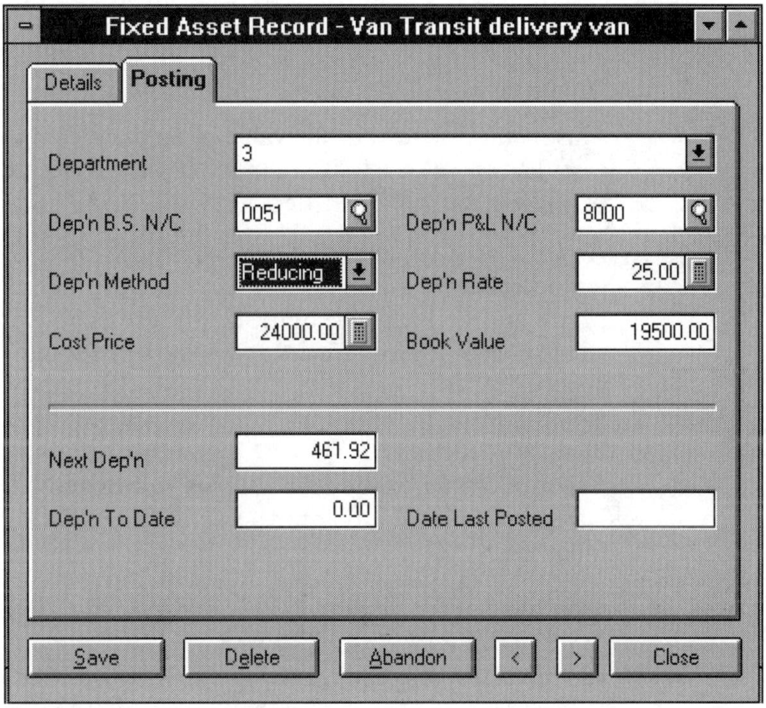

Fig. 6.15

amount is *credited* to account 0051 (Provision for depreciation on motor vehicles), while account 8000 (Depreciation) is *debited* by this amount. Consequently, the Provision for Depreciation Account records all accumulated depreciation on the asset, while the Depreciation Account records each separate year's depreciation as an expense incurred in that year.

Straight line

This method depreciates an asset value by the same amount each year in what is referred to as straight-line depreciation. For example, if furniture valued at £18 000 is depreciated by 10 per cent each year, this amounts to £1800 per year. When divided by 12 to give a monthly value, it would become £150 per month. Eventually, the asset will have no value.

Reducing balance

This method of depreciation calculates depreciation on the last value of the asset rather than a percentage of the whole amount. In Fig. 6.15, the van cost £24 000 with a book value of £19 500. This method means a year's depreciation is calculated as 25 per cent of £19 500.

Each year the 25 per cent will be applied on a smaller figure. At the start of each year, the 25 per cent rate will be applied on the new book value of the van rather than what it originally cost. This method means most of the depreciation occurs in the earlier years of the life of an asset, which is usually a better method of depreciation than straight line for such fixed assets as cars, plant and equipment.

Writing off

This method writes off the value of an asset completely and is used when an asset has no value left at all. In other words, when a period end is carried out on the asset, it will be written off.

As with prepayments and accruals, once the system has been set up, the period ends will automatically carry out the work. This is a far more appropriate and convenient solution to these problems than having to make a whole host of journal entries at the end of each month.

Month end

The month-end routine now allows you to activate the procedures that you have already set up. Before you activate this facility you must carry out the following:

- Create a back-up disk of the current month and then label it as a month-end backup with the date on it.
- Make sure that the recurring entries have been done. This was shown in Chapter 5 and is done via the Bank part of the program.

To carry this out, make sure all windows are closed other than the main Sage window. If any windows are left open, then Sage will alert you to this fact and ask you to close any open windows before proceeding with a period end. From the main pull-down menu, click on the **Period End** option and then, from here, the **Month End** option. If any other windows are still open or recurring entries still need to be processed, Sage will tell you at this stage. If not, then a new dialogue box will appear on your screen as shown in Fig. 6.16.

Figure 6.16 shows that you are required to click on the month-end features you require. The facilities are:

- to post all accruals and prepayments as they were set up earlier;
- to post the depreciation as it was set up earlier;
- to clear all turnover figures.

One of the purposes of the month end, apart from ensuring the prepayments, accruals and depreciation have been carried out, is to clear out of the system all those transactions that have been completed – such as invoices fully paid. This will prevent your system from becoming cluttered up with out-of-date information. However, it is essential to have a backup prior to each month end. Apart from the fact that something might go wrong, you may need to reinstate the month so that you can check on an earlier transaction. The backup facility followed by a restore allows you to jump back in time to an earlier month. This, of course, requires good backing-up practice.

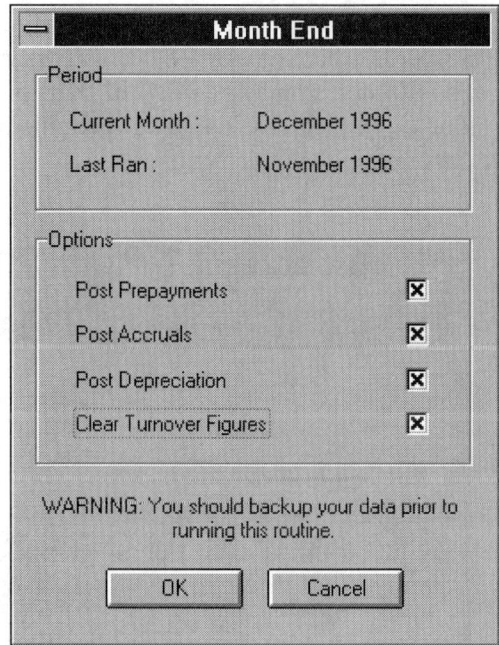

Fig. 6.16

When you have selected the month-end options required, click on the **OK** button to start the process. When the activity is under way, Sage will reveal a number of bars filling up to indicate that the files where the data are stored are being altered as requested.

When carrying out the month end, each option can be done separately at different times rather than all at once, as demonstrated here. However, once the job has been done, you will see some changes in the trial balance have been carried out. The expense accounts against which you placed accruals and prepayments will have been adjusted along with provisions for depreciation and an increase in the amount of depreciation on the Expense Account.

It is now worth considering the effect the month end has had on the value of the fixed assets using a different report. From the Sage main menu, click on the **Fixed Asset** icon and then click on the **Asset Valuation** icon. The resulting window, as shown in Fig. 6.17, shows the cost of the assets along with the accumulated depreciation and the book value. As each month passes, the monthly depreciation will reduce the assets while any purchase of new fixed assets, through the **Bank** or **Nominal Ledger** options, will increase their value.

Suspense accounts

A suspense account is an account that stores transaction figures that cannot otherwise be accounted for. For example, you can offset the opening balances in customer accounts against the Suspense Account. Hence, the Debtors Control Account would have been debited and the Suspense Account credited. At the end of the month, you will need to decide what to do with these Suspense Account entries, because they cannot remain in such accounts. In this example it may be decided that the balances represent sales of various kinds, in which case the sales accounts need to be credited and the Suspense Account debited to clear it.

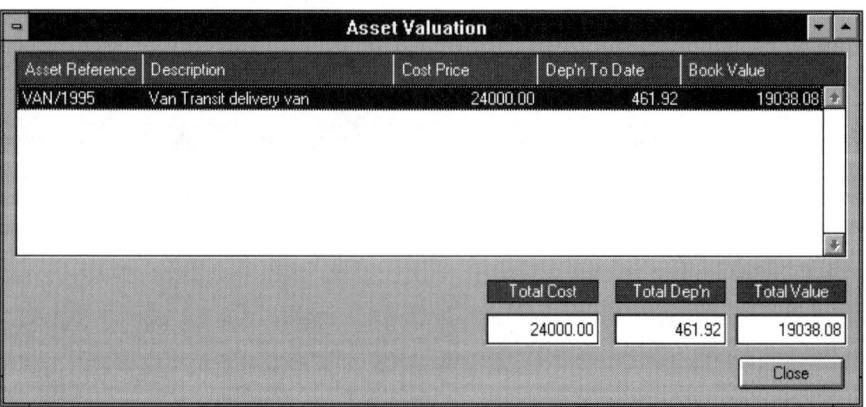

Fig. 6.17

Suspense accounts are often used when it is not known how to enter a figure. An operator can then get on with processing transactions quickly and return to the problem at a later stage – or give the problem to someone else!

At some time after Sage has been installed, you will have to ensure the trial balance is correct. Although Sage allows you to begin using the package immediately, as soon as you have a trial balance that is correct, you should adjust the account via the journal to bring it up to date. This is often left until the end of a year when a firm's accountant has agreed the final accounts.

VAT procedures

VAT, as mentioned in earlier chapters, is a tax on consumers rather than on a business. The tax is collected from sales and then passed on to HM Customs & Excise. Any VAT paid by a business can be claimed back from Customs & Excise. In practice, therefore, the difference between tax collected and tax paid is settled between a business and HM Customs & Excise.

Sage refers to tax collected in its reports as *Output taxes*, as these have to be paid out. Tax is calculated from sales invoices, sales credit notes, bank receipts and cash receipts. It is important that when the tax forms are completed the reports show how and when the tax was collected.

Sage refers to tax paid out in its reports as *Input taxes*, as these will be claimed back. Tax is calculated from purchase invoices, purchase credit notes, bank payments and cash payments.

All transactions that do not involve VAT, such as salaries and bank interest, should have been given the tax code T9.

At the end of the month, you should go through the process of clearing your VAT in preparation for future settlement. The effect will be to extract all VAT reports for a given month and determine whether you owe money to Customs & Excise or are owed money by them. To do this, you could undertake the following monthly routines:

1 *Finish posting all transactions for the month.* This can occupy a good deal of an operator's time, trying to chase up invoices and receipts that have not yet been entered to the system.

2 *Check the inputs and outputs by extracting VAT reports.* This will be necessary to check that all transactions have been entered along with their correct amounts of VAT.

3 *Correct any errors or enter omissions so that your VAT is correct and complete.* This may involve having to check invoices and other documents. A useful report to extract may be an audit trail giving details of all entries made in sequence of entry. The audit trail is available as the first in the list of reports from the main **Reports** option.

4 *Carry out the month-end routines mentioned in the previous section.* Some of these may affect the VAT figures.

5 *Extract a final set of reports needed for VAT.*

The next two stages will be used to clear the Tax Control Account of any balances left and is only a suggestion to help you to keep a month-by-month check on VAT liability. From the main Sage window, click on the **Financials** option and then click on the <u>V</u>AT icon.

From Fig. 6.18, you will see something similar to what is required. This VAT window will attempt to calculate the VAT. The Output tax, which is collected and has to be passed on, is calculated from:

- sales invoices (less any credit notes);
- bank and cash receipts;
- journal credits.

The Input tax, which is paid out and can be claimed back, is calculated from:

- purchase invoices (less any credit notes);
- bank and cash payments;
- journal debits.

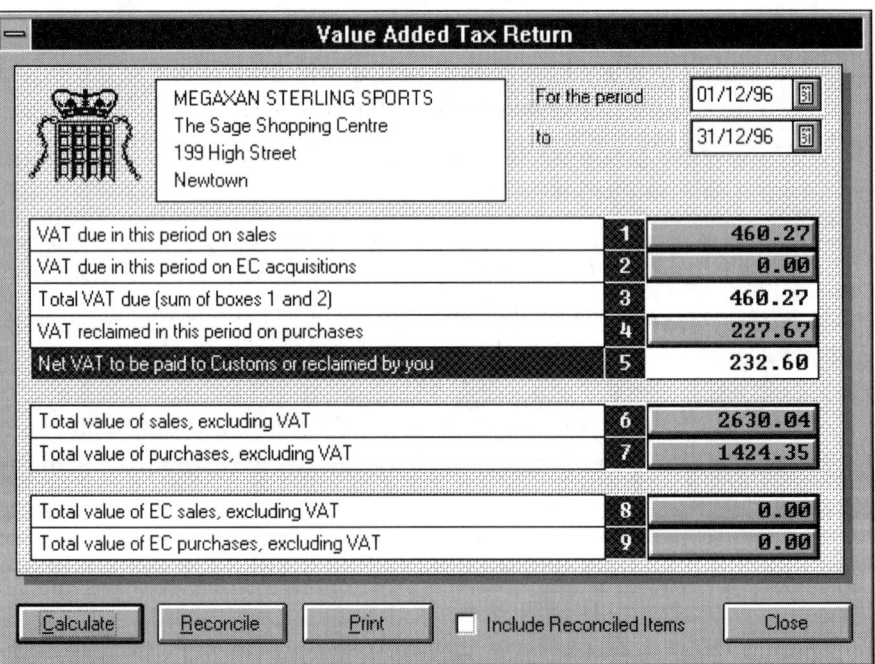

Fig. 6.18

At this stage the window will probably show a series of zeros because no calculations have yet been carried out. Click on the **Calculate** button to start the process. Sage will begin by informing you of the number of transactions that it has found to process for the final VAT report. On the same window, you may see a number of transactions that Sage has found that are either unreconciled or do not appear in the specified period. Do not worry too much about the messages at this stage. Click on **Yes** to include all transactions in the report. When you are able to examine the final reports, it will become clearer to you how the data in the accounts have been used to make up the VAT reports. When complete, Sage will ask you if you want the transaction flagged for VAT. Click on **Yes** to avoid the transactions being included again in a future VAT calculation.

At this stage you can print out a detailed report of the VAT returns by first clicking on the **Print** button in this window. Figure 6.19 shows the Print window that appears allowing you three different types of report along with two choices of output.

If you click on the **Printer** output option, select **Detailed** and then click on **OK**, the printout will be detailed and will provide:

- a summary (the data that appears on the VAT window);
- VAT due on sales and EC (European Community) acquisitions;
- VAT to be claimed on purchases;
- Total value of sales, purchases, EC sales (excl. VAT), EC purchases (excl. VAT);
- Unreconciled transactions.

If these prove to be incomplete or inaccurate, then you will need to go back and repeat the processes until they are correct. When you have finally reconciled the VAT on the computer with what actually happened then you can:

- Activate the **Financial VAT** again.
- Run the **Calculate** option.

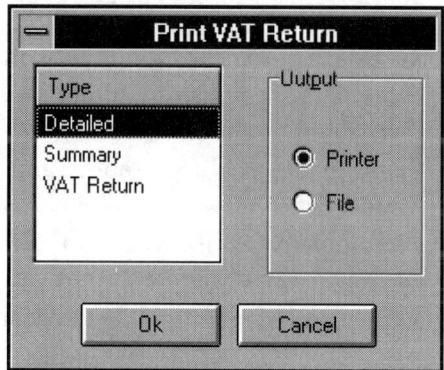

Fig. 6.19

- Click on the **Reconcile** option from the VAT window.
- Run the detailed report.
- Complete the VAT returns to be sent on to HM Customs & Excise.
- Run the **VAT Print** option for the VAT return.
- Pay Customs & Excise the VAT owing.

When the whole operation is complete, you are then in a position to pay off HM Customs & Excise what is owed. This involves a straightforward bank transaction. The cheque and VAT return are then despatched to HM Customs & Excise.

Processing VAT can be a long and laborious job. When using a computerised accounting system for the first time it will be a particularly long and difficult job. As each VAT period passes, the job should get easier. Whatever system is used, this should demonstrate the need for accurate data processing at all levels of business activity.

THE FINANCIAL YEAR

Each business will have a financial year for tax and accounting purposes. The start of a financial year will depend on when the business was formed, but will normally be the first day of a month and run for 12 months. At the end of the year there are many important activities that have to be carried out.

At the end of the year the business must draw up a statement of profit and loss. This can be carried out for you by Sage if your accounts are correctly structured. Before doing this, the business ought to carry out the following tasks:

1 Finish posting all transactions for the year. This can occupy a good deal of an operator's time in trying to chase up invoices and receipts that have not yet been entered into the system.

2 Back up onto a floppy disks all data files for the year, being careful to label your disks as data files as at *end of year* with a date. The need for backing up cannot be over-emphasised. Once a computer system has been running for some time, it is often the case that the data generated is worth more in value than the entire computer system. Once data is properly backed up, there should be no possibility of a disaster in terms of data processing.

3 Print an aged debtors report and check the outstanding debtors total against the Debtors Control Account in the Nominal Ledger.

4 Print statements of account or Sales Ledger transaction histories so that customers can be notified of the state of their accounts.

5 Extract all required Purchase Ledger listings.

6 Print out transaction histories for all the accounts in the profit and loss section. *When the new year is started, all profit and loss accounts will be cleared of their transactions.*

7 Extract an audit trail to give a complete set for the year.
8 Print any analysis reports and the Tax Control Account listing.
9 Run the **Year End** routine from the **Period End** part of the Sage pull-down menu.
10 Back up data files again, being careful to label your disks as data files as at *beginning of year.*

If backing up has been done properly at both stages and it is found that a mistake or omission has been made, then you will always be able to restore the backup and start the end-of-year process again.

Running the year-end program

To run this part of the program you will need to make sure that all windows, other than the Sage main window, are closed and that all recurring entries have been carried out. When this is complete, click on the **Period End** option from the main pull-down menu and follow this by clicking on the **Year End** option. A window will appear as shown in Fig. 6.20.

The four options that appear in Fig. 6.20 are:

- *Transfer all your actual spending figures to next year's budgets.* This will save time if you want to set up budget figures for the future.
- *Increase your budgets by a percentage.* The example in Fig. 6.20 will put all actuals into the budgets *after* increasing the figures by 5 per cent.

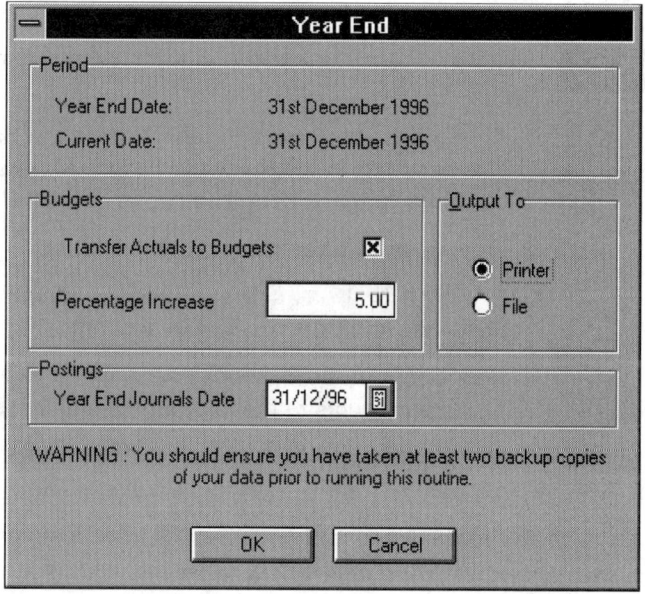

Fig. 6.20

- *Output the resulting report to a file or printer.*
- *Set the date for the heading on the printed report.*

When this program is run, a report is produced which will list the journal entries Sage has gone through to complete the year end as described.

Start of the next year

The accounts will now be ready for the start of the new year with the following state of affairs:

1 All profit and loss accounts will have no entries in them other than accruals and prepayments on expenses that will be brought down to be included in the expenses of the new year.

2 The remaining balance sheet accounts will have a single figure of balance carried down from the previous year rather than a long history of transactions.

The balance sheet in Fig. 6.21 shows an example of what appears at the start of a new financial year.

The figures for this month will all be zero until transactions have taken place. The opening balance sheet represents what makes up the business in terms of assets with net assets excluding any debt. The share capital represents the owners' equity while the reserves figure was derived from last year's profit.

This balance sheet and the profit and loss account are available in the **Financials** part of Sage.

EXERCISES

As a way of gaining a greater knowledge and skill with the ledgers, try the following questions.

1 Create four new customer accounts in the Sales Ledger and three new supplier accounts in the Purchase Ledger. Make sure that two of the accounts are the same so that a contra entry can be made later.

2 Enter opening balances into each account.

3 Extract a trial balance showing the amount that has been posted to the Suspense and Debtors Control accounts.

4 Now clear out the Suspense Account by using the Journal Entries facilities to post the amounts to the relevant sales and purchase accounts.

5 Make a contra entry between the two accounts of a customer who is also a supplier.

6 Process three returned cheques from customers where one is a refund and the other two are 'bounced' cheques.

7 Write off an account as a bad debt.

MEGAXAN STERLING SPORTS

BALANCE SHEET

Date: 03/01/97
Time: 9:42
Page: 1

Default Layout of Accounts

Selected period: January 1997 Mth 1

	This month	Year-to-date
Fixed assets		
Property	0.00	60 000.00
Office equipment	0.00	62 300.00
Furniture and fixtures	0.00	18 000.00
Motor vehicles	0.00	25 538.08
	0.00	165 838.08
Current assets		
Stock	0.00	4 100.00
Debtors	0.00	5 078.71
Deposits and cash	0.00	3 367.10
Bank Account	0.00	1 622.21
	0.00	14 168.02
Current liabilities		
Creditors: short term	0.00	11 489.80
Creditors: long term	0.00	35 000.00
VAT liability	0.00	289.97
	0.00	46 779.77
Current assets less liabilities:	0.00	(32 611.75)
Net assets:	0.00	133 226.33
Capital and reserves		
Share capital	0.00	127 000.00
Reserves	0.00	6 226.33
	0.00	133 226.33

Fig. 6.21

8 Mail a letter to all those suppliers to whom you owe money, announcing that you now have a new telephone number and a new fax (facsimile) number.

9 Pay a supplier a sum of money and issue a remittance advice note.

10 (a) Using the examples set out in the chapter, set up the following recurring entries:
- a bank payment by standing order for rent;
- payments of wages by cheque.

(b) Set up a prepayment for water rates and an accrual for electricity consumption.

(c) Carry out a month-end activity to show the processing that results from 10(a) and 10(b).

(d) Extract a trial balance showing the outcome of 10(c).

CHAPTER 7

Stock control

INTRODUCTION

In this chapter you will examine the way in which a computer records information about stock and how such information can assist a business in determining efficient management of stock. Up until now you have been buying goods and selling goods and have not yet asked the computer to manage the stock itself. This chapter will assume that you have stock to manage and that you are working as a trader or manufacturer.

One aim of controlling stock is to keep stock at its lowest level without impeding either sales or production. If a business holds more stock than is necessary for the running of the business, then the business may well find itself with an unnecessarily high cost for holding stock. For example, suppose you have invested £10 000 more in stock than is needed. This £10 000, if placed in a deposit account at a bank, is capable of earning money in interest payments. There are some advantages, however, for certain businesses in holding high stocks.

The costs of holding stock include the cost of capital tied up in that stock or money that could be used elsewhere in the business. Furthermore, for certain stock, such as frozen foods, there is the high cost of simply storing and looking after such stock. With other types of stock, such as fashion wear, the stock can become obsolete if it is kept too long and not sold. For businesses such as greengrocers, stocks have to be low because goods will perish or become impossible to sell in a short time.

On the other hand, holding large stocks can have real benefits. The cost of capital tied up in stock can be paid for by the rising value of stock through inflation. Holding high stocks for this purpose can be risky if the value of stock fluctuates a great deal. Often businesses derive the benefit of being able to supply customers quickly and at short notice if their stocks are high – sales which might otherwise be lost. Stock of certain items may be high because there are large quantity discounts available from suppliers. High stocks also assist production managers because they are not continually switching production to meet orders that cannot be met with goods in stock.

What is an efficient level of stock will vary quite considerably from one business to another. Sage Stock Control will not be able to make decisions about what represents efficient stock levels. You will have to give the computer this information. What the computer will do is to advise you, with its reporting facilities, of what stock either needs replacing or is too high.

THE STRUCTURE OF SAGE STOCK CONTROL

The stock control function can be broken down into three broad areas:

1 *The setting up of the stock records* that hold information about description, cost, selling price, how stock is sold, when to re-order more stock and how much to order. These records need to be set up for each stock item.

2 *The day-to-day updating of stock*. Every time stock is sold, the quantity has to be deducted from the stock held. The stock records will also need to keep a check on what replacement stock has been ordered and whether any has already been allocated to customers.

3 *The reports*. These are needed to help a business keep adequate stock levels and give it information about what stock has been selling quickly or slowly.

An outline of the stock control function is shown in Fig. 7.1.

From Fig. 7.1 you will see that there is a two-way data relationship between invoicing, sales order processing and purchase order processing. These activities will directly affect stock and are covered in Chapters 8 and 9. When customers are invoiced, the goods they are invoiced for will be removed from stock. Furthermore, sales order processing will have the effect of allocating stock to a customer. In addition to this, purchase orders will inform the stock control function about what stock is on order.

PREPARING STOCK RECORDS

The first job you will need to undertake is to set up details on every item of stock. This can be a major undertaking for a business computerising stock control for the first time as it can involve many hundreds of items of stock. Sage stores details about stock by organising stock into categories. For example, a jeweller may have a category for watches, one for clocks, another for rings and so on. Into each category will go details on individual items of stock.

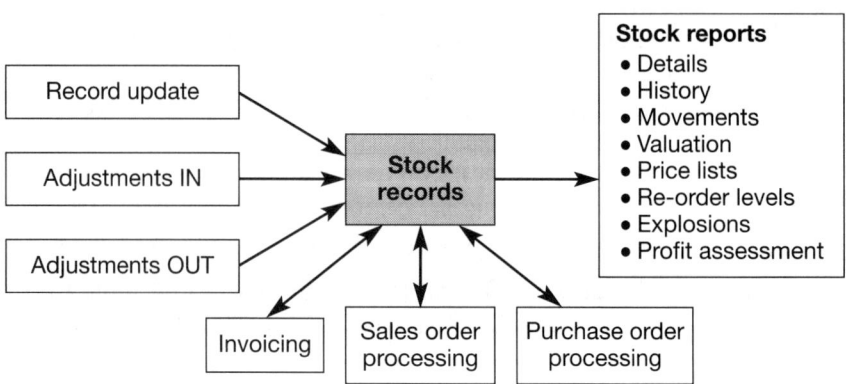

Fig. 7.1

After this has been done, the actual quantities in stock will have to be entered. Figure 7.2 gives an outline of the stages in preparing the stock control system.

To begin with, you will set up a number of stock categories for the stock records to be grouped into. From Fig. 7.3 you will see that six categories have been set up for this purpose. To do this, click on **Defaults** from the main Sage pull-down menu and then click on the **Pr_o_duct Categories** option. Figure 7.3(a) shows an example of the window with the categories set up for the stock records to be inserted. To enter these categories, highlight the category number by clicking on it and then click on the **_E_dit** button. Enter the new category name, as shown in Fig. 7.3(b), and click on **OK**.

```
┌─────────────────────────────────────────────┐
│      Identify the catergories of stock      │
└─────────────────────────────────────────────┘
                       │
                       ▼
┌─────────────────────────────────────────────┐
│   Enter the stock records into their categories   │
└─────────────────────────────────────────────┘
                       │
                       ▼
┌─────────────────────────────────────────────┐
│         Enter the opening stock levels         │
└─────────────────────────────────────────────┘
                       │
                       ▼
┌─────────────────────────────────────────────┐
│ Keep stock records updated as stock enters and leaves │
│  as well as keep details of what is on order and what │
│              customers have ordered              │
└─────────────────────────────────────────────┘
```

Fig. 7.2

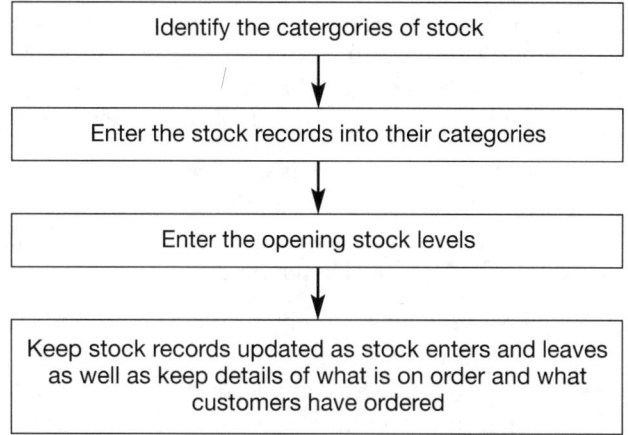

Fig. 7.3

Although categories can be added, altered or deleted in the future, it is important to note that each stock record is identified with a category number. If you feel you do not need to divide your stock into categories, then you can ignore this activity and all stock will be assumed to be in category 1.

In addition to the categories, you can define a default nominal code using the **Product Default** option from the Features menu. This will enable any sale of stock to be credited to a different sales nominal account depending upon the category of stock sold. For example, a different sales code could be used for the sale of sports clothing items as opposed to cricket supplies.

The next stage is to enter details of stock. From the main Sage window, click on the **Products** icon to reveal the main Stock Control window. From here, click on the **Product Record** icon. You will see a blank entry window on the screen which needs to have some of the details completed. Each detail is a field, making up the stock record. Some of the fields are left for future processing. Figure 7.4 shows an example of a stock record prepared with the opening fields.

In this option, there is no need to concern ourselves with the amount in stock, just the details about an item of stock. The stock **Code** is used to represent the way an item of stock is identified and will have to be unique to each item of stock. The **Description** describes the item.

The **Tax Code** is used to assist you in adding VAT to an item when you wish to invoice a customer against such stock. It can also serve as a useful source of information when you need to find out whether to add VAT to an item and at what rate. The small arrow to the right of the field means you can click on this

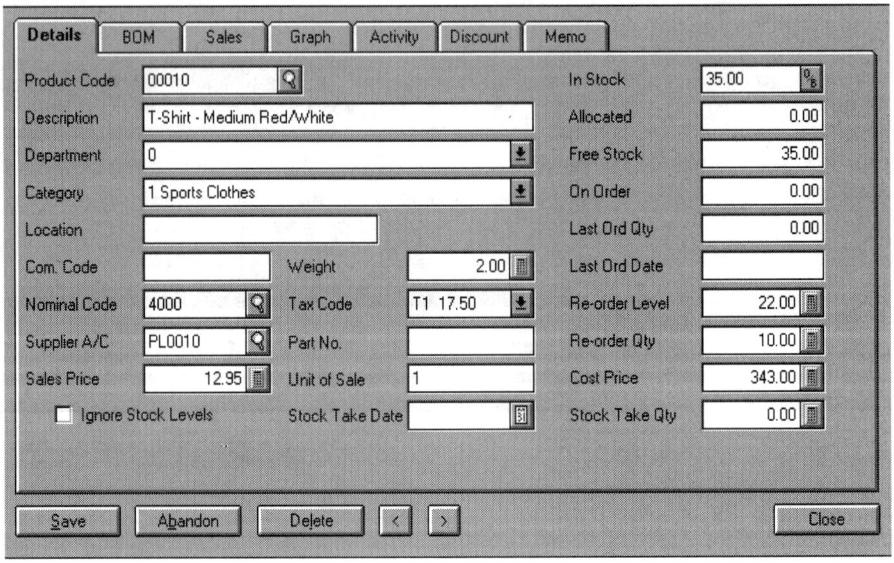

Fig. 7.4

and select from the available list of tax codes. The **Sales Price** serves much the same purpose as the tax code, in that it provides information for invoices and a price list. The **Sale Price** is the price at which you sell each unit, with **Unit of Sale** being how many items you sell at that price.

The **Location** field is used to identify the location of a product. For example, it may be used to store the exact position of the product in a warehouse or the bin number. Such details will often provide useful information that can be provided via a report.

The **Nominal Code** is needed if you are to integrate the invoicing with stock and the Sales Ledger. The nominal code will refer to the nominal account that is to be used when a sale is made. It is a good idea to have nominal codes matching the categories of stock. For example, if you have six named stock categories, then it would make your work much easier if you had exactly the same number of nominal sales accounts and gave them the same names. You can click on the small icon to the right of this field to select from the list of nominal codes.

The **Category** is one of the categories you set up earlier. This is also similar to the **Department** code which would also need to be set up if the business is to be organised into departments each with its own stock-holdings. In both cases, you can select from an available list, if applicable, by clicking on the small **Finder** icon to the right of the field. Again, the use of departments has been left out in order to keep the reports simpler. If departments are to be set up, they really need to be set up as part of the installation and preparation process.

The **Details** page contains details of who supplies the stock to you. This can contain a main or sole supplier but does not restrict you in future from buying stock from any other supplier. Entering data into the relevant records can help when you are required to produce a purchase order later.

The **A/C Reference** can be selected by clicking on the **Finder** icon to the right of the field which will give you a list from the Purchase Ledger to select from. The **Part Reference** will be supplied by the supplier and is also used when producing a purchase invoice. You will not be asked for **Cost Price** until you enter some opening stock.

The **Re-order Level** is the stock level at which a purchase order should be placed. This is going to be crucial for assisting a business to keep a check that adequate stocks are maintained. One of the reporting facilities will need to produce this information to establish what should be ordered at any given time. If this is left blank, the re-order level check will not be performed. The **Re-order Qty** is the amount that is normally ordered once the re-order level has been reached. The **Last Order Date** and **Last Order Qty** will automatically be updated by the program as you process the stock; this is done via the Sales Order Processing part of Sage.

The **Commodity Code** and **Weight** fields are used if you either sell goods to other European Union countries or buy from them. The commodity codes are available from HM Customs & Excise and will be required when submitting VAT returns.

The panel regarding stock levels has fields in it that are updated when the stock is added to, deducted from, allocated to orders and ordered from suppliers.

At this point you should click on **Save** to post the record to the stock file. However, if the stock item you have entered is an assembly of other stock items, it will require a little more processing.

PRACTICE Add some other stock records of your own or as suggested in the appendix at the end of this chapter. The list of suggested stock records in the appendix is a list of the stock items which this book has used and this may help you to build up some stock records to work with.

STOCK ASSEMBLY

Many stock items may be an assembly of other stock items. For example, if you work in a television factory, then a television set, when completed, forms a part of your finished stock. Meanwhile, the components of the television set are also stored in stock as either semi-finished goods or raw materials.

Sage will allow you to define an assembly or bill of materials that make up any stock item. In future processing you are then able both to increase the number of finished goods in stock and remove from stock all the semi-finished stock and raw material stock required to make the finished goods. Sage will also calculate for you how many of the finished stock you can make from existing stocks.

To see how this works, you will need to create a set of product records similar to that listed in the appendix at the end of this chapter. When this is done, from the main Products window use the **Product Record** option to bring the Tennis Kit record onto the window. When this is done, click on the page tab at the top of the screen labelled **BOM** – Bill of Materials. A new window will appear that requires you to enter the products and their quantities that make up this stock line. Figure 7.5 shows such a window.

This example shows that a stock item called 'Tennis Play Kit' is made up of two components of stock. At a later stage, you will be able to return to this window, click on **Calculate** and the program will work out how many tennis kits can be made up with the available stock.

Constructing a complete stock database can be a very long process for a business and needs careful planning. In Chapter 11 you will have a chance to consider how a business may go about this in a practical way.

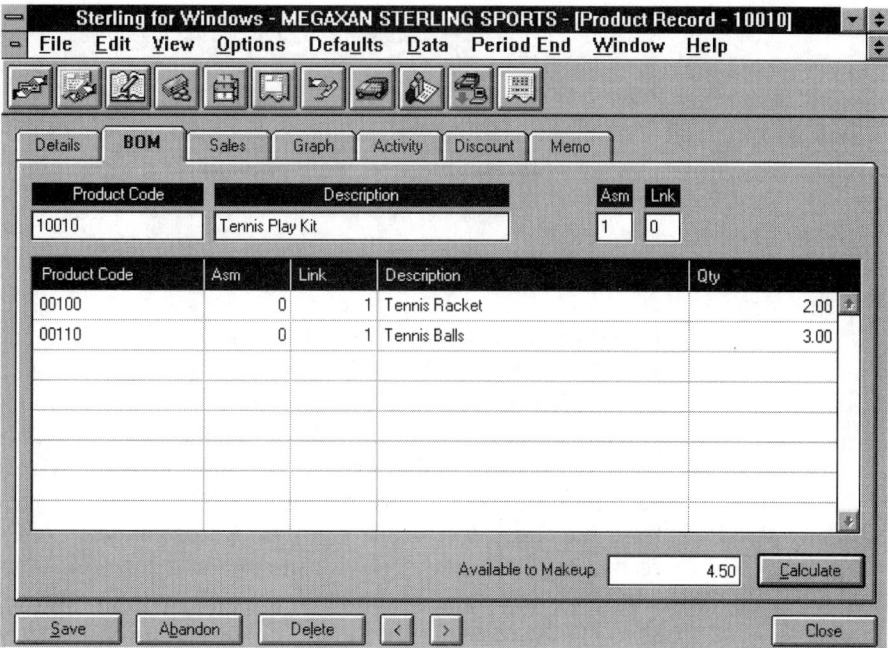

Fig. 7.5

STOCK MOVEMENTS

The next step is to examine stock movements. Stock movements are recorded through the main Products window using the **Adjustments In** and **Adjustments Out** options. If stock control is integrated with invoicing and sales order processing, then the issue of an invoice will result in automatic adjustment of stock, thereby avoiding the need to record a stock movement in this section. Furthermore, when goods are received after a purchase order has been issued, the acknowledgement of this must be recorded both as a stock movement and within the purchase order system – a topic to be covered in Chapter 9.

Before you can start using the stock control function for recording movements of stock, you will need to enter an opening balance. In practice, a business will need to do a complete stock-take at a given point in time and enter all the details immediately. This can be a complicated affair as speed is of the essence. If a business is too slow in entering the details into the computer, the stock quantities can be badly out of date before the process is finished. To enter opening stock, click on the **Record** icon from the Product window and then select a stock record from those already created. Now click on the **O/B** (Opening Balance) button that appears in the **Stock Levels** panel. A small window will appear superimposed on the Record window, as shown in Fig. 7.6.

Fig. 7.6

If the record was not saved before clicking on **O/B**, then Sage will ask you to save the record first by clicking on a **Yes** button. You will see from the window that the **Ref** field has been set up as O/BAL. This is done for you as the amount you enter will be the opening balance stock amount. You are then required to enter the **Date** and the amount you have in stock (**Quantity**) and how much each item of this stock cost (**Cost Price**). When you have done this, click on **Save** and you will return to the main Record window. You will then see that the record has been updated with the quantity in stock. Figure 7.7 shows such a window where stock items are listed with their amounts in stock and a column showing the sales prices. The lines that are in red on the screen (in lighter type in Fig. 7.7) indicate that the current stock level is below the required re-order level and is an indication that more stock ought to be ordered.

Fig. 7.7

To adjust the stock levels so that stock is increased, make sure you are back at the main Products window and then click on the **Adjust-In** icon. Figure 7.8 shows the Adjustment In window where two items of stock have been added.

You need to select, for each line, a stock code which can be selected from a list by clicking on the small **Finder** icon to the right of the text **Code**. The **Details** is available for you to enter a description of how the adjustment came about, such as a purchase of stock. The **Quantity** should be the amount of stock to be added to, with the **Cost Price** being the cost for each individual item of stock. If you purchased your existing stock at more than one price, then you should make a separate entry for each cost price. This is used later to assess how much profit you have been making in buying and selling the stock and to value the stock. When you have entered the adjustments, click on **Save** to record the transaction and update the stock history.

Adjustments Out are done in exactly the same way, but using the **Adjust-Out** icon. If you are not using the invoice system for recording stock issues, then each time stock is issued or despatched to a customer, you should record this movement as an Adjustment Out. The **Details** field would then be used to reflect something about the invoice that was sent or something like Cash Sales. The reference could be used to record the invoice number or receipt number.

It is important that entries of stock movement are made as soon as possible after the event has occurred. Failure to do so will render the reports meaningless.

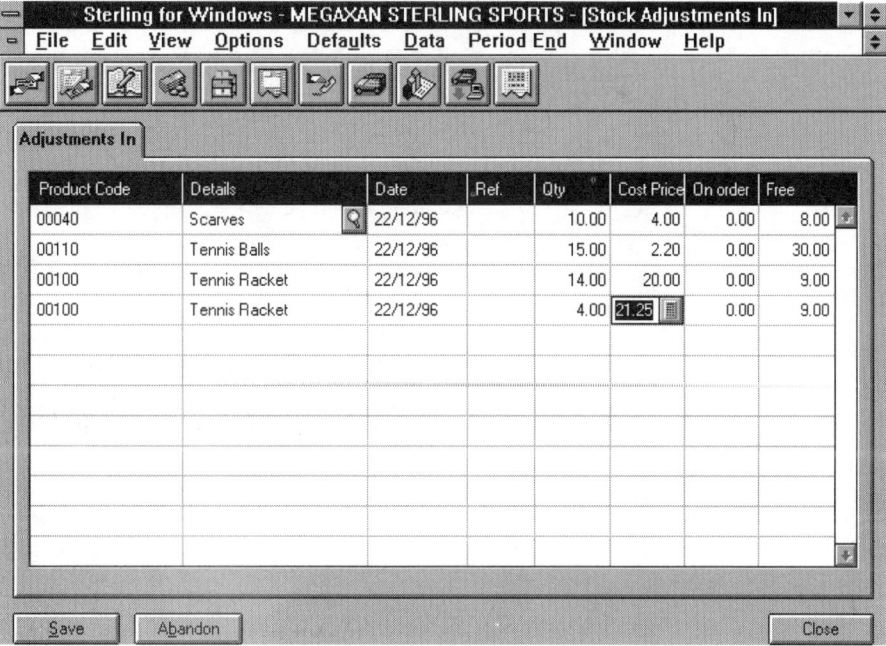

Fig. 7.8

EXTRACTING STOCK REPORTS

The **Quantity Allocated** and **Quantity Re-Ordered** columns, that appear in many reports and on some windows, will not come into use until you have worked through Chapter 9 on sales and purchase ordering. The **Re-order Level** is the amount you enter and you will observe that the report only lists those stock items where the re-order level is below the actual level.

Once some stock processing has been done, you are soon able to extract some useful management information about stock. Figure 7.9 shows the window that contains the reports available at this stage. From the main Products window, click on the **Report** icon.

The Product Reports window shown in Fig. 7.9 has been maximised to fill the screen and reveal all the reports available. The **Status** of these reports is shown as Fixed, which means they are a part of your Sage package and cannot be removed. The Product Details report that appears near the bottom of the list is the same as that shown in the appendix to this chapter. The other reports from this list that will be of use now are:

- *Product list.* This will give a simple list of products showing the products, their prices and nominal code details.
- *Product price list.* The example in Fig. 7.10 shows a product list with the prices you entered when creating the records.

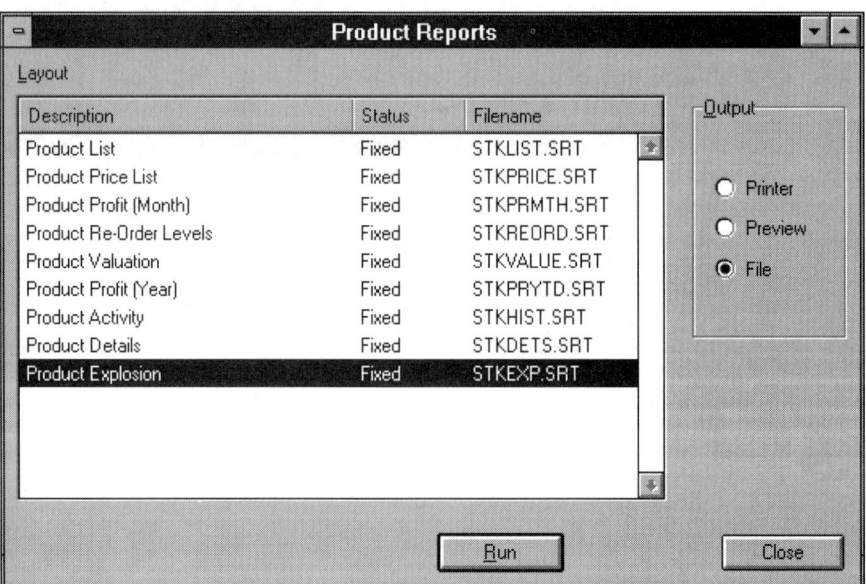

Fig. 7.9

```
                    MEGAXAN STERLING SPORTS

    Date: 22/12/96
    Time: 10:55                                                Page: 1

                          PRODUCT PRICE LIST

    Product From:                                  Category From: 1
    Product To: ZZZZZZZZZZZZZZZZ                   Category To:  999
    -----------------------------------------------------------------
    Product Code       Product Description           Sales Price
    -----------------------------------------------------------------
       00010           T-Shirt – Small Red/White         12.95
       00020           T-Shirt – Medium Red/White        18.00
       00030           T Shirt   Large Red/White         18.00
       00040           Scarves                           12.00
       00050           Cricket Pads                      23.50
       00060           Cricket Bats – Large              48.00
       00090           Soccer Ball                       18.00
       00100           Tennis Racket                     28.00
       00110           Tennis Balls                       5.00
       10010           Tennis Play Kit                   78.00
```

Fig. 7.10

- *Product profit (month)*. This report will show you what profit each line of stock has made by showing the cost of goods sold and how much they were sold for. This is effectively the gross profit figure. As you have not sold any stock yet, this report will be of little use.
- *Product re-order levels*. This will incorporate details about all items that have a quantity in stock below their re-order level. This is discussed further later in the chapter.
- *Product valuation*. This values the stock you have by giving a report that lists the amount you have in stock and how much it all cost.
- *Product profit (year)*. This is the same as the monthly one, but calculates gross profit for the year to date.
- *Product activity*. This will give a detailed account of each stock record's history. When you have done some work on invoicing and order processing, this report will prove to be useful when analysing the performance of an item of stock. Figure 7.11 is an excerpt from the report for tennis rackets.
- *Product explosion*. This shows how certain stock records are broken down into components. For example, the explosion report for the tennis kits, which were made up of tennis rackets and tennis balls, would look like Fig. 7.12.

```
                              PRODUCT ACTIVITY

   Product Code: 00100                    Product Description: Tennis Racket
   ----------------------------------------------------------------------
   Tp   Date      Refn     Details      Quantity  Qty Used  Cost Price  Sale Price
   ----------------------------------------------------------------------
   AI   22/12/95  O/BAL    Bfwd Stock      9.00      0.00     180.00       0.00
   AI   22/12/96           Tennis Racket  14.00      0.00      20.00       0.00
   AI   22/12/96           Tennis Racket   4.00      0.00      21.25       0.00
   ----------------------------------------------------------------------
   Quantity In Stock     27.00
   Quantity On Order      0.00
   Quantity Allocated     0.00
```

Fig. 7.11

```
                              PRODUCT EXPLOSION
   ----------------------------------------------------------------------
   10010     Tennis Play Kit   Quantity   Last Cost   Location   Makeup Cost
   ----------------------------------------------------------------------
   00100     Tennis Racket       2.00       21.25                   42.50
   00110     Tennis Balls        3.00        2.20                    6.60
                                                                   ------
                                                                    49.10
                                                                   ======
```

Fig. 7.12

PRODUCT TRANSFERS

The option **Product Transfers** allows you to add to finished stock from the components you hold in stock. In the example with tennis kits, the packs are made up of two tennis rackets and three tennis balls. If ten packs of kits are to be made, this would require a stock transfer of 20 tennis rackets and 30 tennis balls. A transfer will work this out for you and perform the necessary stock movements.

From the main Products window, click on the stock item 10010 Tennis Play Kit in the list of stock items so that it is highlighted. Now click on the **Transfers** option. Figure 7.13 shows the window completed in which stock will be transferred to make up ten Tennis Play Kits.

Stock control 141

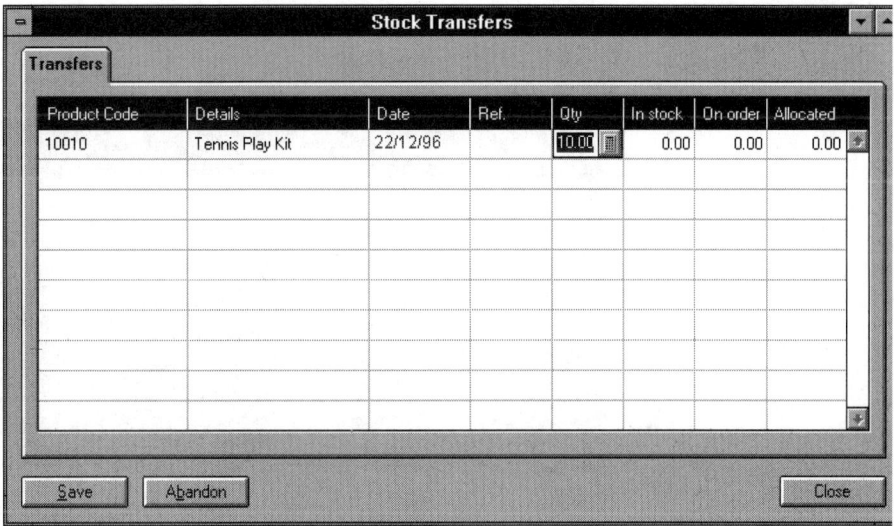

Fig. 7.13

By selecting to make ten kits, you will instruct Sage to add these to the stock *and* remove all the components from the other stock records. As each kit comprised two tennis rackets and three tennis balls, for the ten new kits it will remove a total of 20 tennis rackets and 30 tennis balls from those stock items. This has to be done because if stock were not removed from the other records, the stock valuation report would show stock being counted twice and would give a valuation of stock that is too high. Sage will only allow a stock transfer to be made if there is sufficient stock to make up the requested number.

If you attempt this, then it is worth investigating stock activities for all records affected. Figure 7.14 shows two such activity reports where the report in (a) shows a Movement Out (**MO**) of the tennis rackets to 10010 and report in (b) shows Movements In (**MI**) of the tennis rackets.

This report shows how stock has moved in and out as well as the quantities involved. The movement types are shown with the following abbreviations:

Stock Inwards: AI   Adjustments In
                  MI   Movement In via stock transfer
                  GR   Goods Returned
                  GI   Goods In via purchase orders

Stock Outwards: AO   Adjustments Out
                  MO   Movement Out via stock transfer
                  GO   Goods Out via sales orders or invoices

In later chapters you will generate more of the movement types in stock movement reports.

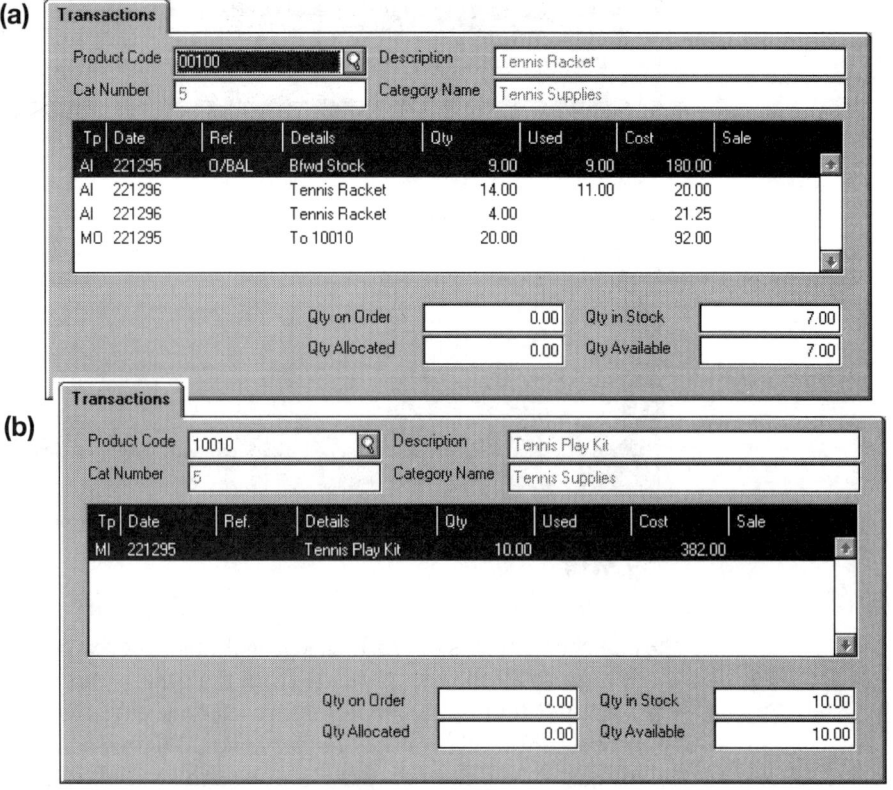

Fig. 7.14

RE-ORDERING STOCK

When you created the stock records, you also entered re-order levels into one of the fields. These re-order levels are suggested stock levels at which, when reached, you should put in a purchase order for more stock. The re-order levels should take account of the time it takes from placing an order with a supplier to the stock reaching your business. The time taken is called the *lead time* and, generally, the longer the lead time, the higher will be re-order level. Another factor that needs to be considered is the quantity sold. If the average stock held will clear in a few days then you need to re-order early enough so as not to run out of stock.

The re-order report will list details about all items that have a quantity in stock below their re-order level. This report will tell you what you need to order of stock so as to bring stock levels back to what you would require, to operate properly. The report will also give you the appropriate supplier code of the supplier who normally supplies the stock. Figure 7.15 is an example of such a report.

		PRODUCT RE-ORDER LEVELS					
Supplier	Description	Quantity Re-Order	Qty Alloc	Qty On-Order	Re-Order Level	Last Pur Qty	Purchase Price
PL0050	Cricket Pads	4.00	0.00	0.00	30.00	0.00	14.00
PL0040	Soccer Ball	12.00	0.00	0.00	20.00	0.00	12.00
PL0030	Tennis Racket	7.00	0.00	0.00	25.00	0.00	20.00
PL0060	Tennis Balls	15.00	0.00	0.00	60.00	0.00	2.20

Fig. 7.15

All the details have been extracted from the stock records. The **Re-order Quantity** was entered when the records were created. The **Quantity Allocated** and **Quantity On-Order** will be discussed in Chapter 10. The report itself is available from the list of reports in the **Reports** option from the main **Products** window.

EXERCISES

Try the following exercises in order to give yourself a thorough understanding of what activities are available with the stock control function.

1 Create another ten stock records and enter opening stocks for them, adding one new category of stock to the list of categories already made up.

2 Add two more stock records that are made up of components from other stock records.

3 Make some adjustments in and adjustments out to at least two of the records in order to build a history for these stocks.

4 Perform a transfer of stock to one of the stock items which is made up from stock components.

5 Now extract the following reports:
 – Stock details
 – Stock history
 – Valuation of stock
 – Stock explosion
 – Re-order levels.

APPENDIX

The following stock records are the basis for this chapter and have been limited to keep the book to a realistic size. You are advised to add some of your own to this list.

Stock Code:	00010:	T-Shirt – Small Red/White			
Category:	1	In-Stock:	35.00	Units of Sale:	1
Category Desc.:	Sports Clothes	On-Order:	0.00	Sup. Part Ref.:	T-Shirt Sma R/W
Department Code:	0	Allocated:	0.00	Supplier A/C:	PL0010
Tax Code:	T1	Bin Location:		Purchase Price:	9.80
Nominal Code:	4000	Selling Price:	12.95	Re-Order Level:	22.00
Date Last Pur.:		Last Purchase Qty:	0.00	Date Last Sale:	

Stock Code:	00020:	T-Shirt – Medium Red/White			
Category:	1	In-Stock:	24.00	Units of Sale:	1
Category Desc.:	Sports Clothes	On-Order:	0.00	Sup. Part Ref.:	T-Shirt Med R/W
Department Code:	0	Allocated:	0.00	Supplier A/C:	PL0010
Tax Code:	T1	Bin Location:		Purchase Price:	10.50
Nominal Code:	4000	Selling Price:	18.00	Re-Order Level:	15.00
Date Last Pur.:		Last Purchase Qty:	0.00	Date Last Sale:	

Stock Code:	00030:	T-Shirt – Large Red/White			
Category:	1	In-Stock:	29.00	Units of Sale:	1
Category Desc.:	Sports Clothes	On-Order:	0.00	Sup. Part Ref.:	T-Shirt Med R/W
Department Code:	0	Allocated:	0.00	Supplier A/C:	PL0010
Tax Code:	T1	Bin Location:		Purchase Price:	14.80
Nominal Code:	4000	Selling Price:	21.00	Re-Order Level:	15.00
Date Last Pur.:		Last Purchase Qty:	0.00	Date Last Sale:	

Stock Code:	00040:	Scarves			
Category:	1	In-Stock:	11.00	Units of Sale:	1
Category Desc.:	Sports Clothes	On-Order:	0.00	Sup. Part Ref.:	Scarves
Department Code:	0	Allocated:	0.00	Supplier A/C:	PL0010
Tax Code:	T1	Bin Location:		Purchase Price:	4.00
Nominal Code:	4000	Selling Price:	12.00	Re-Order Level:	13.00
Date Last Pur.:		Last Purchase Qty:	0.00	Date Last Sale:	

Stock Code:	00050:	Cricket Pads			
Category:	2	In-Stock:	16.00	Units of Sale:	1
Category Desc.:	Cricket Supplies	On-Order:	0.00	Sup. Part Ref.:	C-P332
Department Code:	0	Allocated:	0.00	Supplier A/C:	PL0050
Tax Code:	T1	Bin Location:		Purchase Price:	14.50
Nominal Code:	4001	Selling Price:	23.50	Re-Order Level:	30.00
Date Last Pur.:		Last Purchase Qty:	0.00	Date Last Sale:	

Stock Code:	00060:	Cricket Bats – Large			
Category:	2	In-Stock:	12.00	Units of Sale:	1
Category Desc.:	Cricket Supplies	On-Order:	0.00	Sup. Part Ref.:	BL-5422
Department Code:	0	Allocated:	0.00	Supplier A/C:	PL0050
Tax Code:	T1	Bin Location:		Purchase Price:	32.00
Nominal Code:	4001	Selling Price:	48.00	Re-Order Level:	20.00
Date Last Pur.:		Last Purchase Qty:	0.00	Date Last Sale:	

Stock Code:	00090:	Soccer Ball			
Category:	3	In-Stock:	16.00	Units of Sale:	1
Category Desc.:	Soccer Supplies	On-Order:	0.00	Sup. Part Ref.:	78-9192
Department Code:	0	Allocated:	0.00	Supplier A/C:	PL0040
Tax Code:	T1	Bin Location:		Purchase Price:	12.00
Nominal Code:	4002	Selling Price:	18.00	Re-Order Level:	12.00
Date Last Pur.:		Last Purchase Qty:	0.00	Date Last Sale:	

Stock Code:	00100:	Tennis Racket			
Category:	6	In-Stock:	30.00	Units of Sale:	1
Category Desc.:	Tennis Supplies	On-Order:	0.00	Sup. Part Ref.:	R-92991
Department Code:	0	Allocated:	0.00	Supplier A/C:	PL0030
Tax Code:	T1	Bin Location:		Purchase Price:	20.00
Nominal Code:	4101	Selling Price:	28.00	Re-Order Level:	25.00
Date Last Pur.:		Last Purchase Qty:	0.00	Date Last Sale:	

Stock Code:	00110:	Tennis Balls			
Category:	1	In-Stock:	52.00	Units of Sale:	3
Category Desc.:	Sports Clothes	On-Order:	0.00	Sup. Part Ref.:	Tennis Ball/3
Department Code:	0	Allocated:	0.00	Supplier A/C:	PL0060
Tax Code:	T1	Bin Location:		Purchase Price:	2.20
Nominal Code:	4101	Selling Price:	5.00	Re-Order Level:	60.00
Date Last Pur.:		Last Purchase Qty:	0.00	Date Last Sale:	

Stock Code:	10010:	Tennis Play Kit			
Category:	6	In-Stock:	20.00	Units of Sale:	1
Category Desc.:	Tennis Supplies	On-Order:	0.00	Sup. Part Ref.:	
Department Code:	0	Allocated:	0.00	Supplier A/C:	
Tax Code:	T1	Bin Location:		Purchase Price:	33.00
Nominal Code:	4101	Selling Price:	75.00	Re-Order Level:	0.00
Date Last Pur.:		Last Purchase Qty:	0.00	Date Last Sale:	

CHAPTER 8

Sales invoicing

INTRODUCTION

The main objectives of sales invoicing are to produce invoices and credit notes as well as to maintain up-to-date stock files and customer records. In this chapter we assume that you have now worked through the preceding chapters. In particular, you will have to have a set of customer records and stock records.

Until now, you have been processing sales invoices in a somewhat unusual manner – invoice details have been entered directly to the Sales Ledger with all invoice details required, but with no invoices! One of the principal objectives of this chapter, therefore, is to show you how to produce invoices automatically, extracting all customer information from the customer records in the Sales Ledger and performing all calculations automatically, including totals and VAT. Ultimately, you want the computer to update the customer records automatically, rather than for you to post invoices one at a time through the Sales Ledger. In addition to this, you will invoice customers with stock that is held in the stock records. Consequently, this part of the Sage package requires integration with both the Sales Ledger function and stock control function.

Figure 8.1 depicts the invoicing and credit note functions, integrated with other functions. Each invoice will extract from the Sales Ledger the details about the customer who is to receive the invoice. When the invoice is despatched with the goods, the customer records will be updated with the

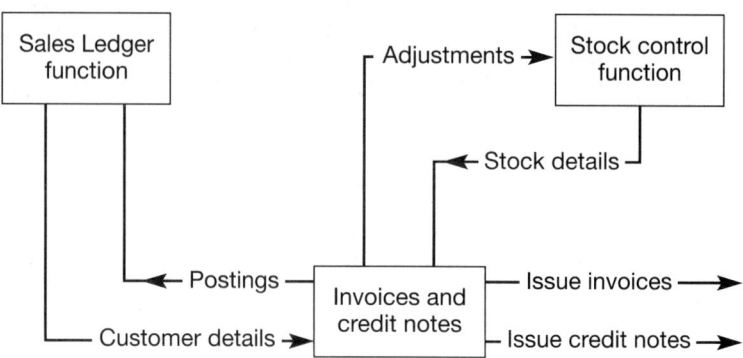

Fig. 8.1

details of the invoice. Each invoice and credit note will need to extract from the stock records details about the stock being sold, and subsequently stock records will need to be updated to show the stock movement.

THE STRUCTURE OF THE INVOICING FUNCTION

From the main Sage window, click on the **Invoicing** icon to reveal the Invoicing window. As shown in Fig. 8.2, there are seven elements to this function. The blank panel within this window, will contain a list of all invoices along with their status – something that will be developed later in the chapter.

Before making a start, a brief overview of these seven elements will help develop a better understanding of how invoicing fits in with the rest of the Sage package.

- **Product Invoice** will be used to prepare the invoices using the stock and customer records.
- **Service Invoice** will allow you to prepare invoices for customers that are not receiving stock.
- **Product Credit Note** is used for the return of goods. It allows you to prepare a credit note that has the opposite effect on a customer record and product record to preparing an invoice.
- **Service Credit Note**, as with a product credit note, will credit a customer but does not represent a return of goods.

These four parts of the invoicing function have a common characteristic in that each is being used to *prepare* the documents rather than actually to process records. This will mean that once the initial documents have been prepared, they can be altered before any customer and stock records are updated.

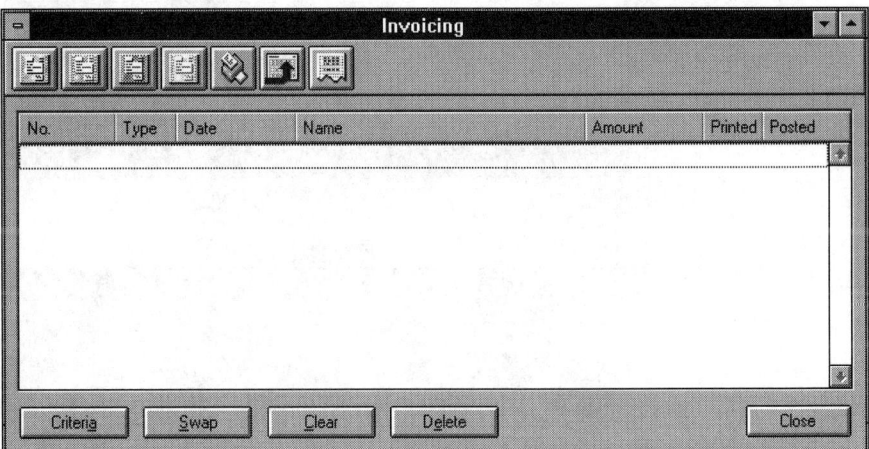

Fig. 8.2

- **Print Invoice** will print the above invoices as a batch rather than your having to print each invoice individually.
- **Print Credit Note** will print the above credit notes as a batch.
- **Update Ledgers** will use the prepared documents to update the customer and product records. This part of the function will normally be used after all the documents have been carefully checked and, where appropriate, altered.

PREPARING DOCUMENTS

When generating invoices, you will find that most of the work was carried out when you set up the customer details in the Sales Ledger and the product details in the stock control system. The principle of invoicing is that you first produce all the details of an invoice and store these details in a file. You will then produce the invoices when they are needed. After checking them through, you will make any amendments and then print off the invoices. When all the invoices have been printed, they are ready to be despatched with the goods. The final stage in the process will be to post the details to both the Sales Ledger and stock control.

To produce an invoice using the details held in stock, click on the **Product Invoice** icon to reveal a blank entry window. Figure 8.3 shows an invoice window that has been completed with customer and stock details.

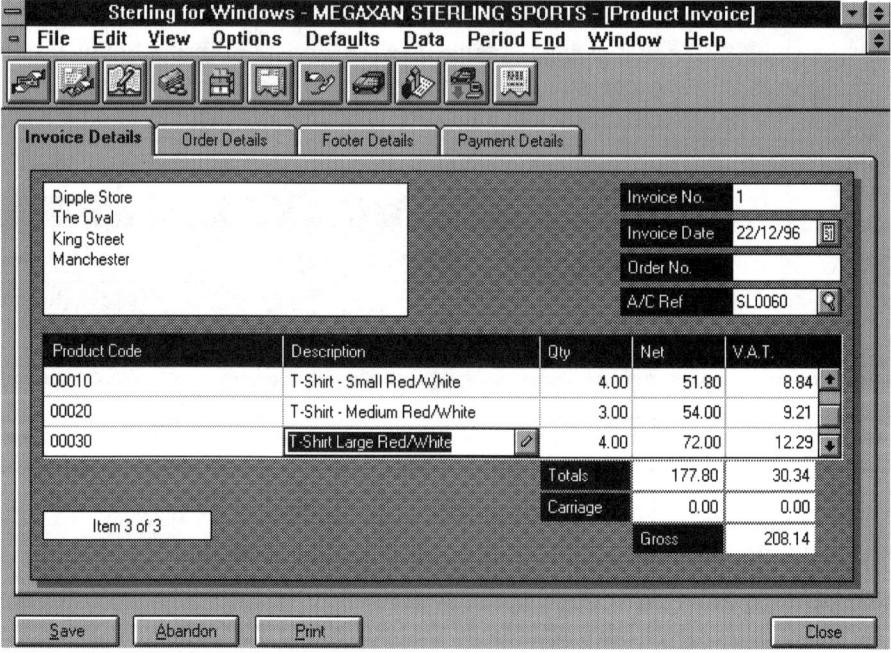

Fig. 8.3

Select from the list of customers the name of the customer to whom you want to send the invoice (**A/C Ref:**). If you click on the **Finder** icon, you will reveal a list of customers and this allows you to create a new customer. The Invoice Number (**Invoice No.**) is generated by the computer. If this is the first invoice to be produced, then Sage will generate the number 1. If you wish to enter a different number to this, then Sage will start at the new number you enter, with the next invoice being incremented by one. The **Date** is again the date of the computer system and can be changed. Once the header details have been entered, you can progress to the detail lines.

To begin with, if the details for each line are exactly as they appear in the stock records, then the task of making up the lines is simple. For each line either enter the **Product Code** as it appears in the stock records or use the **Finder** icon to select a stock record. The **Description** will display automatically what is stored in the stock record, but this can be altered if you wish. The quantity (**Qty**) needs to be entered and the rest is done for you automatically. Variations from this will be dealt with later in the chapter.

At the bottom of this window are a set of buttons that will allow you to further process your invoice. The **Save** button will save what you have entered but will not update the sales and stock records. This means you can later print it or amend it. If you wish to print the invoice at this stage, then click on the **Print** button.

At this stage, click on **Save** and move on to the next invoice taking into account the next few sections are variations away from the more simple invoice preparation.

Changing invoice details

The entry of the invoice shown in Fig. 8.3 assumes no deviation away from what you have in stock and set prices with no discounts. In practice, there will be many instances where you need to enter more than this. Begin another invoice and, after you have entered the product code, click on the **small backslash** icon to the right of the description. This means you will only be able to activate this button when you have entered a product code into a line. Figure 8.4 is an example of the resulting entry window being filled in.

The **Product Code** is as it appeared on the detail line and cannot be altered. The **Description** and **Quantity** also appear and can be altered in this window instead of the main Invoice window. The **Unit Price** can be entered and the total **Net** price will appear in the relevant box below as being quantity multiplied by unit price. The **VAT** will be added to this total by default but, if the total is inclusive of VAT then you can click on the **Calculate Net** button and the VAT will be taken away from the gross amount.

Figure 8.4 also shows that a **Discount** of 20 per cent has been allowed to this customer. When the percentage amount is entered in the box, the new price to the customer is calculated for you.

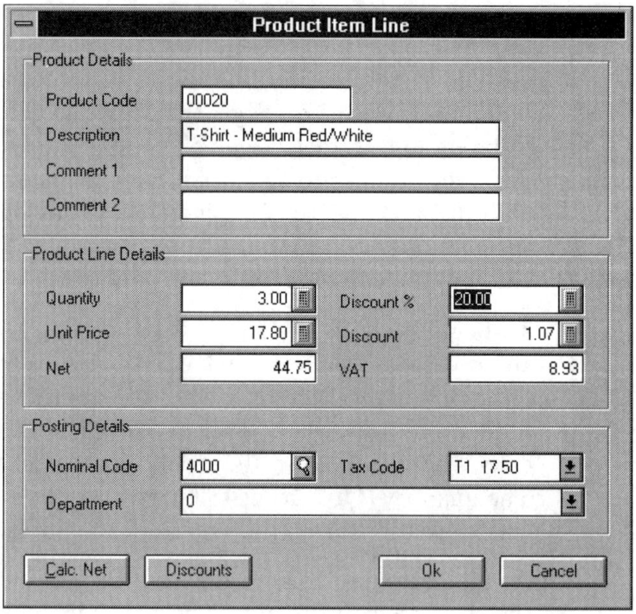

[Screenshot of "Product Item Line" dialog box showing Product Details (Product Code: 00020, Description: T-Shirt - Medium Red/White, Comment 1, Comment 2), Product Line Details (Quantity: 3.00, Unit Price: 17.80, Net: 44.75, Discount %: 20.00, Discount: 1.07, VAT: 8.93), Posting Details (Nominal Code: 4000, Department: 0, Tax Code: T1 17.50), with buttons Calc. Net, Discounts, Ok, Cancel.]

Fig. 8.4

The **Nominal Code** is used to identify the sales account in the Nominal Ledger that will be credited when the invoice details are later used to update the ledgers. This too can be changed, as can the **Department**. Both of these would have been stored within the stock records when they were created.

When this detail line is complete, click on the **OK** button to return to the Invoice window ready for the next detail line.

Entering order details

From the **Invoice Details** page, you will see a set of page tabs at the top of the windows. There are four in all, with Invoice Details highlighted. Click on the **Order Details** tab to enter details about the order you received from the customer. Figure 8.5 shows an example of one completed.

The **Delivery Address** indicates that the goods are to be delivered to a different address than the invoice. The **Notes** are for your own use and may serve as a memory jogger later or any other form of future reference.

The **Customer Order Number** is filled in from the document the customer sent. However, in Chapter 9 you will see that this can be prepared using a different part of Sage. The **Customer Telephone Number** and **Contact** is extracted from the customer file. The **Order Taken By** field can be used if you need to record this information.

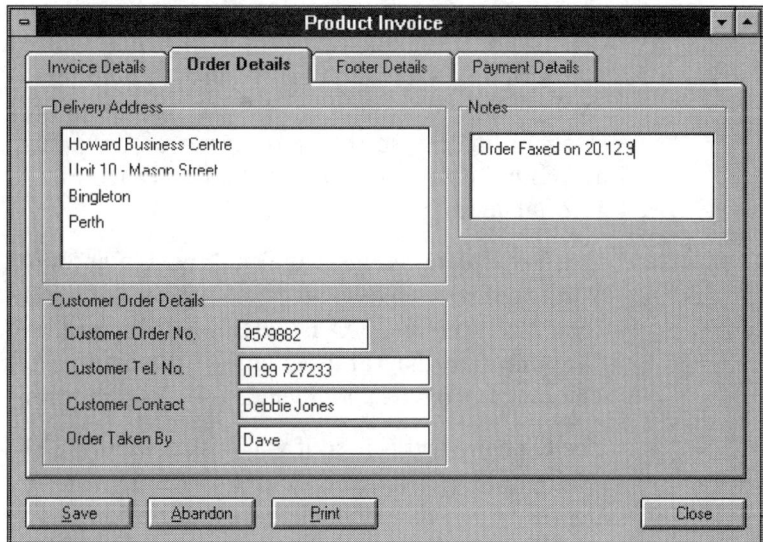

Fig. 8.5

Entering carriage and discounts

Sage has the facility to allow you to enter both carriage details (cost of postage and packing) and any settlement terms you might want to offer your customer. To activate this facility, click on the **Footer Details** page tab that appears at the top of your Invoice window. The result of this will be to display the required entry window similar to that shown in Fig. 8.6.

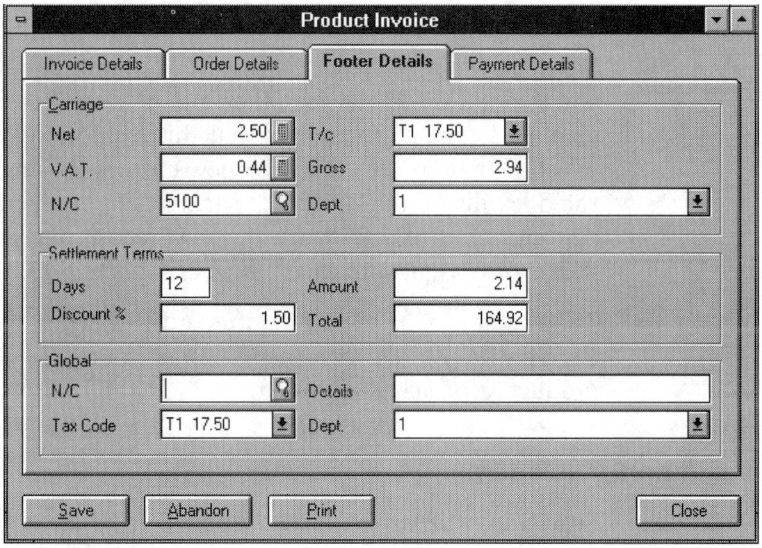

Fig. 8.6

There are three panels on this window. The first panel requires any **Carriage** details. From Fig. 8.6 you will see that this invoice has a **Net** carriage amount of £2.50, plus **VAT** of £0.44, giving a **Gross** figure of £2.94. The nominal code (**N/C**) will be required because carriage should not be treated as part of the sales figure, and so the amount net of VAT must be credited to a carriage account (5100). You can use the **Finder** icon to select the required nominal account code.

The **Settlement Terms** panel in Fig. 8.6 shows that if this customer pays within 12 **Days**, a **Discount** of 1.5 per cent of the invoice amount will be available. The **Amount** box is calculated for you and shows the value of the discount with the **Total** being the amount to settle if the discount is taken. The Items Gross will *not* include the carriage costs.

The **Global** panel is used if you wish to apply VAT (**Tax Code**), nominal code (**N/C**) and **Department** code to all of the invoice rather than line by line. The **Details** box in the panel allows a description of your choice to be stored with the Nominal Ledger posting.

Payment Details should be used only if you have already received payment for the goods. Once used, the Customer Account will be credited with the amount and the chosen bank account debited.

Creating new product records and customers

When an invoice is being created, you are expected to select an existing customer and then select stock items for which a product record has already been created. If a customer or product item does not exist, then you can create new records using the Invoicing part of the package rather than going into the other functions.

When you first create a new invoice, you are required to select a customer. If you click on the **Finder** icon then a panel listing the existing customers will be displayed. The dialogue box that this Finder creates also has a **New** button which allows you to create the new customer as required. When **New** is activated it calls on the Customer part of the package that allows you to create a new customer record. When this new record is saved, you will be returned to the Invoice window to carry on entering details to it.

The creation of a new product record is done in exactly the same way. If you click on the Finder icon that belongs to the **Product Code** field, then a new product record can be created.

Invoices of non-stock items

Situations will arise where you need to raise an invoice to a customer for non-stock items, such as a special delivery for services rendered. To create such an invoice make sure you are back at the main Invoicing window and

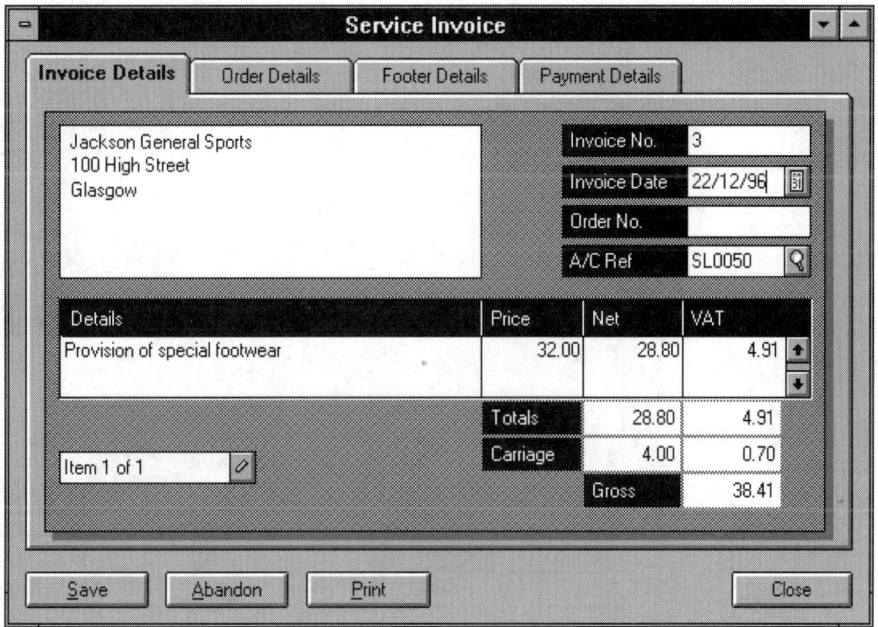

Fig. 8.7

click on the **Service Invoice** icon. This will reveal an invoice window very similar to the Invoicing From Stock window. Figure 8.7 shows an example of such an entry window.

The order details and footer options are exactly as before. To alter any individual line, the **Backslash** icon will appear below the **Details** lines – in Fig. 8.7 it reads *Item 1 of 1*. When saved, the invoice will appear in the list of invoices in the main Invoicing window.

Credit notes

A credit note is prepared in the same way as an invoice. From the main Invoicing menu, click on the **Product Credit Note** icon to reveal an entry window similar to that shown in Fig. 8.8.

The effect of **Product Credit Note** is to return goods to stock that have been previously sent to a customer, and then to credit the customer with the credit note amount. The **Description** line shown in Fig. 8.8 shows how a product item can be replaced with a non-stock item. At this stage you should experiment a little with the creation of invoices and credit notes in order to build a few documents to work with later.

The fourth document icon from the main Invoicing window is **Service Credit Note**. This works in exactly the same way as the **Product Credit Note** – the difference being that goods are not being returned.

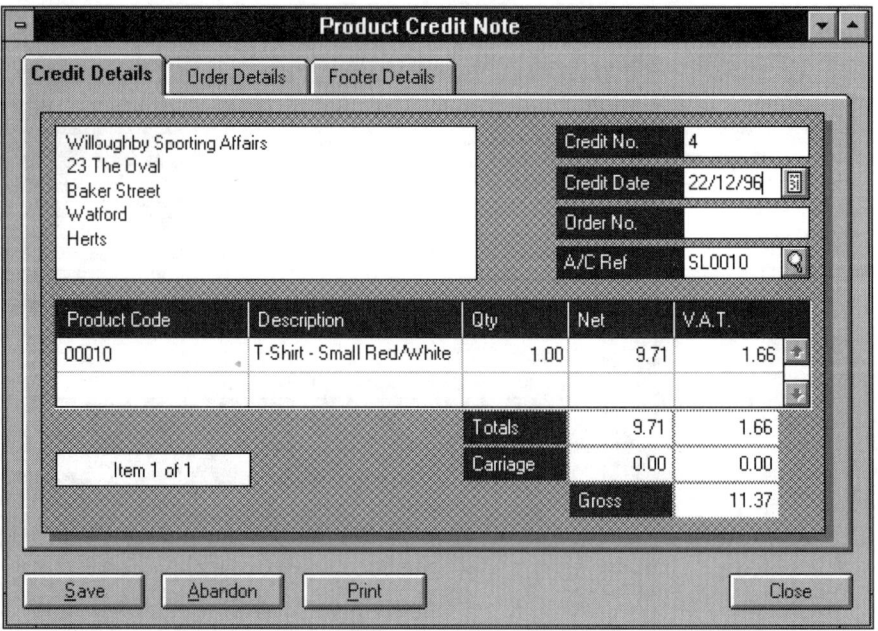

Fig. 8.8

Amending or deleting documents

To amend an invoice or credit note, you need to be at the main Invoice window. Click on the document line you want altered, so that it is highlighted, and then click on one of the four icons that is relevant to the type of document. You cannot, for example, highlight a credit note and then click on an invoice icon.

The effect of this will be to place you in the Invoice or Credit Note window with the document back on screen. You can then alter the details as many times as you wish, providing the details have not already been posted to the ledgers.

To delete an invoice you need to be at the main Invoice window. Click on the document line you want altered so that it is highlighted. Now click on the **Delete** button at the bottom of the window.

PRINTING INVOICES

Setting up the invoice format

You can go on adding invoices any time you want. The printing of these invoices is normally done separately at a later stage. When you were creating invoices, the invoice menu had a **Print** button that allowed you to print the invoice you were creating. It is assumed in this section, however, that this will be done as a batch run – that is, all at once rather than one at a time. This approach has the advantage of saving time in setting up your printer for each invoice. For example, you can enter invoice details many times in a week but need allocate only one time in the week to print them. The strategy should be to enter batches of invoices fairly regularly in order to keep the stock files updated and the customer records and nominal accounts well posted.

Your first step will be to prepare the format of the invoice so that it can be printed in a form suitable to your business. This can be a time-consuming and awkward job but it normally needs to be done only once. To help you, Sage sells preprinted stationery with a layout exactly tailored to the way the invoices are set up when the package is purchased and installed.

Whether you are using Sage-produced stationery or your own, you will still have to make some changes to the stationery layout. From the main Invoicing menu, click on the **Print Invoices** icon to reveal a new dialogue box similar to the one that appears in Fig. 8.9.

This contains further options and the **Layout** box contains a list of file names, each for varying forms and different types of stationery. These are the names of the standard layout files for invoices and credit notes that fit on to Sage stationery. The file name **SRVDIS11.SLY**, for example, is used for service invoices. A similar arrangement was used when you mailed customers with a set of standard files that could be amended. It is now worth spending more time investigating further how Sage allows you to create and amend such documents.

The dialogue window that appears (*see* Fig. 8.9) has a number of options:

- **New** allows you to create a new invoice format of your own.
- **Edit** allows you to edit an existing format to better suit your own stationery.

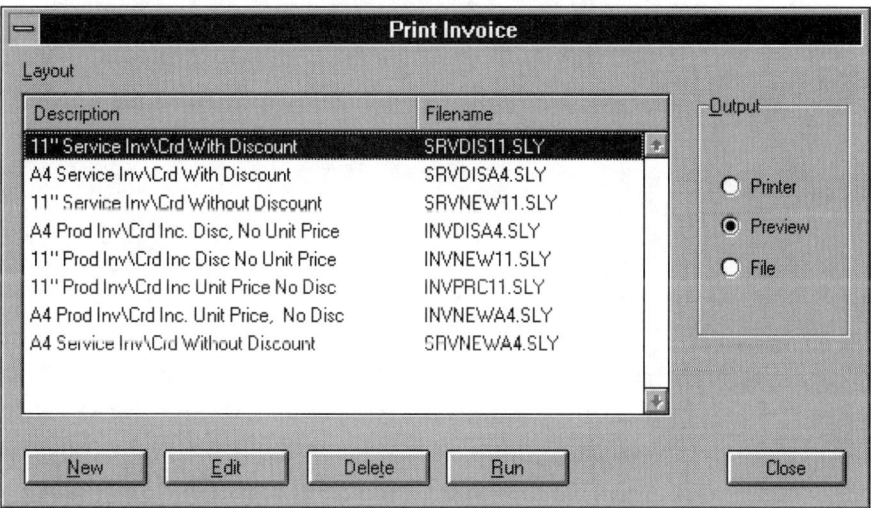

Fig. 8.9

- **Delet̲e** will delete an invoice format.
- **R̲un** is used to run the invoice printing. Before selecting this option, you will need to select the output required as being **Printer**, **Preview** or **File**.
- **Close** will end the Print Invoice session and return you to the main Invoicing window.

Rather than try and create a new invoice layout from scratch, you can use the **E̲dit** facility to see how such a document is created just as effectively. Click on the **E̲dit** button to generate a new window similar to that shown in Fig. 8.10.

If you use the scroll bars down the right-hand side and at the bottom of this window, you can view other parts of the file. The items inside the lightly dotted rectangles are variable names and refer to data held by the Sage package in the accounting records. Text outside these brackets will appear on the invoice in exactly the same way as it appears in the file. If you were to start with a blank file, you could enter text by clicking on the **Insert** option from the pull-down menu, as shown in Fig. 8.10, and then selecting **Text**. This creates a text box to place on the document which can, using your mouse, be stretched to create a suitable text box. You type in the text required into the text box as though you were typing text with a word processor.

To enter variables, you have to select them from a list, available as a drop box to the right of the window and just below the row of pull-down menus. If you require on-screen help for this, then pressing function key **F1** while in this

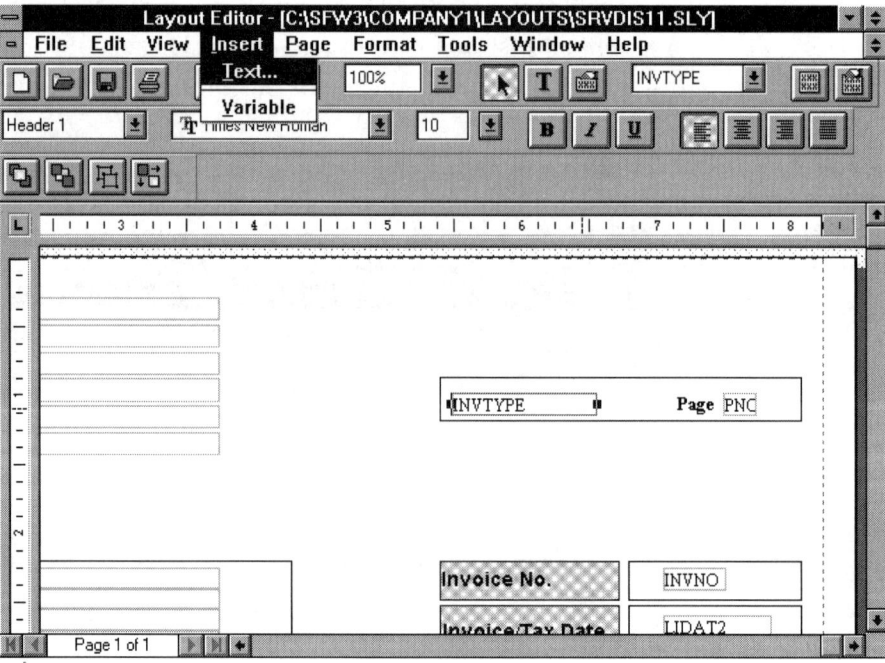

Fig. 8.10

window will give you help specific to this word processor. To see the available list of variables, click on **Tools** from the pull-down menu, then select **Variable List**. This will reveal a dialogue box as shown in Fig. 8.11. If you are going to create your own document or amend an existing one, then a printout of this would serve as a useful reference.

PRACTICE At this stage, it may be worth creating a new file and experimenting with entering variables and text. To do this, you need to exit from this file (**File** and **Exit** from the pull-down menu) and select **New** to create a new invoice layout. Please note, that the output will make no sense until you are actually ready to print an invoice.

Printing the invoice

Once the invoice layouts have been prepared, it is a good idea to print a few invoices simply to check that the output is as required. You can print off invoices as many times as you wish. However, Sage does record the fact that invoices have already been printed after the first print run to help you decide which invoices you want printed. After an invoice has been printed, it will appear in the list of invoices as having been printed.

Making sure you are still in the Print Batch window, which is part of Invoicing, select one of the product invoices by highlighting one of them in the **Layout** box. Now click on **Printer** for the output required and then click on the **Run** button to print the invoice. Sage will begin by preparing the report for you and then printing it. Before you start the printing, you are given the opportunity to set up the printer. Figure 8.12 shows the Print window that allows this.

The default **printer** will be exactly as set up through Windows; if you have another printer on your system, click on the **Printer** button to obtain a list of printers from which you can make your selection. The **Print Range** can be

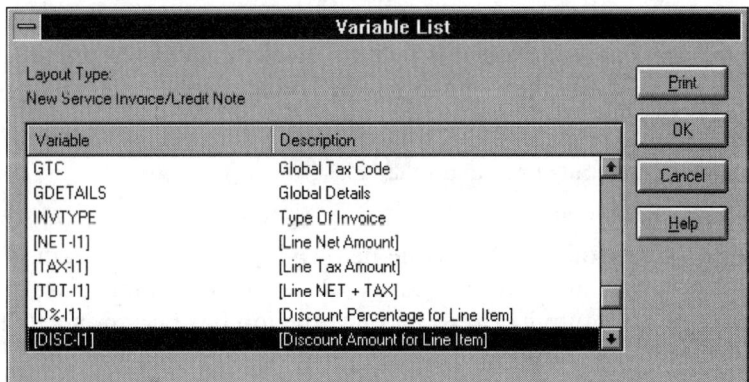

Fig. 8.11

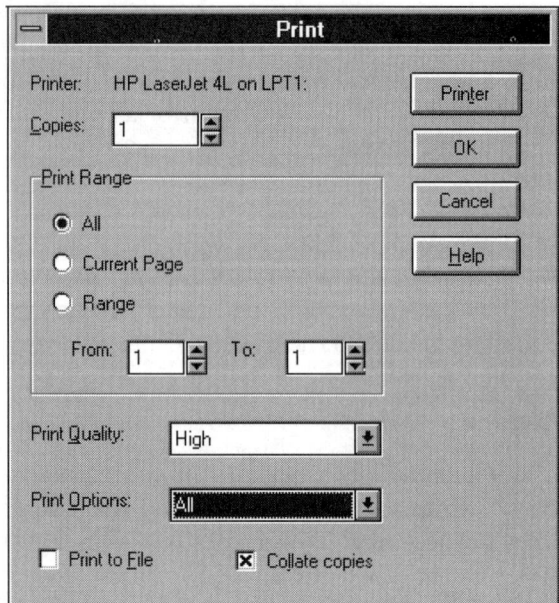

Fig. 8.12

altered if you wish to all invoice, current page or a range of pages. Sage will assume **All** pages are printed unless you decide to specify otherwise. The **Print Quality** can be altered but is again assumed to be as high as your printer will allow, unless you choose otherwise.

The **Print to File** box at the bottom of the window can have its box clicked so that a cross appears in it (often referred to as a toggle being on). This will send output to a file for future printing rather than doing the whole process immediately.

If you choose to **Collate copies**, then invoices will be printed one customer at a time, rather than all page ones, followed by all page twos and so on. If the invoices only consist of one page, then this option will not matter.

Click on **OK** to start the printing. Sage will now start to send the invoices to your printer. When the invoices have been printed, the Main invoice window will flag them as having been printed.

Figure 8.13 is an example of an invoice created using one of the invoice layouts provided by Sage.

If this invoice is not suitable for your stationery, then you should return to the editing of the invoice layout and try again. When businesses use their own stationery, a good deal of time and effort is often taken tailoring the output. However, once the job has been done, it should not be necessary to return to it.

```
                    MEGAXAN STERLING SPORTS
                      The Sage Shopping Centre
                      199 High Street, Newtown
                     Co. Heppershaw, NH88 9ZZ

                              INVOICE

  To:                                                          Page: 1

  Dipple Store                    Invoice No.:   1
  The Oval                        Invoice Date:  22/12/96
  King Street
  Manchester

  987 6666 555                    Your A/C No.: SL0060
  ----------------------------------------------------------------
  Quantity   Product Description        Unit      Net        VAT
                                       Price    Amount     Amount
  ----------------------------------------------------------------
  4.00       T-Shirt – Small Red/White  12.95    51.80      8.84
  3.00       T-Shirt – Medium Red/White 17.80    42.72      7.29
  4.00       T-Shirt – Large Red/White  18.00    72.00     12.29

  Net Amount      166.52
  VAT Amount       28.42
  Carriage          0.00

  Invoice Total   194.94
```

Fig. 8.13

The problem of insufficient stock

You are allowed to create an invoice for stock that you do not actually have available to sell. If this happens, then Sage will generate a message on the screen with a window telling you that there is insufficient stock to despatch the goods. You will then be given the option to either not enter this line on the invoice or go ahead with it. If you pursue an invoice in this way, you will not be able to update the ledgers with it in the next section. When the stock does arrive, however, the invoice can then be used to update the stock records in the usual way.

A situation can arise where there is enough stock on the shelves to meet an invoice but some of it has been allocated to an order. Order processing will be covered in detail in Chapter 9.

UPDATING THE LEDGER

The update routine

Until now the Sales Ledger and stock control have not been informed of the invoices and credit notes that have been produced. Soon after you enter the invoice details, it is a wise policy to amend the ledgers in order to keep the customer and stock records up to date. Before you start, ensure you are in the main Invoice window and highlight those invoices and credit notes you want posted to the ledgers. If you leave all lines clear, Sage will ask you if you want all documents posted.

From the main Invoicing window, click on the **Update** icon to reveal a new small window, as shown in Fig. 8.14. When the **OK** is clicked, Sage will process each invoice and undergo the following ledger updates:

- Remove invoiced items from stock in accordance with the quantity issued. If the stock on an invoice cannot be issued because of insufficient stock, then Sage will abort that invoice and report it to you.
- Debit the account of the customer for the invoice amount. This indicates what is owed by the customer.
- Perform the following double entry:

    1 Debit the Debtors Control Account by the *gross* amount on the invoice.
    2 Credit the Sales account(s) by the net goods charged to the customer.
    3 Credit the Carriage Account by the net amount charged.
    4 Credit the VAT Control Account by VAT on the invoice.

This update process will also process the credit notes in the same way, but having the reverse effect on stock levels, the customer's account and the double entry.

Once the update routine has been done, it cannot be reversed. If an invoice later needs to be amended, then you will have to issue a credit note on the old invoice and then issue a new invoice. It is important, therefore, that all invoices are carefully checked for completeness and accuracy before the

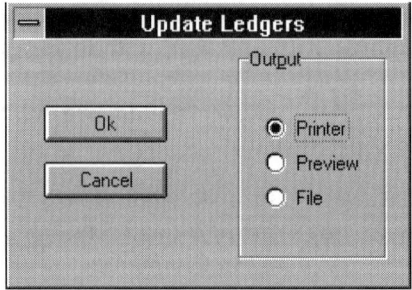

Fig. 8.14

process is carried out. Invoices should also be checked carefully before they are sent out to customers, as changes later are bad business practice and give a poor impression to customers.

The Update window, as shown in Fig. 8.14, has an **Output** panel that allows you to set where you want the output report sent. A printout is wise, just set the output to either **Printer** for direct printed copy or **Preview** which shows the output on screen before printing. Selecting **File** will allow you to print it out later or use the Windows Write program to word process the document. Selecting **Display** will only show the report on screen, leaving you with no reference later, other than working through the ledgers.

From Fig. 8.15 you will see that the **Printed** and **Posted** columns are flagged with a 'Yes' if they have been carried out. This will guide you in deciding what you want deleted. You can also see whether they have been printed. When invoices have been completed in this way, there is little point in leaving them on the computer indefinitely. During the period-end routines, as described in Chapter 6, all those invoices that have been printed and posted will automatically be deleted. If you want to delete them at this stage, simply highlight those you want deleted and click on the **De̲lete** button.

CONCLUSION

By now you will appreciate that, once the system has been set up, most of the data entry functions can be avoided. For example, once the system knows about your customers and your stock, invoice production is quicker and involves less effort. In fact the only real data entry often needed in the Sales Ledger is when a customer settles a debt or you need to make alterations to a customer's record or add new customers.

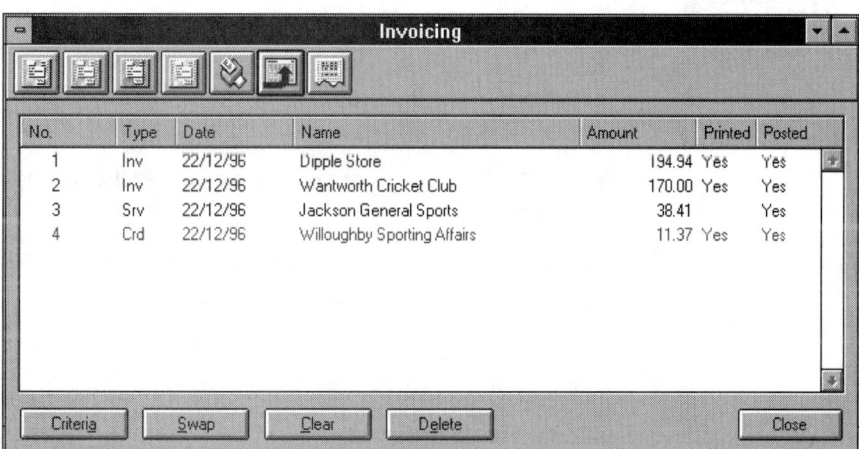

Fig. 8.15

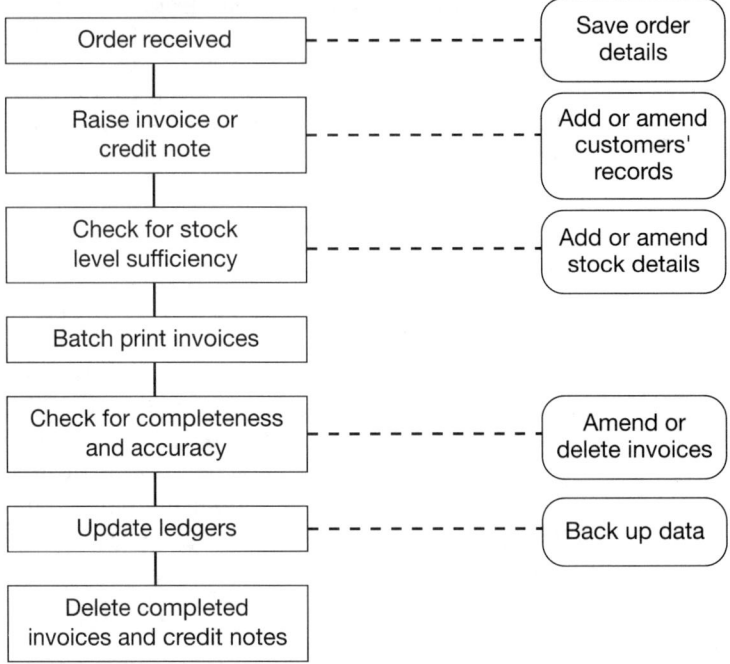

Fig. 8.16

With respect to invoicing, Fig. 8.16 depicts the set of procedures that might be adopted from the receipt of an order to the point where the ledgers are updated.

In Chapter 9, you will have the chance to put into place the final piece of the system – the handling of customer orders. This will take the process one step forward so that even the invoice can be generated automatically.

EXERCISES

1. Create at least:
   - five product invoices
   - two service invoices
   - two product credit notes
   - one service credit note.

   When working on these, experiment with description details, order details and footers details.

2. Amend two of the product invoices to include discounts and carriage.

3. Amend an invoice to record that payment details have been received. This can be done by using the Payment Details page.

4. Delete one of the product service credit notes.

5. Print out your documents.

6. Post them to the ledgers.

CHAPTER 9

Sales and purchase order processing

INTRODUCTION

This final chapter on the actual accounting functions in Sage concentrates on the ordering side of business activities.

The purpose of sales order processing is to process orders placed by customers. Basically, an order is placed by a customer and processed by the business and is then completed by the despatch of the goods or the carrying out of the service, accompanied by or followed by an invoice. The order will, in fact, form the basis of the invoice, thereby avoiding the need to create an invoice from scratch.

In purchase order processing, on the other hand, the business sends an order for stock to a supplier. In both cases, such order processing will have an implication for stock and so relies on stock records being up to date.

Both sales and purchase order processing need to link to other functions of the Sage package if they are to be of use. It is important that customer, supplier and stock records are all in place before you can proceed. Consequently, this chapter has to assume that you have worked through the preceding chapters.

SALES ORDER PROCESSING

This function will help a business to maintain efficient and adequate stock levels. When an order is received and entered into the computer, stock records are adjusted to indicate that certain stocks have been allocated against an order. Sales order processing can be handled in four distinct ways:

- When the order is received by the business from its customer, the order could now be invoiced immediately and the goods despatched. This has the effect of *reducing* stock levels. The problem may arise where there is insufficient stock to meet the order.

- If an order cannot be fully met because of insufficient stock, then the business may decide to partially meet the order by despatching and invoicing for the goods that are available and then sending the rest of the order out when the outstanding goods become available. Although perfectly acceptable in many businesses, it is important to keep a record of what has been delivered and what still has to be sent.

- The business may decide to hold on to an order until it can be met in full. For this to work properly, it is necessary to keep stock *allocated* against an order. The purpose of doing this is to ensure that, as the business awaits sufficient stock to complete the order, it does not despatch what goods it does have available to another customer.

- It is common business practice that when a customer places an order, immediate delivery is not preferred as it creates too high a stock level for the business. In this instance, the details of the order can be recorded and the despatch of the goods scheduled for a future specified date.

When an order is received, a stock allocation is made to indicate that items of stock will be needed to meet the order. The stock file record, therefore, is updated to reflect this. The stock is not recorded as physically absent until the invoice is raised *and* used to update the ledgers. As a consequence, when decisions have to be made about stock, a more rational decision can be made because it is possible to see what stock is required to meet sales orders. When stocks are available to meet an order or complete an order, the stock levels have to be reduced by what has been despatched, and the allocation details must be removed from the stock records. In other words, an allocation becomes an adjustment out when the goods are despatched to the customer.

The sales order elements

From the main Sage window, click on the **Sales Orders** icon to reveal a window similar to that shown in Fig. 9.1.

A brief overview of the six elements behind the row of icons will help develop a better understanding of how sales order processing fits in with the rest of the Sage package.

- **Sales Order Entry** will create an order. When the order is received from the customer, the order details are entered through this option.

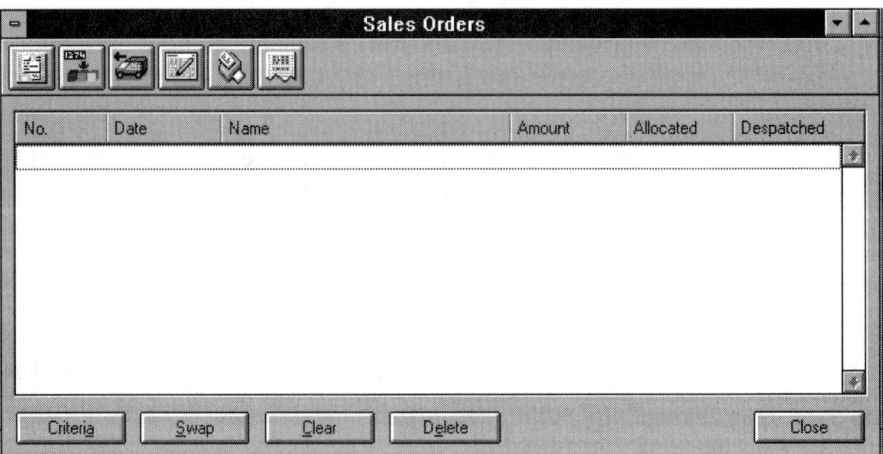

Fig. 9.1

- **Allocate** will allocate stock in the stock file to an order ready for despatch.
- **Despatch** will indicate that the goods have now been sent to the customer and, if required, generate a delivery note and invoice for the goods.
- **Amend Despatch** allows you to find out about the status of an order and gives details of how much of the order has been completed and allocated against stock.
- **Print Sales Orders** allows you to print the order acknowledgements in the same way as invoices were printed in Chapter 8.
- **Report** will produce details about the status of your orders on the system.

Entering orders

When an order is received it may appear on your own order form stationery or on the customer's own order form, depending on the policy of the customer. Increasingly, orders are placed by fax (facsimile telegraphy), which allows orders to be reproduced on the recipient's fax via a telephone line. Many businesses will also accept orders by telephone, with the operator entering details straight on to the computer. Sage has the facility for sending out sales order acknowledgements and purchase orders in this way – a topic that will be covered in Chapter 10.

Whatever method is used, the receipt of the order will be the point of *data capture* and it will have to be placed on to the computer. For most businesses, it

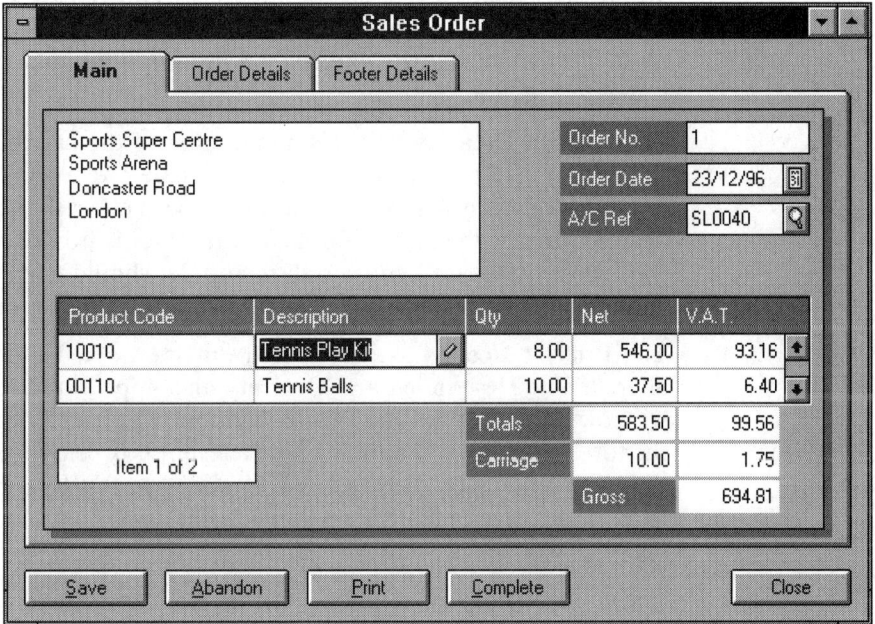

Fig. 9.2

will involve an operator entering the order onto the computer using an order form to gather the initial details.

From the Sales Orders window click on **Sales Order Entry** and a blank entry window will appear on your screen, looking very much like the entry screen for an invoice. Figure 9.2 shows an order form with customer details entered.

The similarity between this and the invoice is largely to be expected because all the details that will appear on the eventual invoice will be generated from the initial order.

The information you will need to complete the entry window that makes up a sales order record includes the **Customer Account Number**, which will appear in the Sales Ledger. As with the invoice, you can use the **Finder** icon for this – it also enables you to add new customers. For example, you may receive an order from a new customer and this order may require you to create the new customer in your records. Meanwhile, you can hold onto the order and check out whether the new customer is creditworthy, before allocating any stock or despatching any goods.

The **Order Number** will be displayed as 1 greater than the previous order processed, which can be changed if you wish. The product lines are exactly the same as for an invoice and, if you use the **Finder** icon to enter the **Product Code**, new product items can be created here too. The situation may arise where a customer requires a product item which you have never held in stock; if the order is to be honoured you might have to create a new stock record and place a purchase order for the stock.

When the **Product Code** has been entered and the **Description** field is highlighted, as shown in Fig. 9.2, click on the forward slash that appears to the right of this field. This will display a Product Item dialogue window as illustrated in Fig. 9.3.

The Product Details window is no different to the one for an invoice and will be used to create the invoice later. It is, therefore, worth taking care to get it right first time. Once the information has been entered, there will be no further need to re-enter the same information. In other words, once data is captured in the form required – its entry to the computer should never have to be repeated, an important principle to be adhered to in any information processing system.

The **Product Code** is as it appeared on the order detail line and cannot be altered. The **Description** and **Quantity** also appear and can be altered in this window instead of the main Order window. The **Unit Price** can be entered and the total **Net price** will appear in the relevant box below as being quantity multiplied by unit price. The **VAT** will be added to this total by default but, if the total is inclusive of VAT, then you can click on the **C̲alculate Net** button and the VAT will be taken away from the gross amount.

The comment figures, as shown in Fig. 9.3, can be used as you please. Figure 9.3 also shows that a 12.5 per cent **Discount** has been allowed on this item to this customer. If you click on the **Di̲scounts** button at the bottom of this

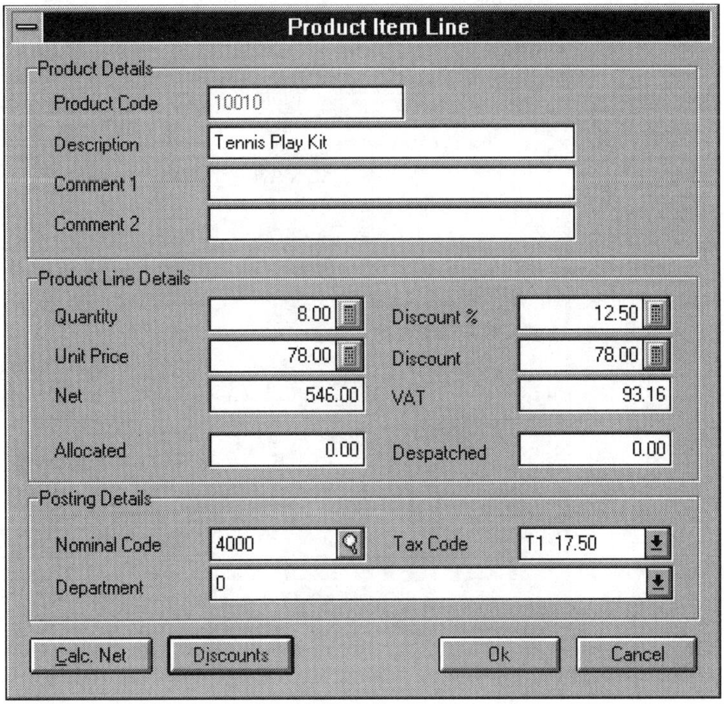

Fig. 9.3

window, you will see a breakdown of how this discount has been arrived at. The **Nominal Code** is used to identify the Sales Account in the Nominal Ledger that will be credited when the invoice is created and later used to update the ledgers. This too can be changed, as can the **Department**. Both of these would have been stored within the stock records when they were created.

When this detail box is complete, click on the **OK** button to return to the Invoice window ready for the next detail line.

If you place a quantity on order but you do not have enough stock available, then a message window appears, as shown in Fig. 9.4.

This informs you that you do not have enough stock to meet this order. Although there may appear to be enough stock in your storeroom or warehouse, what you have may have been already allocated to another order. If you click on **OK**, you can still carry on with the order. This message will alert you, however, to the possible need to order more of this stock.

There are three page tabs at the top of the sales order window. The current page is **Main** and this appears as highlighted. Click on the **Order Details** tab to get a window similar to the one in Fig. 9.5.

This allows you to enter more details about the order as a whole. The data on the Entry window shown in Fig. 9.5 shows how the window can be used to

Sales Order
Main
Order Details
Footer Details
Sports Super Centre
Sports Arena
Doncaster Road
London
Warning
The quantity entered exceeds the amount of available stock.
STOP
OK
Product Code
10010
00110
Totals
549.75
93.80
Item 2 of 2
Carriage
0.00
0.00
Gross
643.55
Save
Abandon
Print
Complete
Close

Fig. 9.4

Sales Order
Main
Order Details
Footer Details
Delivery Address
AS INVOICED
Notes
This company will not take delivery before 9 January 1997
Customer Order Details
Customer Order No.
455/96
Customer Tel. No.
0171 222333
Customer Contact
Mary or Jack
Order Taken By
Dave
Order Status
Due Despatch
16/01/97
Invoice No.
Allocation
Despatch
Save
Abandon
Print
Complete
Close

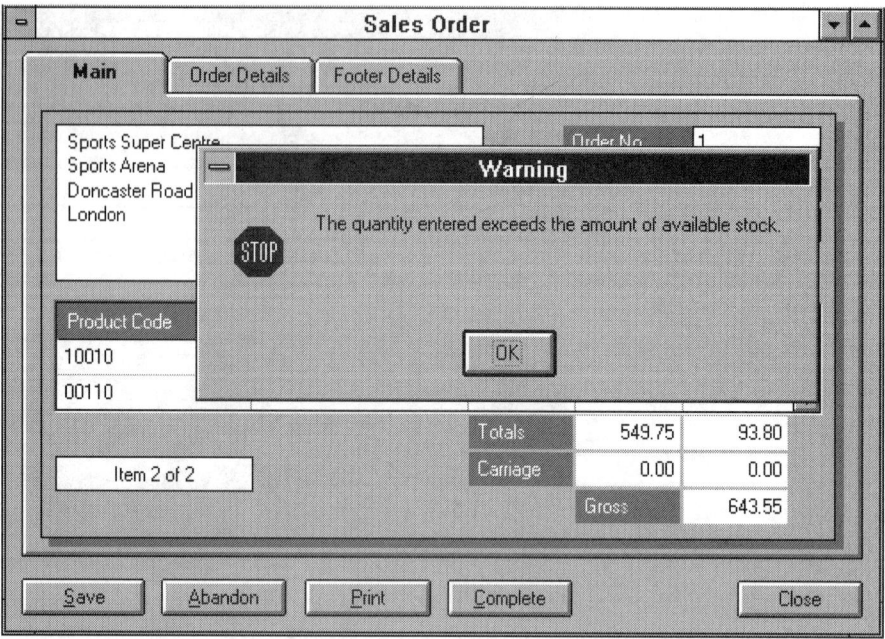

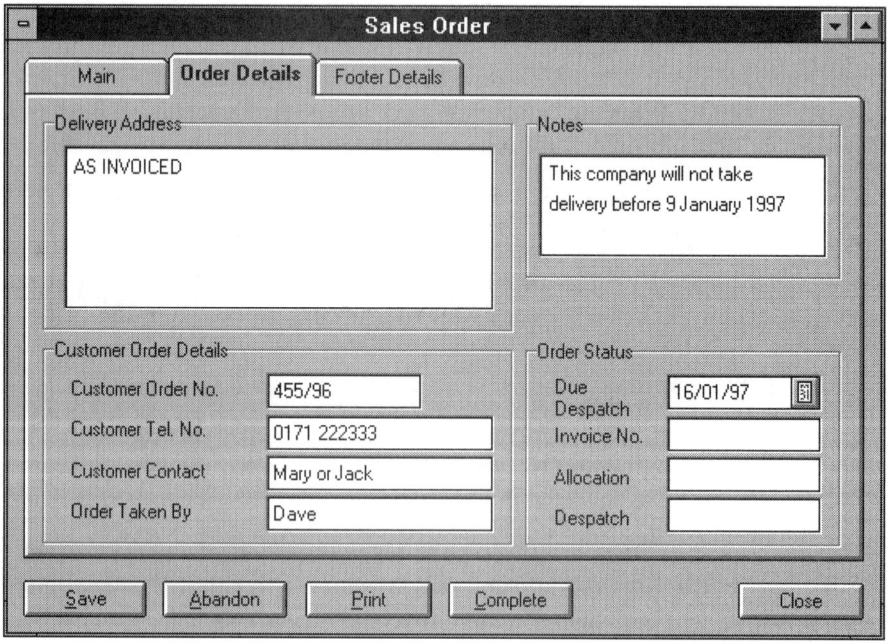

Fig. 9.5

enter details about where to deliver the goods when the delivery address is different to the address held in the Sales Ledger. Most details on this page are the same as the order details that you used when creating invoices in Chapter 8.

The **Due Despatch** date is the date on which you expect to fulfil the order or is the date the customer expects you to despatch the goods. This will be important for future monitoring and decision making regarding priorities for the allocation or despatch of stock. The **Order Taken By** field can be used by the business for any purpose. It can be used to indicate which person in the business processed the order or how the order was received, e.g. by post, telephone or fax. Once this window is complete, click on the main page tab to return to the main Order Create screen.

As with invoicing, you have the facility to enter both carriage details (cost of postage and packing) and any settlement terms you might want to offer your customer. To activate this facility, click on the **Footer Details** page tab that appears at the top of your Order window. There are three panels on this window. The first panel requires any **Carriage** details, the second panel is for **Settlement Terms** and a **Global** panel is used if you wish to apply **VAT**, **Nominal Code** and **Department Code** to all of the invoice rather than line by line.

Once the order is complete, click on **Save** and the details will be entered into an orders file which, at this stage, will have no effect on either the stock records or customer accounts in the Sales Ledger. Consequently, any errors or omissions can be put right without affecting on the accounts. As with invoicing, there is a lot of sense in batch processing the entering of orders rather than doing these one at a time. The stock items are not allocated until you are ready to update the stock items as a separate activity later.

PRACTICE Before moving on, enter a few more orders and experiment with the sales order features that can be used to create and save orders.

Allocating stock against sales orders

This process is used to allocate product items in the stock files to orders. Once the stock has been allocated to an order, the stock is no longer available for other orders or for invoicing. Consequently, you need to be cautious about which orders you decide to allocate stock against, if stocks are in short supply. To perform this operation, begin with the main Sales Order window and highlight those orders against which you wish to have stock allocated. When this has been done, click on the **Allocate** icon. This will reveal a small dialogue box as shown in Fig. 9.6(a).

This asks you to confirm the allocations. If you are still satisfied that this is what you want, click on the **Yes** button. If there is insufficient stock to meet an order, then Sage will inform you of this fact with another dialogue box, as shown in Fig. 9.6(b).

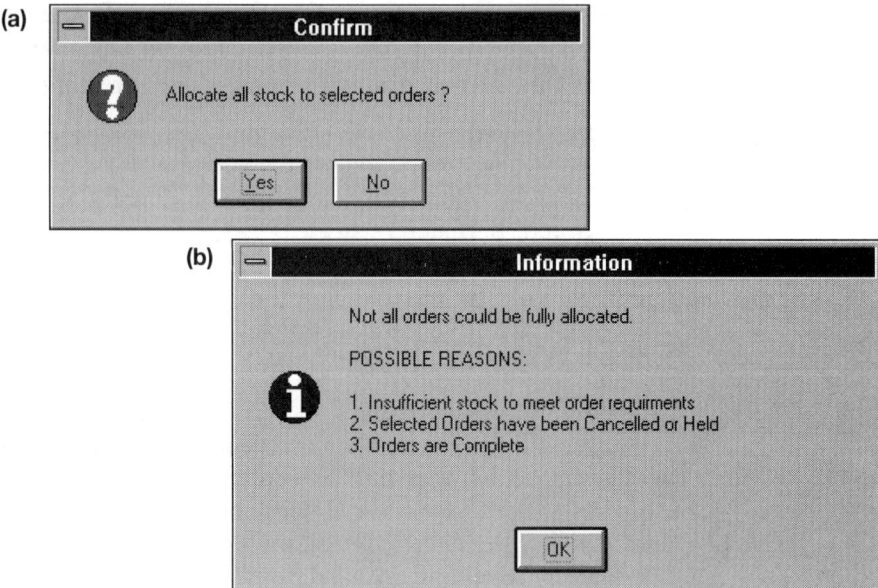

Fig. 9.6

Although the stock that you have now allocated cannot be used for another order or invoice, you still have the option of de-allocating this stock. This will be explained later when you look at amending a despatch. If you decided to choose **Amend Despatch** followed by **Complete**, then all goods that can be despatched will be *removed* from the stock quantities rather than simply allocated.

The main Sales Order window will now show that stock has been allocated against an order. In the **Allocated** column the name FULL will appear on a line to indicate that the order has had stock fully allocated to it and is now ready for despatch. Alternatively, if the words PART appear, then not all of the order has had stock allocated to it and it is not fully ready for despatch.

Despatching orders

The goods will now be despatched to the customer, thus reducing stock levels and debiting the customer. This operation will also create an invoice for you based on the order details. From the main Sales Order window, begin by highlighting an order that you have now entered and which has had stock fully allocated to it. The first message will ask you if you wish to create a delivery note for this despatch, as shown in Fig. 9.7(a).

If you click on the **Yes** button, you will be able to print the delivery note in exactly the same way as an invoice was produced. Sage will suggest one of two file names; if you select **Run** and output to the printer, a despatch note will be produced. This will normally go out with the goods – often physically attached to the packaging.

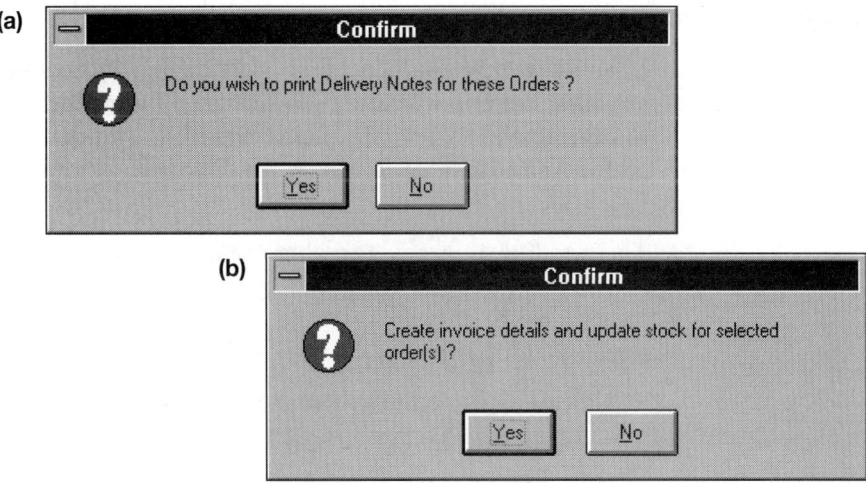

Fig. 9.7

Once the despatch note has been printed, click on the **Close** button from the window to complete the process. The next message that will appear will ask you to confirm whether the invoicing should be done (*see* Fig. 9.7(b)). When you click on **Yes**, Sage will generate an invoice, update the customer account and update the stock.

Figure 9.8 shows a typical despatch note produced by Sage using this system.

```
                MEGAXAN STERLING SPORTS
                 The Sage Shopping Centre
                  199 High Street, Newtown
                  Co. Heppershaw, NH88 9ZZ

                       DELIVERY NOTE

                                                         Page: 1

Sports Super Centre                 Order No.:    1
Sports Arena                        Date:         23/12/96
Doncaster Road                      Your ref:     455/96
London                              Your A/C No.: SL0040
```

Qty Despatch	Product Code	Product Description	Qty Remaining
8.00	10010	Tennis Play Kit	0.00
10.00	00110	Tennis Balls	0.00

Fig. 9.8

Amending allocations and despatches

If, subsequently, the allocation and despatch details need to be altered, then you have the opportunity to do so. Begin by highlighting the orders you wish to have amended from the main Sales Order window. When this is done, click on the **Amend Despatch** icon. A new dialogue window will appear, as shown in Fig. 9.9.

This window allows you to alter the amount of stock to allocate to the order and the amount you wish to despatch at the next process. When the amendments have been made, you then have a set of buttons at the bottom of the screen that allow you to do one of the following:

- **Allocate** the stock in accordance with the details set out in this window.
- **Despatch** the amounts set out in this window.
- Make this **Off Order**, which will remove from the order any balance due to be despatched and, with it, de-allocate that stock. You may want to use this in a situation where you urgently need the stock for another order and wish to release the stock for that purpose. When you have pressed this button, an order will appear, giving you the chance to return to a position where you can allocate stock again.

Sales order status

Figure 9.10 shows a window of orders with different types of status, with respect to their allocated and despatched status. This will appear from the main Invoicing window.

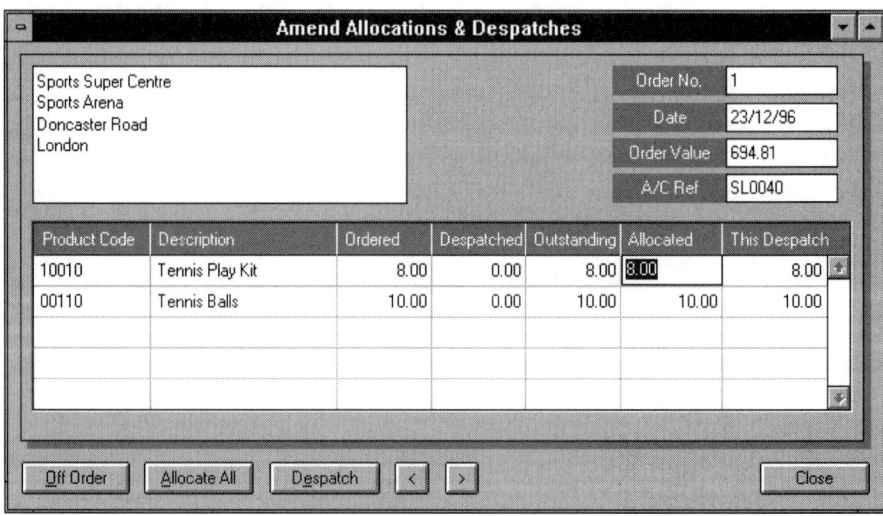

Fig. 9.9

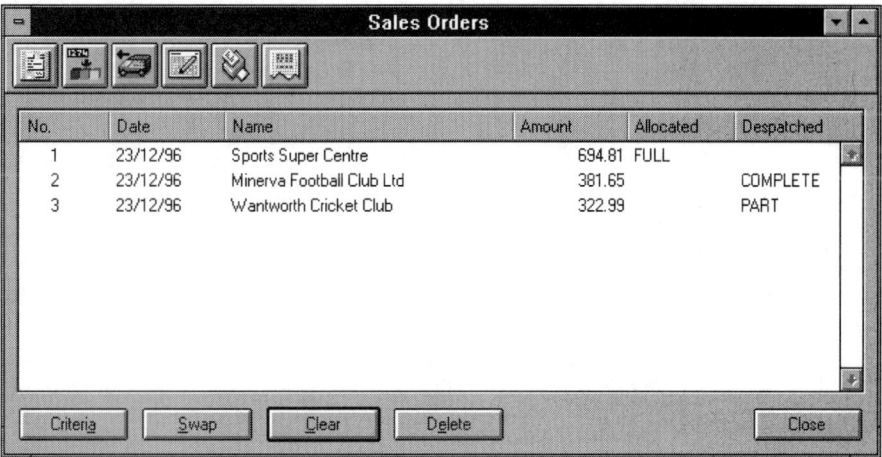

Fig. 9.10

The following types of status can appear on such a window:

- In the **Allocated** column

    FULL   The order has had stock fully allocated.
    PART   The order has been partly allocated.

- In the **Despatched** column

    COMPLETE   The order has been completed.
    PART   The order has had stock partly allocated.
    PART-CAN   Parts of the order have been cancelled.
    CANCEL   The order has been cancelled.

Acknowledging sales orders

When an order is received from a customer, the business may acknowledge receipt of the order by sending the customer a sales acknowledgement document. This document will need to be set up in the same way as the invoices, credit notes and despatch notes. From the main Sales Order window, begin by highlighting all those orders that you wish to acknowledge and then, click on the **Print Sales Orders** icon to reveal a window that is similar to the many other windows used to print documents.

Sage presents you with four layouts to choose from and the ability to create new ones or edit existing ones. A sales acknowledgement would look something like Fig. 9.11.

The order acknowledgement would normally be sent to the customer as soon as the order is received and before goods are despatched. It is this document that can be faxed rather than posted. If you have the correct hardware, then Sage can fax this direct to your customer.

```
              MEGAXAN STERLING SPORTS
               The Sage Shopping Centre
                199 High Street, Newtown
                Co. Heppershaw, NH88 9ZZ

                 SALES ACKNOWLEDGEMENT
                                                     Page: 1

Sports Super Centre              Order No.:      1
Sports Arena                     Date:           23/12/96
Doncaster Road                   Your Order No.: 455/96
London                           Your A/C No.:   SL0040
--------------------------------------------------------------
  Qty                                      Unit     Net
Ordered   Product Code   Product Description Price  Price   VAT
--------------------------------------------------------------
  8.00      10010        Tennis Play Kit   78.00  546.00  93.16
 10.00      00110        Tennis Balls       5.00   37.50   6.40

Total Net Amount   583.50
Total Tax Amount   101.31
Carriage            10.00

Order Total        694.81
```

Fig. 9.11

Sales order reports

At this stage, an explanation is required of the different kinds of order referred to by Sage.

- A *back order* refers to an order that has only been placed onto the system and has had no stock allocated to it. This may be because there is insufficient stock to meet it or because the business is holding back on further processing due to a customer exceeding its credit limit. Alternatively, it may simply be because the order has only just been placed into the file.

- An *outstanding order* refers to an order that has had stock allocated to it but has not yet been despatched. In many cases, part of an outstanding order may have been despatched with the remainder of the order awaiting further stock. The situation then arises where such orders have been processed, but not completed.

- A *completed order* is one where all the goods that have been ordered have been despatched. In this instance, you can remove such details as they are no longer needed except for reporting or information purposes.

What is often needed is a report giving you details about the state of orders you have with your customers. From the main Sales Order window, click on the **Report** icon to reveal a window of which Fig. 9.12 shows a portion.

Sage offers four reports:

- **Back Orders** – as explained earlier.
- **Despatched Sales Orders** – which lists all orders that have had goods despatched.
- **Outstanding Sales Orders** – as explained earlier.
- **Sales Orders Shortfalls** – listing those orders for which there is insufficient stock to fulfil.

PRACTICE Try running these reports after you have entered and processed a few more orders.

Deleting orders

Deleting orders helps keep the size of the files small and speeds up many of the activities carried out later. When sales orders have been completed, there is

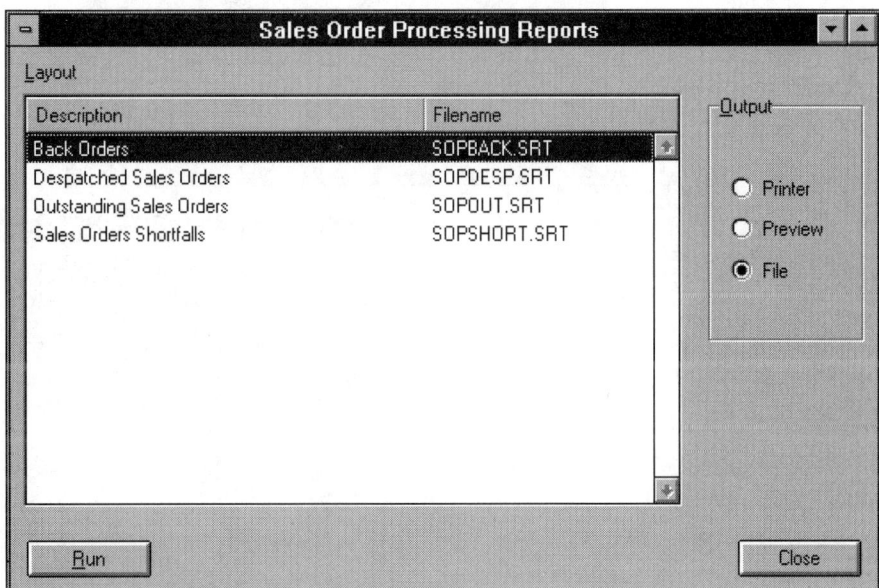

Fig. 9.12

little point in leaving them on the computer indefinitely. To delete an order you first need to be at the main Sales Order window. Highlight those sales orders you want to delete. If any are not completed, then this will have the effect of cancelling them. When this is done, you should click on the **Delete** icon. Sage will ask you to confirm the sales order deletions via a window, as shown in Fig. 9.13(a). When you click on **Yes**, the orders will be deleted and they will be removed from the Sales Order window and the rest of the system.

If an order has not been completed, then Sage will inform you of this and give you the chance to change your mind (*see* Fig. 9.13(b)). If you click on **Yes**, then Sage will reverse the stock allocations and delete the order. If you click on **No**, then the deletion will be ignored.

Before deleting sales orders, it is a good idea to do a backup, especially if you are clearing out a large number of sales orders.

Effect on invoicing

On a final point, if you click on the **Invoicing** icon from the main list of icons, you will obtain a list of invoices which include those invoices created from the Sales Order part of the program. Figure 9.14 shows such a window where the bottom two invoices in the list were created via Sales Order.

You can now alter the invoice, print the invoice or perform any operation on the invoice in the same way as you did when working through Chapter 8.

(a)

(b)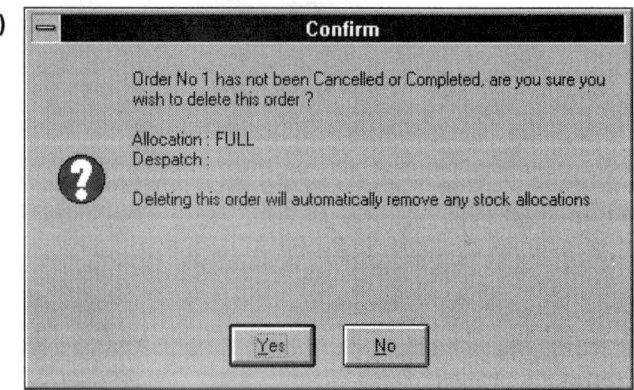

Fig. 9.13

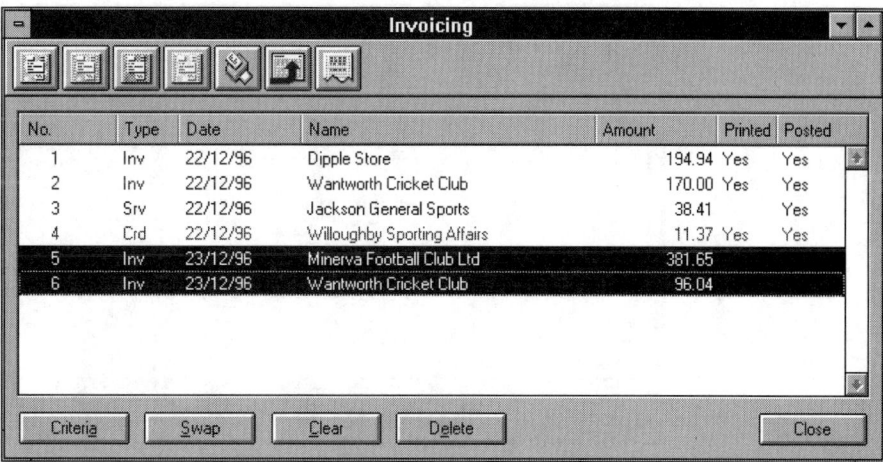

Fig. 9.14

PURCHASE ORDER PROCESSING

By now you should have a good idea of the operation of the Stock Control function and the activities involved in maintaining stock records, entering stock movements and extracting reports. The final stage is to cover purchase order processing, which will make use of both the Purchase Ledger and Stock Control functions. In addition to issuing orders, this function will have an effect on the stock available to be issued and, when a receipt of stock has been recorded against a purchase, will affect the physical stock quantity held.

When ordering goods, you will issue a purchase order and send it to a supplier. In some cases, you may have to send orders to certain suppliers on their own purchase order forms. Whatever way a purchase order is sent, a record must be made and details of the amounts ordered must be stored in the stock records. Each stock record will contain details of what is on order, so that any reference to a stock record will give you an overview of the stock situation. When stock levels are low, it is important to know whether any more is on order, if only to avoid ordering stock more than once.

In addition to keeping stock records updated with what is on order, a purchase order file will also need to be kept so that you are able to keep track of orders placed and report on those orders that are late in being met by suppliers. There will be a record held in the file for each purchase order still outstanding.

Figure 9.15 shows the top part of the Purchase Order window and, as you will see, the window is not significantly different to that of Sales Order Processing. The main difference is that the **Despatch** icon has now become a **Delivery** icon, used to record goods from a purchase order having been delivered. **Allocate** has become **On Order**, which is used to indicate an order has actually been placed. The purchase order processing function also differs very little from sales order

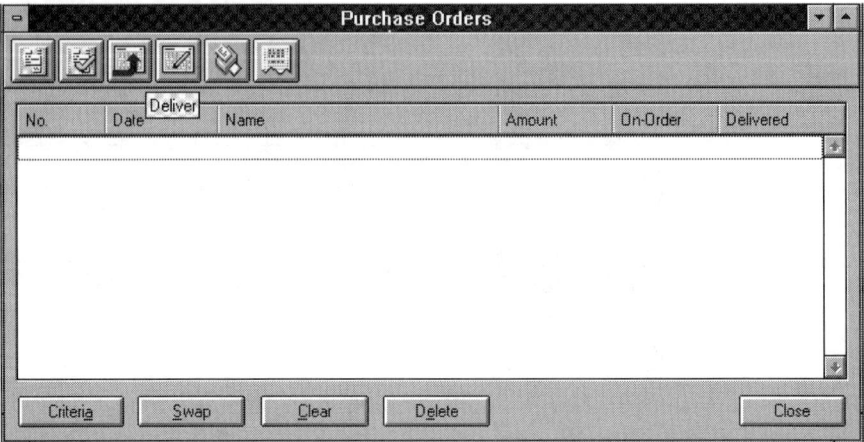

Fig. 9.15

processing in its operations. Consequently, not much will need to be explained in this section of the chapter regarding the operation of purchase order processing. The processes involved are, however, more straightforward as the onus of getting the goods to their destination in time falls on the supplier.

Creating purchase orders

Entering a purchase order is the same process as entering a sales order. When you click on the **Purchase Order Entry** icon, as Fig. 9.16 shows, the order is made up in the same way as a sales order.

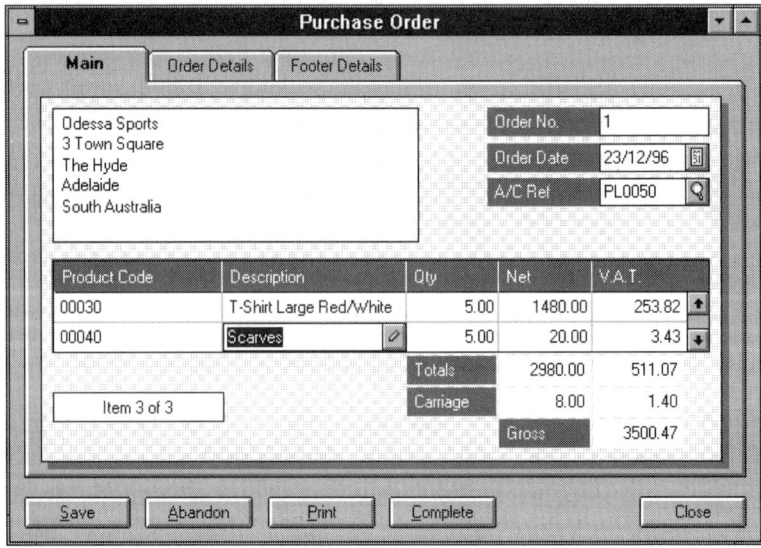

Fig. 9.16

The **Order Number** is again generated by the computer and the **Purchase Reference** is extracted from the Purchase Ledger. The **Order Details** page, **Footer Details** page and **Item Detail** page are used in the same way as for a sales order. You should note that the **Due Despatch Date** that is entered via clicking on the **Order Details** tab button is the date when you want or expect the goods to be despatched to you. Some of the **Settlement Terms** are often agreed with the supplier beforehand and can be entered to confirm the arrangements (again clicking on the **Order** button).

The rest of the order is made up in exactly the same way as for a sales order and is also stored in a file. Once orders have been placed onto the file they should then be processed. The effect of this processing will be to update the stock records with what is on order.

Printing orders

The **Print Purchase Orders** option prints the orders for sending to suppliers. You will be asked to select the file where the order documents are detailed, in the same way as for printing invoices. You will be presented with a choice of four print layouts. When an order is printed using this file, it looks something like Fig. 9.17.

```
                    MEGAXAN STERLING SPORTS
                     The Sage Shopping Centre
                     199 High Street, Newtown
                     Co. Heppershaw, NH88 9ZZ

                         PURCHASE ORDER

                                                      Page: 1

 Odessa Sports                       Order No.:  1
 3 Town Square                       Date:       23/12/96
 The Hyde                            Our Ref:    PL0050
 Adelaide
 South Australia
 -----------------------------------------------------------
  Qty                                   Unit    Net
  Ordered  Product Code  Product Description  Price  Price  VAT
 -----------------------------------------------------------
   5.00     00030    T-Shirt – Large Red/White  5.00  25.00  4.37
   5.00     00040    Scarves                    4.00  20.00  3.43

  Total Net Amount     45.00
  Total Tax Amount      7.80
  Carriage              8.00

  Order Total          60.80
```

Fig. 9.17

Placing stock on order

When the invoices are printed, or output to a file, you are given the option to change the status of the order to being on order. When this window appears, you should click on the **On-Order button**. At this stage, you are also given the option to print the orders again.

An alternative to this, is to click on the **Order** icon from the main Purchase Order window. If you do print the order using Sage, then this is the quickest way of updating the system. When the status of an order is placed On-Order, then the stock file is updated to show that stock is now on order.

Amending deliveries

The deliveries part of the purchase order function does differ from the despatch equivalent in just a few ways. Clearly, you will be receiving goods rather than despatching them.

When you click on the **Amend Deliveries** icon, an entry window appears that allows you to process a purchase order and at the bottom of which there are a number of buttons. The buttons have a different effect to the despatch equivalent in the sales order function. If you click on **Off Order**, the order will be taken off order and the whole process will be reversed, including the changes in the stock file. If you click on **Deliver**, the stock files will show stock movement in and the order will be recorded as delivered. It will also update the Purchase Ledger to indicate that you now owe the money to the supplier.

Figure 9.18 shows such a window and, as you can see, this gives you the chance to manually alter what has been delivered, leaving an order only part-delivered.

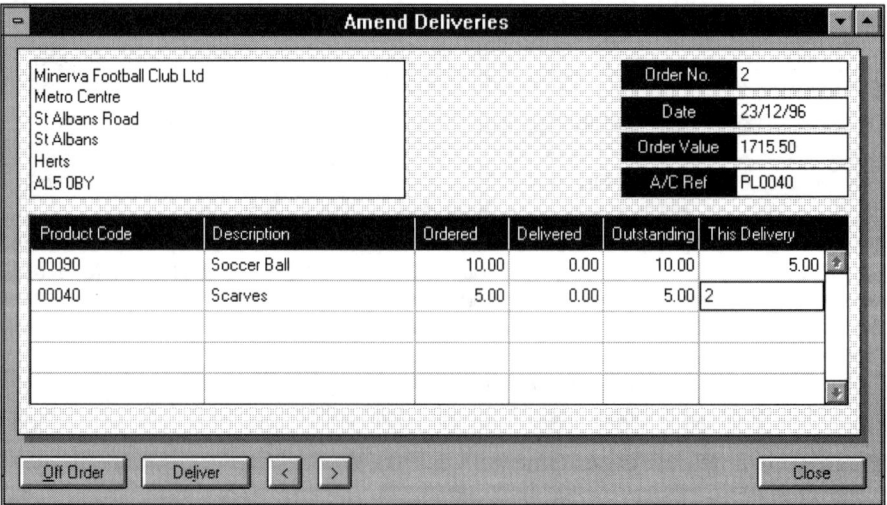

Fig. 9.18

Purchase order status

As with sales orders, the main Purchase Order window will list all orders along with their status. If the status for an order appears blank, then the order has been entered but not placed on order with the supplier. You need to use either **Print Purchase Orders** to place the goods on order or click on the **Order** icon. Over a period of time, you will see the following status indicators:

- In the **On Order** column

    ON ORDER   The goods are on order with the supplier.
    PART-CAN   Some of the goods on the order have been cancelled.
    CANCEL   The order has been cancelled and this too can be deleted.

- In the **Delivered** column

    COMPLETE   The order is complete and can be deleted from the system using the **Delete** facility. (This is done in the same way as you did when deleting sales orders.)
    PART   Some of the goods on the order have been delivered.

Purchase order reports

You can also obtain a printout of order status by clicking on the **Report** icon and choosing from two reports. The **Outstanding Orders** report gives you details of all orders still awaiting stock deliveries of them. The other report gives you details of what has been delivered.

Updating records

One option that does not exist with the purchase order processing is the creation of invoices. Purchasing does not require a business to generate an invoice because the supplier will be sending its invoice with the goods. The result of this is that updating the Purchase Ledger cannot be done automatically. Instead, when an invoice is received, you will have to update the Purchase Ledger by going through the Purchase Ledger function as you did before.

When you examine stock records, you will now get a complete picture as the stock record will show what is in stock, what stock has been allocated to an order and what stock is actually on order with suppliers. With such a complete picture, it now becomes far easier to keep a close check on stock and maintain a better degree of efficiency.

EXERCISES Try the following exercises.

Sales order processing

1 Amend the order acknowledgement document (SAORDER.LYT) by using the editing facility accessed through **Print Batch** from the Sales Order Processing window.

2 Create a number of sales orders by entering imaginary orders placed by customers for goods or services.

3 Cancel and amend one or two of these orders.

4 Allocate any available stock to these orders.

5 Despatch stock to some of these orders.

6 Create invoices for these sales orders using the **Despatch** facility from the Sales Order Processing window.

7 Delete the completed orders.

8 Investigate the effect these activities have had on the stock records, customer accounts and the Nominal Ledger.

Purchase order processing

9 Amend the purchase order document using the Print Batch part of the purchase order processing function.

10 Process a number of purchase orders by entering imaginary details of orders placed with suppliers for goods or services.

11 Cancel and amend one or two of these orders.

12 Print the purchase orders and update the stock records to show that goods are on order.

13 Enter some orders as delivered.

14 Go to the Suppliers part of Sage and update the Purchase Ledger with invoices received. You will need to extract an outstanding orders report to assist you.

15 Delete the completed orders.

16 Investigate the effect these activities have had on the stock records.

CHAPTER 10

Advanced Sage utilities

INTRODUCTION

A good deal of the practical content of this book has involved the extraction of a whole series of reports. Information in the reports available with the Sage package is often not in the required format, however. Generating your own reports is, in effect, another way of extracting reports from the system. The difference lies in the fact that you choose the reports you want and the format in which you want them. Using this facility is rather like programming the computer yourself – you determine the rules and the output.

In addition to being able to print reports, you may want to incorporate a report into a different document that is to be generated by a spreadsheet, word processor, desktop publishing or graphics package. Later in this chapter, you will see how this can be achieved.

This chapter also looks at how you can alter the features, appearance and preferences of the Sage package on your screen. The importance of good file and data management is discussed and further information is included on how to back up and restore your data. Other topics are the use of fax facilities – mentioned in Chapter 9 – how to generate graphs and how to create and use multiple companies in Sage.

GENERATING REPORTS

Audit trails

One report that will prove valuable to any business is the audit trail. This will list all transactions undertaken in the sequence in which they were entered. Throughout your work with Sage, you will have seen a transaction number unique to each transaction, regardless of the function you were operating in.

From the main Sage window, click on the **Financials** icon and then click on the **Audit Trail** icon. This gives you a visual image of the audit trail. To get a print of this, you would need to go to the Nominal Ledger window and then click on the **Reports** icon from there. The audit trail will then appear as one of the report files.

Creating a new report

Sage has a facility called **Report Generator** and this is accessed by clicking on the **Report Generator** icon from the main Sage window. Click on this option to reveal the Reports window. At this stage the window should be empty, as you have not created any reports yet.

Begin by clicking on the **New** button that appears near the bottom of this window to reveal the first of four Layout Wizard dialogue boxes. At this point, you will have to decide from where in the Sage package you want to collect the data on which your report will be based. From the Layout Wizard shown in Fig. 10.1(a), you will see that you have a list of report generator types from which to select.

This example will show you how to generate a list of all stock records that have either stock on order or stock in quantity, or a combination of both. Consequently, you require a report based upon the Stock Control part of the program. The following functions will be the basis of your report:

- Sales Ledger
- Purchase Ledger
- Nominal Ledger
- Management reports (offers a limited combination of the three above)

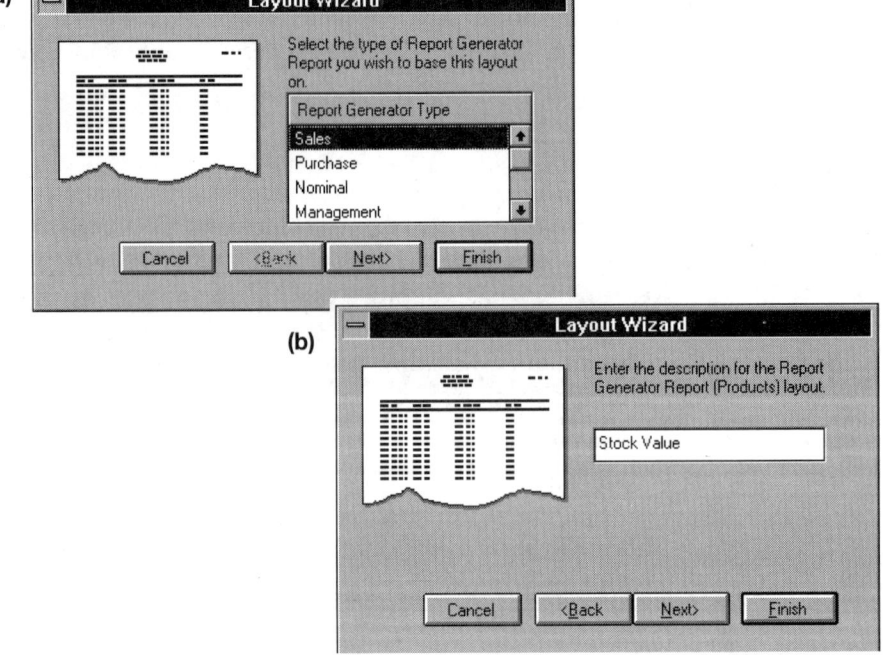

Fig. 10.1

- Products
- Invoicing
- Sales order processing
- Purchase order processing.

Highlight the **Products** option and then click on the **Next** button. When the **Type** has been selected, you can enter a **Report Heading**. This heading can be of your choice but should give some indication as to what is contained in the report. This is because it will be the title that appears in the main Reports window as your main reference to the report. From Fig. 10.1(b) you will see that the report heading *Stock Value* has been entered. When you have typed this in, click on the **Next** button.

The rest of the report now contains the column contents of the report. From Fig. 10.2(a) you will see that the Layout Wizard now requires the list of variables that are contained in the Products file to be selected, so that they appear on the report.

You will see that there are two panels – the **Variables** list indicates what is available while the **Report Variables** indicate what is to be placed onto the report. Highlight the **Variables** required on the report, and click on the **>** (greater than) symbol to place it into the **Report Variables** box. You can keep moving variables to and from these panels until you are satisfied that the ones you have in the **Report Variables** panel are what you want on the final report. The vari-

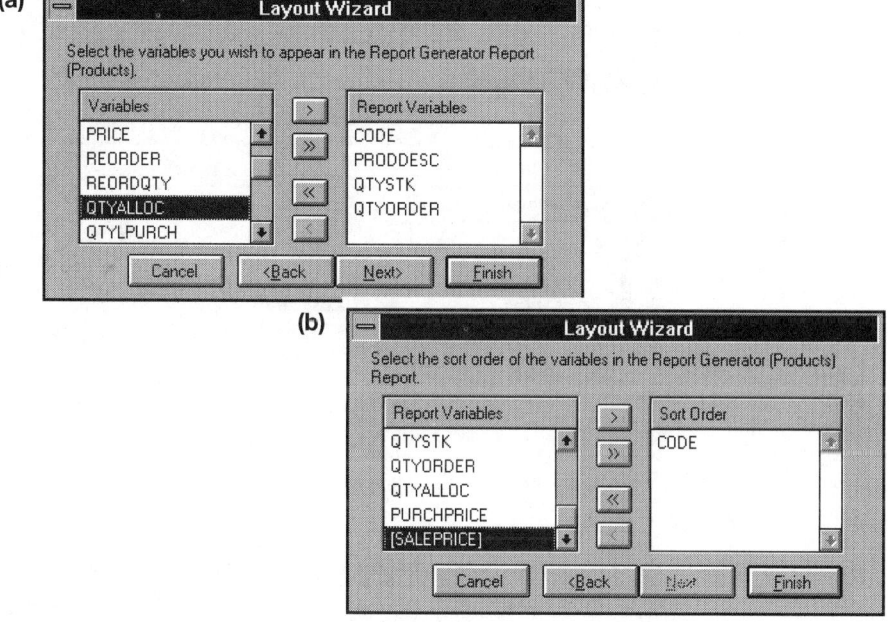

Fig. 10.2

able <CALC> can be entered; this will be used as a variable calculated on two others. The variables used in this example are CODE, PRODDESC, QTYSTK, QTYORDER, QTYALLOC, SALEPRICE and <CALC>.

Some of the field names that appear were placed in square brackets, such as [Transaction Type]. This refers to transaction data types and can appear many times against the other forms of data types, such as the stock reference.

When this is complete, click on the **Next** key to move to the final Layout Wizard dialogue box, as shown in Fig. 10.2(b). Your **Report Variables** will appear on the left and the **Sort Order** required on the right. In this example, CODE appears in the **Sort Order** to instruct Sage to place the report in product code order. When this is complete, click on the **Finish** button.

The Layout Editor window now appears and will help you add the final touches to your report. Figure 10.3 shows such a layout. Do not worry at this stage if your layout takes on a different appearance. You will need to experiment for a while before you can get exactly what is required.

While in the Editor you are able to add fields, more text and edit existing details. The four Wizard dialogue boxes were used to get you started, rather than give a complete solution. The format of the Layout Editor is much the same as that of the window you worked with before when editing document files. The fields are in light-shaded rectangles while the text is not boxed. To

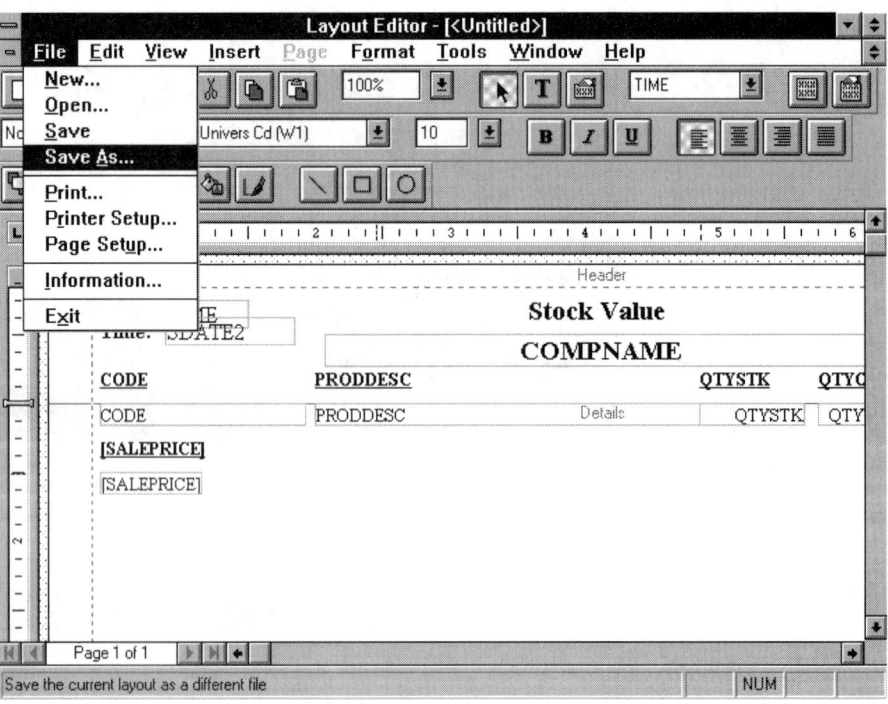

Fig. 10.3

Advanced Sage utilities **187**

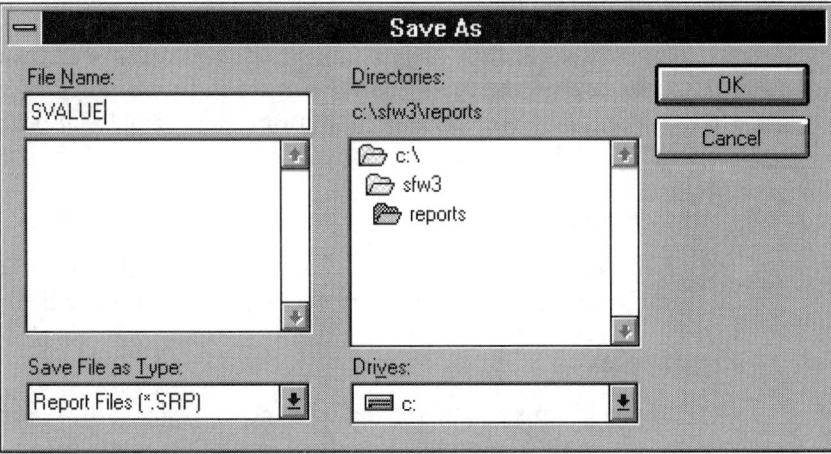

Fig. 10.4

edit any part of the layout, click on the variable or text and, from the Edit pull-down menu, select one of the features. At some point, however, you must save the file with a report name. Figure 10.3 shows the **File** pull-down menu has been dropped to the screen and **Save As** is highlighted.

When these are selected, you will be required to enter a **File Name**, as shown in Fig. 10.4 where the file name SVALUE has been entered. Once saved, any future edits will require you to save the file again using **Save** from the **File** pull-down menu.

Before leaving this Layout Editor screen, click on **Tools** followed by **Report** to reveal a window similar to that shown in Fig. 10.5. This shows the bottom left part of the available column details. On examining this, you will be able to get a good idea of what is possible with regards to the information on a report and what you can do to alter it.

Item	Variable	Calculated	Invisible	Total	Sign	Break
#3	QTYSTK	No	No	None	None	None
#4	QTYORDER	No	No	None	None	None
#5	QTYALLOC	No	No	None	None	None
#6	PURCHPRICE	No	No	None	None	None
#7	[SALEPRICE]	No	No	None	None	None
#8	<CALC>	Yes	No	None	None	None

Fig. 10.5

Item and variable

These are the first two columns and will determine in the report which variables are on the report and the order in which they appear across the report. As the list goes from top to bottom, the variables appear on the report from left to right.

Calculated

This determines whether the field is to be calculated. If the answer is **Yes**, then a **Calculation** field at the end needs to show how the field is determined.

Invisible

If you set this as **Yes**, the data will not appear on the report. This can be of use if you wish to use the contents of one field to help calculate another, but have no need to see the data on the report.

Totals

The **Total** field allows three toggles and will only be of use if you are setting out attributes for a numeric variable type. **Print Total Only** will print a total of columns but not the numbers in each column, while **Print All** does both. **No Total** will not do any adding up for you.

Sign

This applies to numeric data where it allows you to place a sign after the number indicating whether the amount is a debit or credit balance, or both signs can appear. This is obviously limited to account balances, but can be left blank throughout if you simply want the numbers to appear by themselves.

Break

This field allows you to enter a blank line after each variable occurrence, or start a new page.

Break No.

If you set a **Break** in the previous field, then you will need to enter the number of blank lines (or pages) you want to insert after the variable in the field. If you use the **On Chars** toggle, then a break can occur when a character changes in the variable name; the **No.** field determines how many characters into the field name the change of character is to occur.

Sort level

The **Sort** panel will be used to sort the data in the report. Each line must have a different sort number – that is, no two sort numbers can be the same. In the example here, the field CODE will have Level One as its sort level. As no two product codes will be the same, there is little point in having a Level Two.

Sort order

If there is a sort level, you need to set this at either ascending or descending order.

Selection Criteria

The **Selection Criteria** allows you to either filter out lines you do not want in your report, or only include specific lines. For example, if you only wanted stock items that began with the letter C or above, then you would enter:

> C

in the **Code** (Item #1) line,

which, when translated, means greater than C. Alternatively, you could enter:

>= D AND < E

which, when translated, means greater than or equal to D *and* less than E. The complete collection of these symbols (sometimes referred to as *operands*) are:

```
=   Equal to
!=  Not equal to
<   Less than
>   Greater than
<=  Less than or equal to
>=  Greater than or equal to
```

As in the earlier example, you can combine this with the logical operands – AND and OR. You can also include wildcard symbols ? for a single character or * (asterisk) for a group of undefined characters. For example, a criteria that reads:

= T* OR = Z??

would translate to *equal to anything starting with T* or *made up of three characters starting with Z*.

You can also search for a specific piece of text using $ to check that a word exists in a string of characters or !$ that it does not. For example, a selection criteria that appears as:

$ "TENNIS"

would select all variables where the word Tennis (in whatever case) appears.

When the variable and its attributes have been set up, click on the **OK** button to enter the details on the **Report Generator** line and to return to the Report Generator window.

Calculation

If the **Calculation** field is set at **Yes** then you are able to perform a calculation of other fields to create this one. In the example shown in Fig. 10.6, Item 8 (#8) is to be Item 3 multiplied by Item 6 (#3*#6).

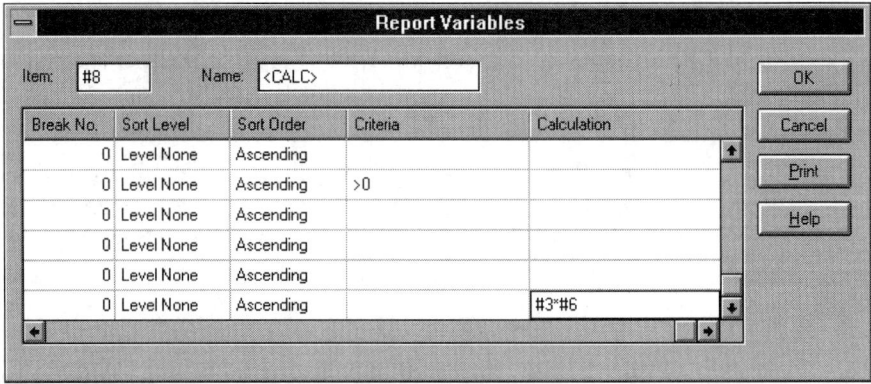

Fig. 10.6

Each variable has to be made up as before – in this example from #1 to #8. If, for example, you had a field that read:

(#3+#4)*#6

this would first add the value of the variables in Item 3 and Item 4 and then multiply the sum by Item 6. The use of formulae in this way will conform to the usual convention of formula manipulation in mathematics – that is, the bracketed calculations take precedence. The complete set of arithmetic symbols are:

+ Add
− Subtract
(Open bracket
) Close bracket
* Multiply
/ Divide

Saving and running the report

When you enter a filename, this is the name Sage will use when you want to select and run the report in future and the name is added to the list of files along with any other report files. Click on **File** from the pull-down menu and then on **Save**. When this is done, pull down the **File** menu again and click on E**x**it to return to the main Report Generator window.

From the Report Generator window, make sure your report name is highlighted and click on **Run**. Fig. 10.7 is an example of a report created in this way.

The report shows how the items are listed and how each variable and its attributes are organised. Again, do not be too concerned if yours differs from this. You can always keep on editing this report via the Report Generator window until you get it right. The Report Generator will offer you a great deal of flex-

		MEGAXAN STERLING SPORTS					
		STOCK VALUE					
Date: 24/12/96							Page: 1
Time: 10.10							
Product Code	Description	Quantity in Stock	Quantity Ordered	Quantity Allocated	Purchase Price	Sale Price	Value
0030	T-Shirt – Large	10	10	5	5	18	50
0040	Scarves	14	3	0	4	12	56
0090	Soccer Ball	17	5	2	10	18	170
00110	Tennis Ball	41	20	5	3	5	123

Fig. 10.7

ibility in what you can extract from your accounts data. You will need to give yourself time to practice this, as much of this can only be learnt with continued practice and a degree of trial and error.

CSV output

The Report Generator allows you the facility to output a file in CSV format – **Comma Separated Variable**. This allows the output to be saved in a file with a line for each record and the fields separated with commas. The purpose of this is to allow a spreadsheet or database package to read them. This will allow yet further flexibility in how you can use the data generated by these reports.

In order to have a report output as a CSV file, you need first to select the report from the main Report Generator window or from the Reports features in any of the other main functions. Sage has created a large number of such reports which you can either use in their current state or edit to your own needs. Click on the report you have just created so that it is highlighted and then make sure that output is to **File**. Now click on the **Run** button. After the report has been prepared, you will see an entry window that requires details about the file to which the data is to be output. Figure 10.8 shows such an example.

You will need to decide on which disk and in which directory to put the file. The information in Fig. 10.8 will output on drive C; the file will be placed in the directory \SFW3\REPORTS. The **Save File as Type** panel now needs to be set so that it is saved as a CSV file and not as a normal report. If you click on the small up arrow key, you can select the CSV type from a small drop-down menu listing the file types, as shown in Fig. 10.8. Once this has been done, you need to enter a filename (file extension is not necessary). Figure 10.8 shows the

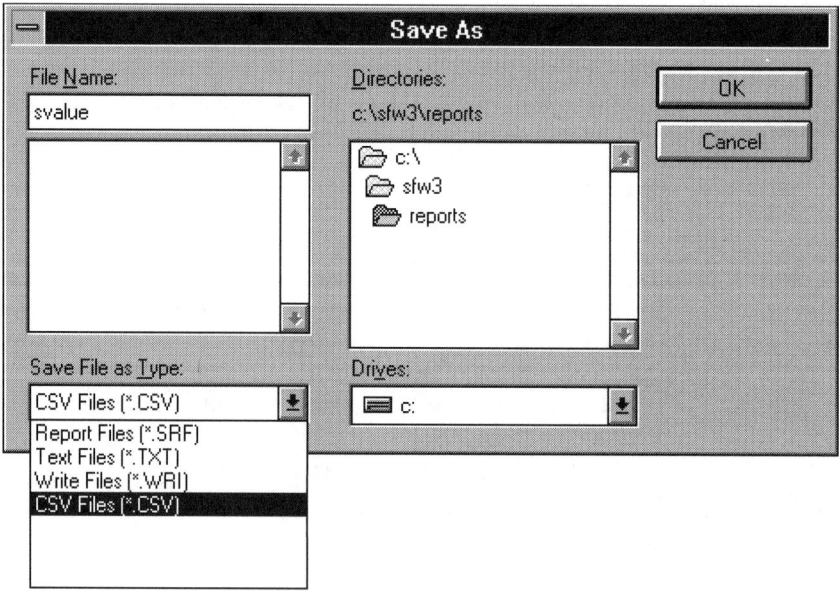

Fig. 10.8

file is to be saved as a CSV file with the name SVALUE. Sage will put the .*CSV* extension at the end of the filename for you. When this is done, click on **OK** to carry out the data output to the file.

You are now able to enter another suitable application package and read the data into that package. From Fig. 10.9, you will see that a spreadsheet has been able to read the file and has placed the data into it.

A spreadsheet is the electronic equivalent of an accountant's ledger – a large piece of paper divided by vertical columns and horizontal rows into a grid of **cells**. In Fig. 10.9 the columns are headed by letters (A,B,C ...) and the rows by numbers (1, 2, 3 ...). Each cell is referred to by its coordinates, like a map reference or point on a graph. For example, cell reference C5 in Fig. 10.9 has the value 14 in it. The user can enter numbers, text or formulae into the cells. Formulae are used to link cells.

	A	B	C	D	E	F	G	H
1								
2	Product	Description	Quantity	Quantity	Quantity	Purchase	Sale	Value
3	Code		in Stock	Ordered	Allocated	Price	Price	
4	0030	T-Shirt- Large	10	10	5	5	8	50
5	0040	Scarves	14	3	0	4	12	56
6	0090	Soccer Ball	17	5	2	10	7	170
7	00110	Tennis Balls	41	20	5	3	5	123
8								
9								

Fig. 10.9

For example, cell H4 shows the value of stock as being the **Quantity in Stock** (cell C4) multiplied by the **Purchase Price** (cell F4). A spreadsheet program then has the facility to copy this formula to all the other rows.

C4*F4   (Quantity in stock *times* Purchase price)

The data, when *imported* into the spreadsheet, will not have the headings that appear at the top of the spreadsheet in Fig. 10.9. These were added subsequently to illustrate what the columns represent.

Once the data has been imported from Sage in this way, you have a further tool to work with. Such spreadsheets have very powerful capabilities with regard to accounting functions such as statistical analysis, forecasting, graphing and the presentation of final accounts.

GENERATING GRAPHS

Sage has the useful facility of producing graphs, although this facility is more limited than for some other packages. Graphs are available in both the Products and Nominal parts of Sage. To begin with, click on the **Products** icon from the main Sage window and, from here, click on **Product Record** to reveal the Records window. Use the **Finder** icon to call up a record that has previously been created and has a set of transactions against it. When the record details appear, click on the **Sales** tab that appears near the top of the Product Record window.

Figure 10.10 shows such a window which has both a sales history and a set of sales budgets for this product. Such a history will take time to build up if you want Sage to update the figures for you. As each month end is carried out, the

Fig. 10.10

monthly history builds up. Each year-end routine has the effect of building up a comparison of sales over the previous year. The budget figures are entered by you, normally as a sales target. Alternatively, if you have all the data for the past two years, then a complete history can be entered. The data in Fig. 10.10 have been made up for the purpose of demonstration.

If you click on the **Graph** tab near the top of this Product Record window, you will reveal a graph. The graph that appears should be similar to the one that appears in Fig. 10.11.

The graph appears in a three-dimensional multiple bar chart plotting actual sales, budget sales and the sales in the previous year – as shown by the legend that appears to the right of the graph. By clicking on the small **Graph Type** drop menu, you will see that there are three other graph types from which to choose. In the panels above the graph, you can de-select **Actuals**, **Budgets** or **Prior Year**, as well as choose between showing a graph of sales by quantity or sales by value.

The **Save** button is used to store an image of the graph in the Graphics file. Once the image is stored in this way, you can then go into another Windows package, such as a word processor or spreadsheet, and *import* the image to that package.

For a further demonstration of graphing, you can produce a graph based upon the same kind of history through the Nominal Ledger. If, for example, a nominal sales account has recorded the entire sales for all products in a certain category, then this can be graphed in the same way. To do this, enter the **Nominal** part of the package and then click on **Nominal Record**. You now need to call up a nominal account to reveal the record details. This window will show an

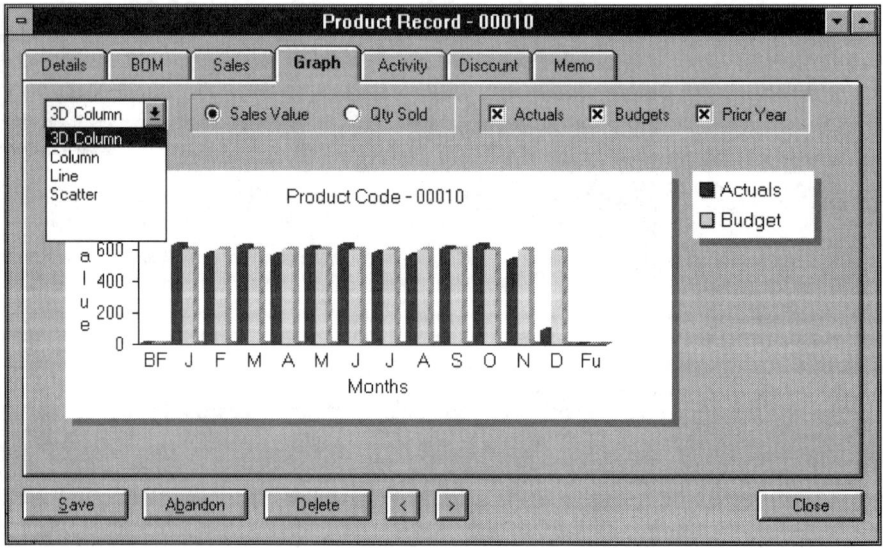

Fig. 10.11

activity history which, as with the products, can be updated to give a fuller history. When you click on the **Graph** tab you will obtain a graph.

MULTIPLE COMPANIES

Sage allows you to have the accounts of more than one company stored on your disk without your having to install the package each time you want such a new company. When a new company is created, a new icon is created for your Windows environment so that you can easily access it. Alternatively, you will be able to access another company from the **File** pull-down menu (**File**, **Open Company**). From the main Sage window click on the **File** option from the main pull-down menu. From here, click on **New Company**. You will now need to re-enter your password for security purposes before Sage reveals the New Company Setup Wizards.

When this is done, you will proceed with the following stages via dialogue boxes:

1 Choose between **Create data files for new company** or **Update files** from a company using an old version of Sage.
2 Enter name and address details. The company name and address is entered as you would want it to appear on the stationery printouts.
3 Define the program group in Windows where the new icon is to be stored and enter a new password for the company.
4 Set VAT defaults and access rights.
5 Decide whether you want a new Nominal structure or you want to create one of your own.

A **Password** that is unique to this company can then be entered. In the **Data Files** field you should enter the directory where the new company files are to appear. If you use a directory path that already has company data in it, then Sage will write on top of them, wiping out any data that used to be stored there. You should then enter the first day of the current **Financial Year** for the new company.

When you have completed this, Sage will create a new set of layouts, reports and data files in the chosen directory for this purpose and finish with the creation of the new icon. You will then be given the option of transferring control to this new company.

Changing the company preference defaults

Many of the features you have worked with can now be altered. Begin by making sure you are in your newly formed company. If you are still in the old one, then exit from this and enter the new one via the new Windows icon. From the main Sage window, click on the **Defaults** option from the main pull-down menu and from there, select **Company Preferences**.

You will now be presented with a Company Preferences window consisting of four pages, indicated by the tabs near the top of the window. The first page, labelled **Details**, contains the details of the company name and address which, if needed, can be amended at any time to suit changing circumstances.

Figure 10.12 shows the second pages – the **Labels**. The **Text Labels** panel allows you to redefine the labels that appear before each box. This will simply help the presentation of your screen and may be used to better guide someone, for example, when entering details about new customers and suppliers. In particular, you may find useful the ability to redefine the analysis labels to something more appropriate to the information needs of the business. For example, **Customer Analysis 1** could be used to express the credit rating of the customer.

The **System** page, as shown in Fig. 10.13, contains a list of toggles that will have the following effects on your company if switched on:

Printing

- **Page Throw**. This affects the standard Sage reports in that each record will start on the top of a new page.
- **Print End of Report Banner**. This will ensure that an end-of-report message is printed at the end of each report to indicate its completion.

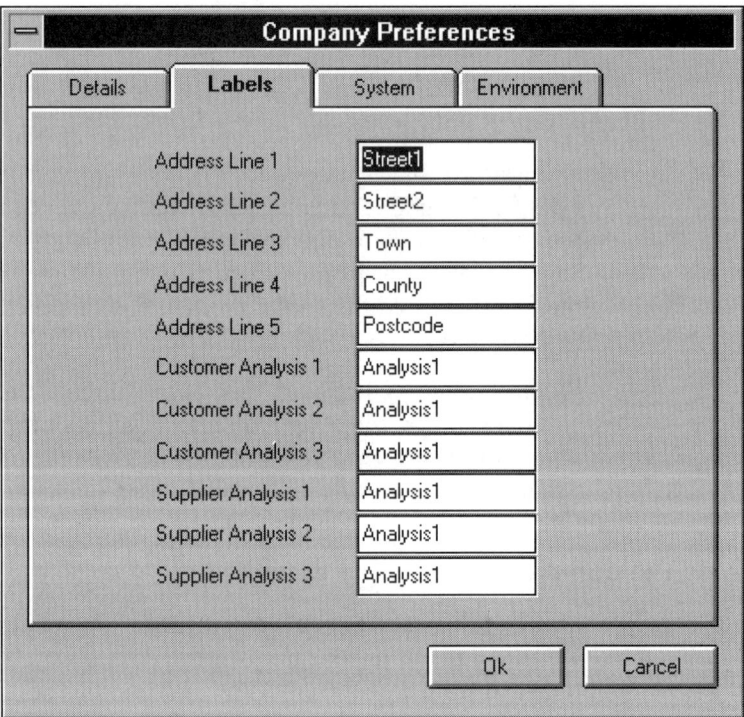

Fig. 10.12

Advanced Sage utilities **197**

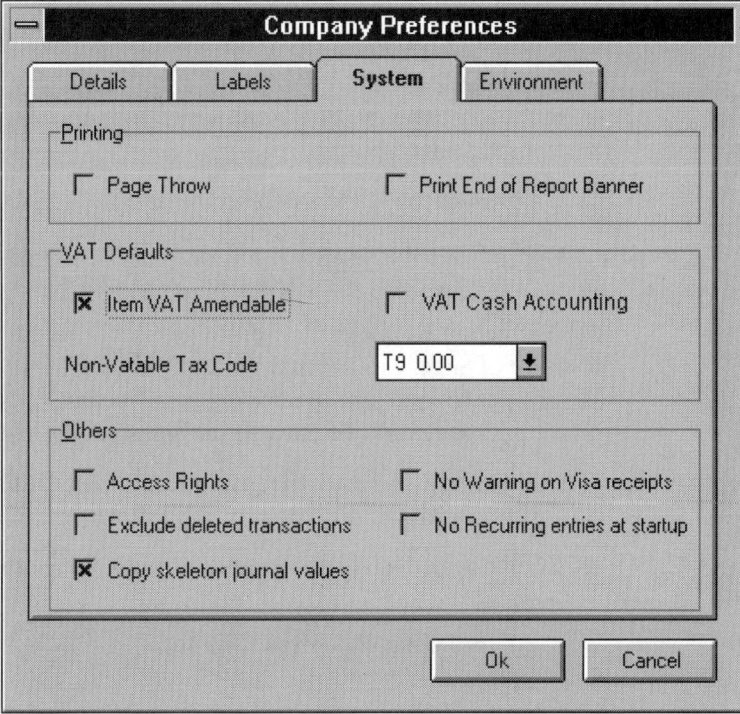

Fig. 10.13

VAT Defaults

- **Item VAT Amendable**. If switched on, this allows you to alter the VAT amounts after Sage has worked them out for you.
- **VAT Cash Accounting**. This alters the way VAT has to be paid and collected. If set on, it will mean VAT is calculated, not on what is invoiced, but on what cash and cheques are received and paid. It only applies to small businesses. Furthermore, this can only be altered if all VAT transactions on the company have been cleared.

Others

- **Access Rights**. This allows you to set up passwords for different users, where each user is restricted as to what parts of the Sage package he or she is allowed to work on.
- **Exclude deleted transactions**. With this switched on, transactions that have been deleted will not appear on your reports or activity histories.
- **Copy skeleton journal values**. With this switched on, you are able to save the values of your skeleton Nominal Ledger journal entries which you make on a regular basis, such as the payment of wages or rent.
- **No Warning on Visa receipts**. Sage has a bank account dedicated to credit card payments. With this switched on, you will be reminded that when

attempting to enter a receipt on a company credit account, this is not allowed as the company credit card is for payment purposes only.

- **No Recurring entries at startup**. If you have any recurring entries outstanding, each time you run Sage, a window appears informing you of transactions that need posting.

The **Environment** tab has two sections to it.

The **Communications** panel sets up the communications details and is needed in order to take advantage of your modem for sending faxes.

The **Function Keys** can be used to gain easy access to other programs that are outside of Sage, using function keys F11 or F12. If, for example, you are using a spreadsheet package to support your accounts, then the name of the spreadsheet package could be entered in one of these fields.

The Defaults also have other facilities in them. Rather than listing all of these in this book you should attempt the following:

1 Click on the **Defaults** menu and select **Change Password**.
2 Press function key **F1** – the **Help** key.
3 Click on the **File** from the new pull-down menu and then on the **Print Topic** option.

This offers you a detailed explanation of this topic and works in exactly the same way for all other topics.

MAINTENANCE OF DATA FILES

Backing up data

This section examines ways of ensuring that your data is both safe and well backed up. If you click on the **Data** option from the main Sage window, you are given seven options to choose from (you have already worked on the last two in Chapter 6). The **Backup** option performs the same back-up routine as backing up prior to exiting Sage. As mentioned at the end of Chapter 3, the need to back up files cannot be overstated, for a number of reasons:

- In the event of lost or corrupt data files, the back-up files can always be restored to use, resulting in only that information input since the last back-up was taken being lost.
- In the future you may want to restore files in order to check on past events.
- You may want to transport data from one machine to another. If, for example, your accountant uses Sage and is happy to work on your accounts data for final auditing, then you could send a copy of a back-up set of your data files. Alternatively, you might have another computer with Sage at home and you are then able to take copies of the entire company's data to your other machine. Remember, it is always safer to move data around rather than the machine!

You should always back up regularly, either using the **Data** pull-down menu or when you exit Sage. For most businesses this will mean daily or even twice daily if they generate a substantial amount of data in a day's work. At the end of each month, you should put a copy of a backup into storage and not use the disk again. When carrying out a routine backup at the end of a day, it is wise to rotate a number of disks (say seven) rather than using the same disk each time.

Restoring from a backup

Restoring from backed-up files is virtually the opposite of the backing-up procedure and is done in almost the same way – that is, pull down the **Data** menu and select the **Restore** option. Before restoring, you should note that the system will copy the files on your floppy disk onto your hard disk, wiping out the existing files in the process. If the existing files are corrupt, then this will normally be the desired effect. If, however, you simply want to look into the past, then the following procedures should be taken:

1 Back up the existing data onto a floppy disk and label it with the *current* date.
2 Insert the old disk into your drive and **Restore** from that.

Now you can work on the old data as required.

3 Restore the disk with the current date on it to bring you back up to date.

An alternative to this, is to restore the old data into a new company set of files.

As a word of warning, do not attempt to use the computer's operating system to restore Sage back-up files. Much of the data in different files will be related in some manner and to restore one set of files and inadvertently not restore another, could lead to the program having severe difficulties in operating correctly. In general, it is wise to back up and restore everything each time, using the Sage package.

Importing data

This option allows you to convert data from other programs into Sage. The data files from the other program have to be carefully arranged to be compatible. Consequently, this is beyond the scope of a book of this nature and you should seek specialist help before embarking on this. If you are familiar with data management, then both the Sage manual and Help pages will show you how the data files for importing have to be set out.

Disk Doctor

From Fig. 10.14, you will see four icons to choose from. Each option is designed to manage the data on your disk – often referred to as good housekeeping measures. Each of these options should be run periodically as a part of good data management (weekly at least). Before carrying out any of these, you are advised by Sage to back up your data first.

Fig. 10.14

The **Check** option reads through all your files to see if there are any errors on them – in other words, whether they are corrupt or not. If any are corrupt, then you can either move on to the **Correct** option from Disk Doctor or **Restore** from an earlier backup.

The **Correct** option will attempt to correct the errors by trying to rebuild your data files. This may not work if the corruption is severe, but it is often worth trying before you have to restore from an old backup.

The **Compress** feature will rebuild your data files but, as the name suggests, pack them more tightly together. This will only be of use if you have been deleting records since installation or the last compression. When completed, your program should run faster and it should release more space on your computer.

The **Rebuild** option will reconstruct your entire data from the audit trail and, in most cases, restore any damaged data structures. Such a measure should only be taken as a matter of last resort. You will still need to check whether any transaction data has been lost after running this program.

Global changes

This allows you to make changes across parts of your company data and will prove to be a major time-saving tool. For example, if you wanted to increase all Nominal budgets by 20 per cent, this would allow you to do it in a few quick steps rather than your having to enter each Nominal account to alter the budgets.

In the following example, you will increase a range of product sales prices by 10 per cent. To do this, there are five simple steps, as depicted in Fig. 10.15.

From the **Data** pull-down menu, click on **Global Changes** and then perform each of the following steps:

Advanced Sage utilities

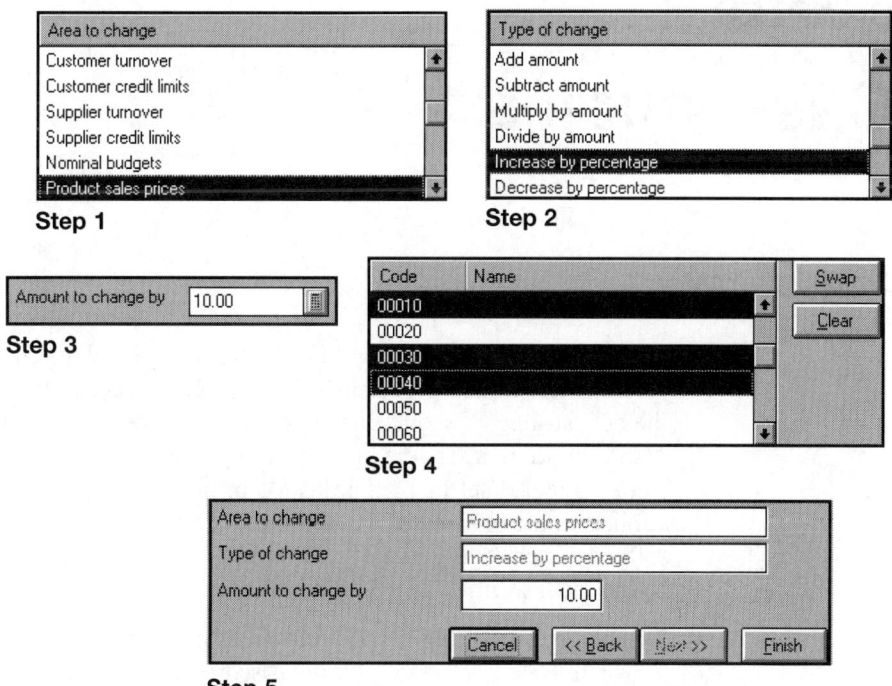

Fig. 10.15

Step 1 Select **Product sales prices** from the list of options and click on **Next**.

Step 2 Select **Increase by percentage** from the list of options and click on **Next**.

Step 3 Enter 10 as the amount by which you want to increase prices. You do not need to enter a % sign. Then click on **Next**.

Step 4 Highlight all those product items for which you want to increase the price and then click on **Next**.

Step 5 Click on **Finish** to confirm the changes.

At any time during the above steps you can go back a step or cancel the whole operation.

CHAPTER 11

Case studies

INTRODUCTION

This final chapter focuses on methods of implementing a computerised system. One of the problems of implementing computerised accounts is that the best strategy for one business may not necessarily be the best for another. Although there are some basic and important rules to observe, it is difficult to state a general set of principles for implementing such a system that can be applied to all businesses. Another problem is that the technology and related software is changing at such a rapid pace that an ideal solution now may not be the ideal solution in a few years' time.

This chapter will present you with three fictitious case histories outlining the way in which three businesses computerised their accounting procedures (and other functions) and the varying degrees of success. At the end of each case study is a series of questions, which are designed to generate thought and discussion.

CASE STUDY 1: BRIGHTER LIGHT LTD

This case study is based on a company that manufactures and markets domestic lighting equipment. The equipment manufactured is quite extensive, but the mainstream of activity involves the manufacture of 30 different ranges of torches, 10 different ranges of light fitting, 10 types of table lamps and a range of specialist lights, often made to customer order.

The company prides itself on meeting orders from retailers and overseas customers promptly and always delivering on time.

The facts

Number of employees

Production shopfloor	15
Production administration	2
Marketing, sales and distribution	5
Despatch	4
Accounts	3
Managerial	4
Total staff	33

Turnover	£12 million
Expected number of orders	400 per month
Number of suppliers	100
Number of regular customers	650
Average stock value on premises	£2.5 million
Number of different items held in stock	5000

Although these figures depict the state of the company at present, they represent a 50 per cent growth in the volume of trade over the five-year period since the company was formed.

Projected growth for the next five years is estimated at about 15 per cent to 20 per cent per annum. With such growth, it is anticipated that more capital equipment will be required and there is likely to be a need to employ more production shopfloor staff (probably two staff) and an extra person to cope with despatch of goods. The company already has its own production staff working on regular overtime and equipment working six days a week when production needs to be high to meet orders – hence the need for more staff and capital equipment.

The problems

All administrative procedures are, at present, carried out manually by clerical staff. Although the company sees no problem in coping with the extra capital equipment and staff, it anticipates a problem in information flows which cannot be overcome by simply employing more administrative staff. In fact, information needs are not being properly satisfied by the current manual system. The company has identified the following information problems which will get worse with the projected growth:

- Maintaining efficient stock levels becomes increasingly difficult. With the more essential stock items, such as differing types of flex (there are 50 in all), the company holds far more stock than is probably needed, because it cannot afford to run out. It is estimated that stock values are £500 000 higher than they really need to be – a figure that will grow rapidly with expansion.
- Keeping track of customer orders is becoming a strain, endangering the reputation the company has built up for meeting customer orders punctually.
- At any one time, there are up to 100 purchase orders with a range of suppliers, some of whom are overseas. Keeping checks on suppliers is becoming difficult because the information on orders still outstanding is coming to the Production Manager too late. On more than one occasion, the manufacture of key products has had to be held up because of shortages of certain components. The problem tends to be resolved by resorting to holding even higher stock levels of key components.
- Information about customers owing money to the company is not forthcoming at the right time. Quite often customer debt is left outstanding

longer than it needs to be and customers exceed their credit limits because of the lack of prompt information. The average total of customer debt is £1.2 million. It is estimated that this figure could be reduced to an average of £800 000 without damaging company sales. Bad debts could also fall by half to about £20 000 per annum.

Despite these problems, it is important to stress that the company is far from struggling. However, it sees that, if something is not done about these problems over the next two years, a serious situation could evolve.

The new system

The decision to computerise was taken as a result of a visit by a computer consultant, who advised that the company should acquire the following:

- *A computer network of four microcomputers*. Each microcomputer has its own hard disk with a capacity of at least 100 Megabytes and the file server, where the main files would be held, holds up to 400 Megabytes of information.
- *The Sage for Windows package*.

The strategy was to computerise the Stock Control function first, as this was identified as the main problem area. A decision to implement all functions simultaneously was felt to be too ambitious. One thing at a time was regarded as the best policy.

When the equipment was installed, one microcomputer was positioned in the Production Manager's office, one in stores and two with the production administration staff. The file server was also positioned in the production office where the two production administration staff were located. The consultant who organised the installation also arranged two days' on-site training for the two production administration staff, the person in charge of stores and the Production Manager. The two-day training was focused towards setting up and running stock control and purchase order systems.

Getting prepared

The next stage was to place all stock information onto the stock control system. This process took the following form:

1. The person in charge of stores had to ensure that all stock cards kept for each item of stock were up to date. There had to be one stock card for each item of stock; the description for each item should be correct; cost prices should be accurate and the location where stock could be found should be correct.

    During this exercise, some errors were found and corrected, with improvements being made.

    The company always noted on stock record cards the estimated lead time for ordering stock quantities, re-order quantities, the usual supplier and stock movement history.

2 The production team, which was to be responsible for maintaining the stock control system, had decided to scan carefully through the stock records, allocating new codes to the stock items. It was felt that this was long overdue and now was the best time to do this. Essentially, the stock codes that were already in existence would still be used, but each code would be prefixed with A, B, C or Z to indicate the classification of stock. Basically, classification 'A' meant the stock was expensive and should be held only when needed in the short term. At the other end of the spectrum, 'Z' indicated very little cost involved in both buying and holding stock. The purpose of this was to arrange stock lists in the order they were required – a technique the team learned during training. The stock code would have a three-digit code, following the classification code, to indicate where in the warehouse the stock would be located. Again, this produced a listing of stock that would prove useful for stores management, providing 'picking lists' from the Sage Report Generator and a quick check on stock.

3 When everything was complete and, as a result, the data was ready for input, the decision was made to create all the stock records on computer over the weekend. The weekend chosen was soon after the manual stock records were ready; there was always the fear that, if this process were delayed for any time, the figures would soon be out of date. A Saturday was chosen, with four operators working through the day on the four microcomputers, to input the information. Two of the staff needed a little training, but by the end of the day all the records were entered on the computer.

At this point, the only item missing from the stock records was the actual stock level. This was intentionally left until last, because a time delay in getting this information onto the computer would render all such stock level figures useless. Before progressing further, a printout of the stock details already entered was extracted and a few alterations were made (three records that were originally omitted were also added).

Another visit from their consultant led to the advice that all such records should be backed up before going any further. It was decided that a backup be made to floppy disks immediately, with the disks labelled and dated. In future, backups would be made weekly onto the microcomputer in the Production Manager's office. The Sage backing-up procedure was regarded as sufficient for this activity. It was also agreed that such a backing-up procedure would be carried out regularly, at the end of each day onto a different machine each time, rotating between the other three machines. The Production Manager has recommended to the Board that, at a future date, the file server should be equipped with a tape streamer that would be capable of backing up everything on the file server at the end of each day within ten minutes.

Getting started

The next stage was to enter all stock quantities and implement the system. It was decided to do this on the following Friday and Saturday. Over these two days, stock levels were checked and stock records adjusted to reflect actual stocks in the warehouse. Each stock record was then given an opening stock using the Sage stock control Adjustments In procedure.

The responsibility of keeping stock levels up to date was that of the person in charge of the stock. As from the Monday, every issue or receipt of stock was entered as a stock movement – Adjustment In when stock was received and Adjustment Out when stock was issued. This implementation went extremely smoothly without too much disruption to the normal business. The company went on using the system almost unhindered for a month. It became apparent to the Production Manager that the ability to sit at a terminal and enquire regarding stock quantities at any time was an invaluable tool for his job, especially when planning production. Furthermore, it was found that the 'low stock' reports were extremely useful when planning what orders to place with suppliers. The consultant had created some special stock reports from the Report Generator to obtain the kind of reports wanted by the Production Manager.

Only one problem occurred when, in error, the stock files were corrupted on the file server. This happened at 10.45 one morning. The Production Manager telephoned the consultant and soon put things right by restoring the stock details from the previous day (which had been backed up onto his own machine) and re-entering the morning's movement figures. The whole process wasted just two hours, soon recovered during the day's work.

At the end of the month, another stock-take exercise was carried out to see how closely it matched the computer system records. The differences were small and easily corrected and new procedures for the collection and input of data were quickly drawn up.

Further developments

During the month, the production administration staff were sent on a computer appreciation course for two days. As a result of this, they requested the facility of a word processing package for their machines to replace their typewriters. The Production Manager, commending them for their suggestion and enthusiasm, promptly purchased two single-user versions of a Windows-based word processing package for their machines. Within one week, both staff were using their packages in preference to their typewriters. In addition to this, they learned the technique of outputting reports to a file and then using the word processing package to incorporate the stock control output into reports and letters to a professional standard.

One of the obvious problems with the computerised stock system was the fact that low stocks could not automatically generate an order for new stocks because the system did not take into consideration what was already on order. It was felt, therefore, that the next stage was to implement the purchase order system.

The first step was to decide on which preprinted stationery to be used. The existing stationery for generating order forms was scrapped and the company ordered its own stationery with its company logo from Sagesoft Ltd. When the stationery arrived, adjustments were made to the stationery layout set up in the relevant Sage files. After a few trial-and-error dummy runs, the printing of orders matched the stationery. One of the production administration staff placed all outstanding orders on to the system. It was found that printing orders to suppliers using this system was relatively quick and easy, and was a substantial improvement on typing orders and placing copies on a file.

Other benefits

Almost immediately, the implementation of the purchase order system enhanced the stock control system and made it easier to see any outstanding orders that had not been received. Furthermore, the ordering of more stock when stock reached re-order levels was much more efficient. Within a few weeks, staff were becoming more capable and confident with the system, and stocks held on the premises could be reduced, as it was apparent there was less need to hold large stocks.

One of the other benefits derived from the computerisation of both stock recording and purchase ordering was that staff had more time to study the supply of stock and 'shop around' for better quotations from other suppliers.

In all it was estimated that the value of stock in hand fell by £200 000 (saving an estimated £13 000 a year in holding costs) and about £10 000 would be saved in a year because of better terms given by switching suppliers.

System evaluation

The company's Board of Directors, at an evaluation meeting, had come to the conclusion that the computerisation project was a resounding success and should be extended into accounts. The Accounts Manager, therefore, was given the job of investigating the feasibility of computerising the sales, invoicing and sales order processing functions of the business. The reason for this was largely that the Production Manager had complained that the effectiveness of stock control was hindered because it was not clear from the computer what stocks were earmarked for sale. If it were clear what stocks were allocated for sale, it would be easier to decide what needed re-ordering and, more importantly, rational decisions could be made regarding production planning. Too much time was still wasted in switching production schedules at the last minute to meet pressing orders.

Computerising the sales function

The Accounts Manager began by using the same consultant to help determine a strategy on computerising sales. The first stage involved acquiring three extra microcomputers and upgrading the existing file server to enable it to be linked to them. Additional printers were also acquired. One microcomputer was installed in the Accounts Manager's office, one in the main accounts office and one with the sales clerk.

As soon as the system was upgraded and the additional hardware installed, four members of staff, one of whom was the Accounts Manager, were trained on using the computer, and in particular the Sales Ledger functions. A trainer came to the company and trained the staff on site. The training lasted two days.

Then the four staff formed a small committee, chaired by the Accounts Manager, to decide on a plan of action. The plan decided upon took the following form:

- Design and order special continuous stationery from Sage for the invoices, credit notes and sales acknowledgement forms.
- Collect details of all customers and input this information to the Sales Ledger, entering an opening balance into each account to indicate how much is owed by each customer.
- Update the stock files already implemented, so that each stock line has the correct selling price as well as the discount details associated with the line. The VAT codes also need updating as the Production Control Department has not entered the codes for all stock.
- Enter every invoice, credit note, debit note and all accounts adjustment details to the Sales Ledger.

These first four stages were implemented smoothly, although staff did not appreciate the benefits of entering such details, other than being able to print customer statements of account. The system was left to run for one month before being extended. Meanwhile, the following preparations were being made:

- Each stock record was being prepared with a departmental code to indicate the categories of lights being sold. For example, all table lamps were given the departmental code 1.
- Each stock item had a VAT code attached to it.

This was all done in conjunction with operating the Sales Ledger by itself for one month. In the second month, the next stage could go ahead.

As each customer was about to be invoiced or sent a credit note, the operator would use the invoicing function to achieve this. This proceeded with remarkable results. It meant that the stock file was now being updated almost immediately the stock had been issued. In addition to this, the whole process of invoicing had been speeded up. The operators soon got into the habit of processing such transactions as a Batch Processing run at 11.00 am each weekday.

The information being supplied to both the accounts and marketing personnel proved invaluable. In fact, for the first time, the Marketing Department could analyse sales performance almost as soon as it happened.

In addition to this, keeping a more effective check on customer credit limits meant fewer customers were being allowed to go over their credit limits without proper authorisation.

Within one month, sales order processing was also implemented. This proved easy because most of the preparation had been done. As a starting point, all outstanding orders were placed on a file and then all orders received from customers were processed through the computerised sales order processing system. Operators soon realised the benefits and found themselves with more time to concentrate on customer relations and to promote the company's policy.

In addition to many of the accounting functions being carried out, those responsible for maintaining stock levels not only knew what was in stock at any time, but also what was on order and what stock had been allocated to sales.

Completing accounts

After six months of computerisation, a number of minor errors had been ironed out and the company was running the system with a good deal of success.

The next stage in the development of the system was to extend the role of computerised accounts to include both the Nominal Ledger and Purchase Ledger.

Starting with the Nominal Ledger, the company soon had this function set up and integrated with the rest of the operation. All journal entries were at first carried out by the Accounts Manager. The first set of automatic postings from the Sales Ledger to the Nominal Ledger caused a few problems, but these were soon sorted out. Most journal entries were set up through recurring entries, depreciation automation, and prepayment and accruals.

Further development

After 18 months the company had seen its information systems develop a long way. One of the main future developments would be to extend the size of the system to allow more users to access the information on the system. The marketing personnel's information requirements were such that they needed a good deal of information on sales. A microcomputer was installed in their office to facilitate this requirement.

Over time, as the system developed, the company organised itself quite effectively in order to get data onto the computer as quickly and simply as possible.

The major problem caused by computerisation is that the company now finds it much more difficult to recruit staff of the right calibre, even when it has increased its staff salaries to reflect the additional skills required to perform the tasks.

At present the company has computer expertise among its managers, who have a number of developments they wish to implement – Payroll almost certainly being the next project. It is anticipated that the information processing requirements over the next few years will continue to change.

The latest evaluation report shows that the company is meeting its information needs well and would be able to cope easily with future expansion.

Case study questions

1. Trace the history of Brighter Light's computerisation, indicating timescales involved. When doing this, try to show the development as a diagram depicting the sequence of events with timescales.

2. What role did staff training take in the development exercise and to what extent did it help?

3. Could the company have started with computerising the accounts function first, followed by stock control, in much the same way as covered in this book?

4. What developments can you see in the future for this company?

5. Outline:
   - the benefits of the new system;
   - the costs of the new system.

CASE STUDY 2: FUTURE STATIONERY SUPPLIES

This case study is based around a firm that supplies stationery through one retail outlet and also distributes supplies direct to a large number of businesses and individuals. The firm has three categories of clientele:

1 customers through its retail outlet;
2 corporate organisations who are supplied in bulk and receive sizeable discounts;
3 small firms and individuals who order goods based on a widely distributed mail order catalogue.

Although this firm has a large customer base, its supplier base is relatively small. There are three large UK-based businesses and about 15 overseas businesses who supply to the firm via agents; this avoids the firm having to handle import procedures.

The facts

The following facts will help give some perspective on the firm.

Number of employees

Retail staff	2
Driving and despatch staff	2
Storekeeper	1
Administrative staff	2
Managerial staff	1
Total Staff	8

Turnover	£2.4 million
Expected number of orders	250 per month
Number of suppliers	18
Number of regular customers	
Corporate	26
Mail order	800
Average stock value on premises	£150 000
Number of different items held in stock	2000

Background

The business has developed over four years of trading and was founded by its Manager, Jack Staples. The business has grown rapidly, with the mail-order side of the business being the latest activity, launched one year ago.

Staples envisages that the retailing and corporate sides of the business will grow by less than 5 per cent per annum over the next three years. On the other hand, if it can get its marketing and distribution right, the mail-order side could double over the next two years.

In order to develop the mail-order side of the business, Staples believes that the sales side of the business will need to be computerised in order to cope with the growth in administrative activity.

Getting started

Staples takes the following action:

- He organises national newspaper and magazine advertisements for his catalogues. The advertisements are designed to appear at the same time in all the publications in one month's time.
- He orders from his printers a new set of catalogues.
- He buys a microcomputer with a 20 Megabytes hard disk, colour screen and a printer. The microcomputer is one of the latest and looks extremely stylish – he is always fussy about appearance.
- He purchases a copy of Sage Accountant through a Sage dealer. He learned about this package from an accountant friend at his Golf Club who used Sage for other business accounts.

After receiving delivery of the computer hardware and software, Staples spent many hours struggling with the manuals to get the system set up and installed. Eventually, with a little help from a friend and a few telephone calls to the dealer who sold him the computer system and software, he got Sage correctly installed.

After two weeks of having the system, he decided to appoint one of his administration staff, Judy Punch, to operate the Sage system. Judy was sent on a three-day course to learn about the Sage package. Because the course did not start exactly when he needed, four weeks had passed before Judy went on the course. This coincided with the advertisements for the mail-order side of the business. On top of the normal business load, Judy was away on the three-day Sage course, and requests for 3000 catalogues had suddenly accumulated. All staff were now working overtime in order to get the catalogues delivered, with some orders from existing customers being held up for a day or two.

When Judy returned from her course she was required to set up the Sage system with a view to implementing the Sales Ledger immediately, to incorporate the new customer accounts on the mail-order side of the business. Judy spent many hours setting up the Sales Ledger and entering all the customer details for existing mail-order customers. The time spent doing this meant further neglect of other processing activities in the firm: again orders were being delayed, because invoices were not being set up correctly.

Crisis management

After another two weeks, new customer orders were coming in at about 90 a day, and the administration could not cope. Staples, in a near state of panic, contacted the local job agency and recruited two temporary staff to help handle the requests for catalogues, production of invoices and some basic accounts work for the shop. In addition to this, he employed the services of a consultant from a neighbouring firm who was experienced in setting up computerised accounts for such firms.

With the help of the two temporary staff, who needed a good deal of supervision, and the consultant, a plan of action was drawn up.

The two staff in the shop concentrated on managing the shop and doing something about sorting out the backlog of work. Many items were low in stock in the shop by now and disgruntled customers were complaining of some stocks not being available. In addition to this, some accounts work had been neglected.

The two temporary staff and the other administrator concentrated on sorting out the backlog of mail-order and corporate customer orders. This largely involved processing orders and making up invoices so that goods could be despatched. The storekeeper and drivers concentrated on coping with the extra despatches. A much larger proportion of despatches had to be sent by post in order to cope with the extra work.

During all this activity, Judy Punch was able to set up the Sales Ledger properly and enter all invoices through the Sales Ledger. By the end of the second month, the processing was up to date and customers received their first computerised set of statements of account.

Getting settled

It was difficult to assess whether any real damage had been caused by the introduction of a computer and the transition period that occurred. However, Staples felt certain that some ground had been lost with some of the mail-order customers, and orders were lost with two large corporate customers. In addition to this, Staples spent a good deal of money employing staff for overtime work, employing temporary staff and paying consultancy fees. It is also certain that his advertising campaign to expand the mail-order side of the business did not have the impact it was designed to have.

In spite of everything, however, growth in business activity was expected, albeit not as extensive as originally planned. With the help of the consultant he hired, the decision was made to start the Nominal Ledger as soon as staff training was adequate. One of the shop staff was trained on the Sage system, along with Staples himself.

Meanwhile, one of the temporary staff left the firm and the other was taken on full-time; Staples felt the growth in the mail-order side of the business now justified the extra member of staff.

Once the training was over, the decision was made to set up and run the Nominal Ledger. On this occasion, the transition went smoothly. It only took a few days to set up the accounts and enter the opening balances. Staples learned from previous experience and from the training course that adequate pre-planning and preparation were important factors when converting manual files to computerised ones.

It soon became evident that the system, with only one microcomputer, was not sufficient for the business information requirements. He was advised to install a network of three microcomputers. Consequently, he needed two extra microcomputers and a file server. The new system was set up with two computers placed in the main office and one with the storekeeper for future development. Staples regretted not being able to anticipate this early on, because the adaptation to a network cost more than if he had started with a networked system, and it meant having to retrain staff for the different skills required of them. It also caused a little staff resentment. In addition to the extra hardware, he had to purchase Sage Financial Controller to upgrade his software for the new environment and demands that would be placed upon it.

Very soon after this, both shop workers familiarised themselves with the computerised system and found that it was saving them time. Staples had also learned how to extract the information he wanted from the ledgers and was soon planning effectively for changes in sales and keeping closer checks on customer debt.

Expanding the system

After two months, the system had settled well and Staples was ready to utilise the Purchase Ledger, sales order processing, invoicing and purchase order facilities. He sent his storekeeper on a Sage course with the aim of learning how to set up and maintain the stock files needed for the operation of the additional functions.

As soon as the storekeeper felt ready, he began to prepare the stock records by ensuring that all stock cards were complete and accurate. It was decided that stores would be kept separate from the shop stock. When goods were moved from stores to shop, it would be treated as a stock issue from stores in much the same way as issuing stock to customers through mail order. The storekeeper converted all records to the computer in about one month and soon learned to keep the records updated, especially with prices.

A major problem then occurred because Judy Punch left the firm for another job; she felt that with so much computing expertise behind her she could command a much higher salary than Staples was willing to offer. Staples had to recruit another employee to bring him to full staff strength. Finding another member of staff with the necessary expertise proved difficult. Eventually he found someone, after increasing the salary offered by 20 per cent. This new person still needed training in Sage and needed some time to be able to get to grips with the way the firm went about its business.

The transition period between Judy leaving and the new person being taken on and becoming able to work fully with Sage lasted about two months.

During this period, some potential trade was lost, along with credibility with a number of customers. Unfortunately the usual backlog of work had built up. Staff morale had also taken a bit of a knock.

It took nearly three months for the expanded system to finally settle and for all the data processing to be up to date. Much of the management information was only just becoming of real use to Staples.

After one year of computerisation, the firm had expanded its business in all fields, especially the mail-order aspect. Staples, on reflection, felt that computerisation was a success but realised that it could have gone much better with more careful planning, better handling of the staffing situation and better use of informed advice.

Case study questions

1 Trace the history of the development of computerisation at Future Stationery Supplies, indicating timescales involved. When doing this, try to show the development as a diagram with the sequence of events and the timescales.

2 In your opinion, did Staples start off correctly? Explain the reasoning behind your answer.

3 To what extent did the lack of staff training and involvement cause some of the problems that occurred?

4 At what stage did Staples really get involved with the package? Did it help matters?

5 What can be done to improve staff morale, performance and the likelihood that staff will stay with the firm longer?

6 What developments can you see for the future at this firm?

7 Outline:
- the benefits of the new system;
- the costs of the new system.

CASE STUDY 3: NATIONWIDE APPLIANCE SUPPLIES PLC

This case study is based on a large company that retails durable goods through a national chain of stores. The company has a central headquarters in the north of England, and five regional centres with depots for distributing to retail outlets in each of its regions. The organisation chart in Fig. 11.1 indicates how the company is set up.

The role of Central Office is to:

- make *all* purchasing decisions and order supplies centrally, to ensure maximum discounts from suppliers;
- define sales policy, which determines exactly what each retail outlet is to sell and at what price, ensuring that the company develops a clear national corporate image and can market its retail outlets in a more effective way.

Each retail outlet is headed by a local manager, with a deputy manager and up to four full-time assistants and part-time staff. The number of staff at each outlet will vary from store to store, depending on the time of year and the size of store.

Local retail managers decide on shop layout, although general guidelines are issued from Central Office. They also order stocks from their regional depot, hire and fire part-time and full-time assistants, and attend weekly regional meetings. Retail managers and their deputies receive basic salaries plus bonuses linked to their retail outlet's sales performance. Retail management can find their bonuses suffering if they recruit too many staff to justify the sales volume.

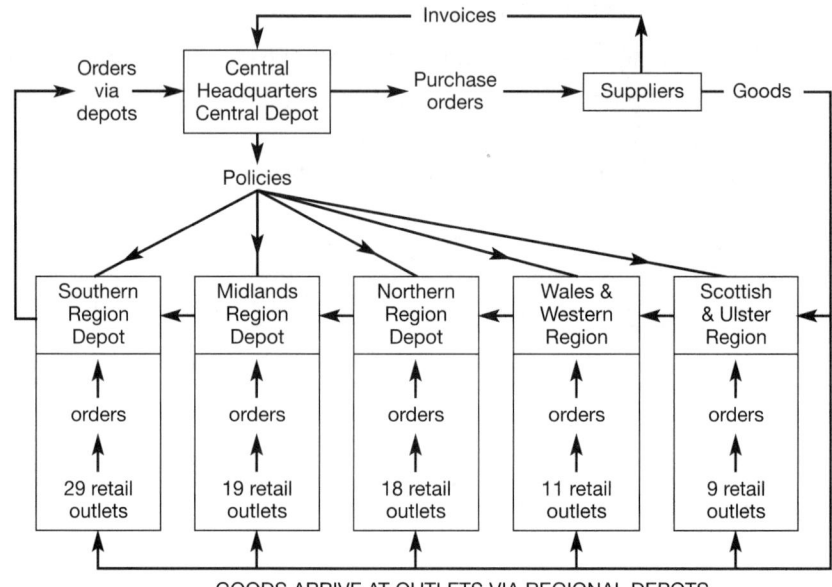

Fig. 11.1

Each region has an area manager and assistant manager, who have the task of co-ordinating the activities within their region, organising and overseeing staff training and development, and managing the distribution of stock. Regional centres manage the depots and are responsible for keeping stocks replenished. It is important to note that all ordering of stock is done through Central Office. However, deliveries from suppliers are made direct to the depots. Area managers meet at headquarters once a fortnight.

The current computer system

Central Office has developed a mainframe computer system based at Central Office, with minicomputers at each regional depot for the purpose of:

- overall company accounts;
- stock control;
- Purchase Ledger;
- monitoring of sales across the regions and within the retail outlets;
- purchase order system;
- payroll – especially developed to ensure that retail managerial staff receive bonuses to match their sales performance;
- monitoring receipts of goods from suppliers to regional depots;
- management information systems.

The system has taken ten years to develop to its current stage and will go on being developed by the company for the foreseeable future. Each regional centre's minicomputer has a direct link with the mainframe at Central Office via modem links. The modems enable data transmission between Central Office and each region in much the same way as any other data communication link. The mainframe has a set of modems – one for each region – so that all regional centres can interact with Central Office simultaneously. The company, therefore, has set up for itself a *Wide Area Network* (WAN).

The software on the system has been tailored by the company's own programming staff. The company employs a Senior Systems Analyst and two junior analysts, whose function is to oversee the entire computer system, its operations and development. There are six computer programmers who work under the supervision and instruction of the Senior Systems Analyst. In addition to this, the company has four maintenance staff who are responsible for ensuring that the computer systems function.

At retail level, there is virtually nothing in the way of computer systems other than electronic tills that keep a simple set of accounts. The retail deputy managers have the responsibility of submitting sales reports each day on specially designed sheets, which are posted to their regional depot.

The problems to overcome

A major problem with the system is that information about stock levels and retail sales can take up to one week to be entered to the computer system. This is because the retail shops have to fill in sales sheets by hand, and then post the sheets to the regional office where the information on the sheets is keyed into the computer. Exactly the same problem occurs when retail managers order stock, as order forms are again completed by hand and sent to the regional depots. In addition to information taking too long to be incorporated into the management information system, it was felt to be too time-consuming for staff at both the regional and retail level.

A feasibility study was commissioned to investigate the possibility of installing computing facilities at retail level with the following terms of reference:

1 To reduce the time lag between sales at retail level and the information being available on the Central Office mainframe computer.
2 To allow retail management to place orders with their regional offices by computer link rather than by filling in stock requisition sheets.
3 To maintain each retail outlet as an entity – that is, to ensure that a complete stock, sales and personnel profile can be kept on each retail outlet. (One of the major functions of the management information system at Central Office is to monitor and compare retail performance, analysing national, regional and local trends and other statistical data that require individual retail performance figures.)
4 To ensure that any new system can be piloted first, and then phased in over time.
5 To provide information for retail managers to assist them in both managing stock and being more effective as a sales centre.

With this brief, a feasibility study team was set up which was chaired by the company's Senior Systems Analyst and made up of the junior analysts, two programmers, three regional area managers and six retail managers.

The feasibility study was carried out, with regular meetings being held each month, and each member of the team being given a different task to perform. At the end of six months the team agreed and recommended a strategy to the Board of Directors, which was accepted, for immediate implementation.

The strategy

1 A sample of five retail outlets would be selected to run a pilot scheme where each shop would be equipped with a microcomputer, a modem, printer and communications software.
2 Each microcomputer would have a copy of Sage Accountant Plus, implementing the functions of Purchase Ledger, Nominal Ledger, invoicing and sales order processing and stock control.

3 Both managers and deputy managers of all retail outlets would go on a week's intensive course in computing with Sage, to be based at one of the regional depots.

4 Managers would then go back to their retail outlets to implement the systems within a specified time.

5 While training was being carried out, two of the programmers would set up the Sage system, with all the required nominal codes and report generation details, in such a way that the reports would reflect what had to be sent to the regional offices. It was vital that all users of Sage should send compatible reports to Central Office. Such reports would be printed to a spool file and then transmitted from the retail outlet's microcomputer to the regional office down a telephone line via a modem.

6 Managers would be required to meet each month for six months to report on the successes and failures of the new system, drawing on their experiences and contributing ideas about how implementation should take effect in future.

7 After this six-month pilot scheme, the team would submit a report on its experiences, along with recommendations about how the scheme should be implemented universally.

The pilot scheme

The first step was taken by purchasing five microcomputers equipped with hard disks, five printers and five data communication kits. Each machine was fitted with the communication boards that would allow the machine to connect to the telephone system. These communication boards were effectively a modem built into the computer rather than having a separate box. The systems staff then installed an operating system onto each hard disk and tested the computers fully. The Sage software was then installed, set up in a way that ensured it was correctly configured for the retail outlets. The analysts also set up with the Report Generator a wide range of reports that would be needed by the regional centres.

The programmers, meanwhile, had to write a suite of programs to enable reports sent down from each retail outlet to be used to update the main computer files as well as being used to transmit details to Central Office.

Five microcomputer systems were quickly set up and distributed to the five retail outlets that made up the pilot scheme. There was a delay, however, because the software that was being developed for the main computer system took longer than expected to write and test. Once the system was fully tested, the five managers and their deputies could then go on a training course.

The one-week training course went off without too much trouble, although three of the managers complained that too much was being taught in too little time and that they feared they could not remember everything expected of them.

Each manager then went back to his or her store with clear instructions and deadlines to implement systems. The instructions, in brief, went as follows:

1 Build up the stock files to reflect current stock situations. Time allowed was one week, after which regular updating would have to be made.
2 In Week 3 implement the purchase order system by first placing current outstanding orders on to file and then processing new orders from a low stock list.
3 From Week 4 all new purchase orders would be printed to a spool file and then, with the aid of company-written software, be transmitted to the mini-computer at regional office.
4 Once the system had settled, each retail outlet should then implement the Nominal Ledger and send a detailed trial balance each day to the regional office in the same way orders were sent.
5 In Week 5 the Sales Ledger would be implemented, which meant placing all credit sales and cash sales onto the computer. Existing debtors did not need to be placed on the system – only new ones. Once completed, these details too would be sent to the regional office.
6 Because credit control was handled at regional level, retail outlets would receive details on a daily basis about those customers who had made payments towards their accounts. This meant having to collect data from the regional office, print it and then use the information to update the Sales Ledger.
7 Sales reports would also be sent to the regional centre on a daily basis as soon as they were available.

In order to ensure that feedback from managers was effective, it was decided that the retail management would meet after the first two weeks to report on their progress.

Feedback

After two weeks the managers met with the systems staff to discuss and share experiences. Out of the five managers, four reported it took longer than one week to get the stock files to a position where they could start regular updating. One of the problems found was that managers were not doing a thorough manual stock-take before building up the files. It was established that the best way to do this was to generate special stock cards which included all the required fields and to fill these in during stocktaking, recording the date on which the information was compiled. With the larger shops it was felt that conversion should be done in four stages by splitting up the stock into four categories and setting up these categories one at a time. Furthermore, stricter checks were needed on sales, and the figures should be entered onto the computer in a more systematic way. In other words, it was necessary to establish a simple routine for updating stock. All retail shops, however, had converted the stock files. The managers decided to meet again in four weeks' time.

At the next meeting all managers reported success in setting up and implementing the purchase orders system. One of the retail outlets attempted to print orders to a spool file and send them down a line to the regional office. The attempt failed because the system at the regional centre had not been set up properly to receive the information. When eventually the orders were sent, the software at the regional centre had not been correctly written to translate the information into orders – that is, there were some bugs in the software. At the meeting, the Senior Systems Analyst reported that the problems had been sorted out and managers could implement the sending of orders by modem to their regional offices rather than sending them by post or courier.

During the next two months, managers had succeeded in meeting the remaining implementation targets, which were achieved within the predicted time span. The only problem managers really found was that of handling the data communications hardware and software. However, after two months they all felt they had just about mastered the skills needed to operate the system.

The scheme ran for another three months before the next meeting. At this meeting plans were drawn up to implement the new system in every retail outlet in all regions. The members of the meeting agreed to form a Steering Committee to draw up a plan for phasing the new system into the retail outlets. From their own experiences they were able to identify some of the pitfalls to look out for and were better able to define training needs. In addition, all the hardware and software problems had been solved.

Corporate strategy

The plan involved starting off with three outlets per month in the Southern Region; two per month in the Midlands, North, Welsh and Western Regions; and one per month in the Scottish and Ulster Regions.

Implementation would take much the same form as for the pilot schemes, with managers and their assistants first going on a one-week intensive training course before actually implementing the system in their shops. Each manager would also have a well documented 'action plan' which formed a corporate strategy to work from during the process of transition.

The implementation went ahead, in most cases, extremely well. A good deal of trouble-shooting was needed, especially in handling equipment. Another problem occurred because a few shops experienced a change in management during the transition period (although the situation fortunately never occurred where both manager and deputy left together). During the project, regional meetings were held between retail managers, and the visiting of each other's shops became far more common because managers felt they needed to share and draw upon the experience of others. This extra liaison between managers had a beneficial side-effect, because managers often learned from each other about new sales skills, marketing techniques and shop layouts.

Case study questions

1 Trace the history of the company's development of computerisation, indicating timescales involved. When doing this, try to show the development as a diagram with the sequence of events and the timescales.

2 How long would the complete computerisation in all retail outlets take?

3 Could the company have either saved time or money developing its own software rather than purchasing a package like Sage to do the job instead?

4 Discuss the role of staff training during the project and how staff training might play a role in the future development of the company.

5 How does this company benefit from having such a large number of retail outlets being computerised, compared with a small business that only has one outlet?

6 From your knowledge of Sage, identify those parts of the package that were not used and examine whether there might be a role in the company for some of the other functions available in Sage.

7 What developments can you see for the future of this company?

8 Outline:
 – the benefits of the new system;
 – the costs of the new system.

INDEX

Accruals	116
Acknowledging sales orders	173
Activity reports	33, 56, 80, 139
Adjustments of stock	135–7, 206
Aged creditors report	57
Aged debtors report	34–5
Allocating stock	165, 169–70
Amending deliveries	180
Asset valuation	120
Assets	79, 87, 92, 93, 116–20
Audit trail	15, 183
Back orders	174
Backing up data	58–60, 118, 196–7, 206
Bad debts	105–8
Balance sheet	87
Bank payments and receipts	65, 96–7
Bank reconciliation	72–4
Bank records	63
Bank statements	74–7
Banking transactions	30–1, 53–5, 61–78, 96–7
Batch credits	
customers	48, 103, 153
suppliers	48, 55
Batch invoice	
customers	26
suppliers	45
Batch processing	15, 38
Benefits of computerisation	2–4
Bill of materials	134
Budgets	89
Calculating fields	186, 190
Calendar icon	64
Cancelling invoices	103
Carriage	151–2, 169, 179
Cascade effect	51
Chart of accounts	89–90
Clear button	81, 84, 108
Close button	17
Closing windows	32–3, 56
Collating	77, 158
Company preferences	195–6
Compressing data files	200

Contra entries	104–5
Control accounts	62–3, 81–4
Credit	80
Credit limits	19, 32, 41, 56, 208
Credit note	
customers	14, 29, 153
products	147
services	147, 152–3
suppliers	48, 55
Creditors	56
Creditors control account	62, 83
CSV output	191–3
Ctrl-F4	44, 50, 56
Current assets	87, 93
Current liabilities	87, 94
Customer accounts	14–36, 100–1
Customer activity reports	33
Customer invoices	24–8
Customer receipts	30–1
Customer records	17–21
Data capture	165
Data file maintenance	199–200
Data Protection Act	6–9
Data pull down menu	101–8
Debit	80
Debtors	14
Debtors control account	62, 82–3
Default settings	25, 62, 89, 195–6
Deleting orders	175–6
Deliveries from suppliers	180
Delivery address	19, 150
Delivery notes	171
Departments	20, 133
Depreciation	92, 116–18
Despatching	170–1
Direct expenses	87
Discounts allowed	35–6, 63, 149, 151, 166
Discounts received	54, 63, 179
Disk doctor	199–200
Double entry	80–95, 101–8, 160
Drag and drop	52
End of period run	38, 119, 124–6
EU commodity codes	134
Exception reporting	3
Exiting from Sage	36
Expense accounts	95, 114–16
Explosion reports	139

Fax (Facsimile)	165
Field names	110–1, 187
File maintenance	199–200
File output	23, 77, 158
Financed by	87, 94
Financial year	124
Financials	84–5, 183
Finder icon	26, 30, 45, 48, 64, 133, 137, 149, 152, 166
Fixed assets	87, 92, 93, 120
Function key F1	43
Function key F6	28
Graphs	193–4
Hard copy	6
Hardware, definition	5, 206, 214, 219
Help windows	43
HM Customs & Excise	121–4
Icon	9, 51
Implementing Sage	202–22
Importing data	197
Ink jet printers	6
Installing computer hardware	2
Installing Sage	8–13
Invoice and invoicing	14, 146–62
Invoices from suppliers	45–7
Invoices to customers	24–8, 54–61, 103
Journal entry	91–2, 95, 121
Key fields	18, 40
Labels	49
Laser printers	5–6
Layout editor	111, 154–7, 186–9
Liabilities	79, 87, 93
Mailing customers	108–11
Manufacturing accounts	95
Margin set up	75
Matrix printers	5
Maximise button	16, 52, 53, 80
Memo tabs	21
Minimise button	16, 51–2
Mispostings account	103
Month-end routine	118–20
Movements of stock	141
Multiple companies	195

Networks	5, 206
Nominal account layout	88
Nominal accounts	50, 63–4, 79–99
Nominal activity	80
Normalise button	17, 50, 52
Object editing	111
Opening balances	20–1
customers	100–1
suppliers	112–13
Opening bank balances	64
Operating systems	4
Order status	172
Outstanding orders	174, 207
Overheads	87, 89
Page set up	75
Paper size and source	75
Passwords	16, 195
Payee	53, 66
Paying suppliers	53–4, 113–14
Period end	119, 124–6
Petty Cash	95–7
Picking lists	207
see also Stock reports	
Prepayments	114–15
Preview outputs	35, 50, 74, 85, 114
Price changes	200–1
Price list	138
Print quality	76
Print to file	23, 77
Printer types	5
Printing	23, 44, 74–5, 196
Printing invoices	157–9
Product categories	131
Product codes	210
Product credit notes	147
Product explosion	139
Product invoices	147
Product list	138
Product profit estimates	139
Product records	131–4, 152
Product transfers	140–1
Profit and loss	87, 94
Profit on stock	139
Provision for depreciation	92
Pull down menus	17, 25
Purchase categories	38, 87
Purchase ledger	37–60

Purchase order processing	163–82
Purchasing a computer	1
Receipts from customers	30–1
Reconciling bank transactions	72–4
Recurring entries	69–71
Reducing balance method of depreciation	118
Remittance notes	35, 113–14
Re-order levels	139
Re-ordering stock	142
Report generator	184–94, 219
Reports	
customers	22, 31–5
sales orders	174–5
suppliers	44, 56–8
VAT returns	121–4
Restoring from backups	197, 206
Returned cheques	101–3
Returns inwards	29
Returns outwards	49
Revenue accounts	95
Sales acknowledgement	173
Sales Ledger	14–36
Sales order processing	163–82
Scroll bar	67
Service credit notes	147, 152–3
Service invoices	147
Settlement terms	20, 42, 56, 152, 169, 179
Sorting fields	186
Spreadsheets	192–3
Stand alone systems	4–5
Statement of account	15, 35
Stock assembly	134
Stock codes	208
Stock control	129–45
Stock explosion	139
Stock movements	135–7, 208
Stock profit	139, 206
Stock record creation	130–4, 152
Stock reports	138–40, 159, 167
Stock transfers	140–1
Straight line method of depreciation	118
Supplier accounts	37–60
Supplier activity reports	56
Supplier invoices	45–7
Supplier payments	53–4
Supplier records	40
Suspense account	101, 120–1

Tax codes	25, 132
Title bar	16
Trade discounts	20
Trading accounts	95
Training staff	6, 202–22
Transaction histories	33, 57
Transfer funds	68–9, 96
Trial balance	84–5
Turnover	32
Updating ledgers	160–1, 181
Utilities routines	183–201
Valuation of stock	139
Variable names	112, 157, 185–6
VAT	24–5, 27, 32, 45–7, 62–3, 81–2, 121–4, 152, 166, 197
Windows manipulation	50–2
Windows set-up	8–9
Wizard usage	8–13, 31, 101–8, 110, 184–6
Write offs	105–8
Writing off assets	118
Year end	124–6
Zoom	74–5, 114

Information Technology Skills for Accounting Students

Ian Robertson

A knowledge of IT packages is an integral part of most accounting courses and this book provides the skills needed to use spreadsheets and accounting packages as tools in accounting. The book is application-specific, based on Sage Sterling 3 for Windows and on Excel 5.

The material takes the student through the packages, keystroke by keystroke, providing case study material on which to work. The spreadsheet section of the text allows the student to build a worksheet from scratch using Excel and become familiar with the fundamental spreadsheet tools. A bank of questions is provided which can be used with Excel or any other spreadsheet package. The answer for each question is provided in the form of a model and an additional worksheet showing the underlying formulae.

- The computerised accounting material is based on a running case study
- The spreadsheet material includes questions for solution on a spreadsheet

Ian Robertson is a Lecturer in the Department of Economics and Management at the University of Paisley, Glasgow.

ISBN 0 273 61714 1

For further information, contact:

The Higher Education Marketing Department,
Pearson Education Ltd, Edinburgh Gate, Harlow, Essex, CM20 2JE.
Telephone: 44 (0)1279 623623.

For an inspection copy, write to:

Inspection Copy Service, at the above address.

giving full details of where you teach.

PEARSON EDUCATION

We have a wide range of publications on Accounting and related subjects. Write to:

Customer Service Department
Pearson Education Ltd
Edinburgh Gate
Harlow
Essex CM20 2JE

Telephone: 01279 623623

for a free copy of any of the following catalogues:

ACCOUNTING AND FINANCE
BUSINESS AND MANAGEMENT
LAW

For details of our publications on Computing write to:

The Marketing Manager
Pearson Education Ltd
128 Long Acre
London WC2E 9AN

Telephone: +44 (0)171 447 2000
Fax: +44 (0)171 240 5771